Prayerfully Yours

PRAYERFULLY YOURS

Qualityprayer for Qualitylife

BENJAMIN A. VIMA

Order this book online at www.trafford.com
or email orders@trafford.com

Most Trafford titles are also available at major online book retailers.

© Copyright 2012 Benjamin A. Vima.

All rights reserved. No part of this publication may be reproduced, stored in a retrieval system, or transmitted, in any form or by any means, electronic, mechanical, photocopying, recording, or otherwise, without the written prior permission of the author.

Printed in the United States of America.

ISBN: 978-1-4669-1060-7 (sc)
ISBN: 978-1-4669-1062-1 (hc)
ISBN: 978-1-4669-1061-4 (e)

Library of Congress Control Number: 2011963674

Trafford rev. 01/04/2012

Trafford Publishing   www.trafford.com

North America & international
toll-free: 1 888 232 4444 (USA & Canada)
phone: 250 383 6864 ♦ fax: 812 355 4082

Contents

Dedication vii
Acknowledgments ix
Introduction xi

Chapter I : What Is Quality Prayer? 1
    A. Prayer in general 1
    B. The Concept of Qualityprayer 7
    C. Foundation of Christian Qualityprayer 31

Chapter II : The Upshot of Qualityprayer 36
    A. The Ultimate Goal in Qualityprayer 36
    B. Shortterm Goals of Qualityprayer 41
    C. Qualitylife: The Endresult of Qualityprayer 48

Chapter III : Ingredients of Quality Prayer 54
    A. According to Jesus' formula "The Lord's Prayer" 54
    B. Other Components of Qualityprayer 80

Chapter IV : The Method of Qualityprayer 100
    A. Settings of Qualityprayer in Jesus' life 102
    B. Church's Traditional Prayer-settings 106
    C. Capsulated Method of Qualityprayer for today's Christian 115

Chapter V : Some Salient Points on Qualityprayer 143
   A. The Power of Qualityprayer 143
   B. Powerlessness of some prayer ventures 151
   C. The misuses of prayer 157
   D. Qualityprayer in Sufferings 159
   E. The Hardships faced in Qualityprayer 167
   F. Prayer of Petition in Qualityprayer 171
   G. Praying With Mary, Mother of Jesus 180
   H. Fasting in Qualityprayer 186

Conclusion 195
Books & Authors Referred 203

Dedication

To my late father, *Susai Manickam*, who was truly my mentor and rolemodel in persistent and faith-filled prayer; thanks to his prayerlife I am what I am today; his qualityprayer still continues to bear fruits in the lives of his children and grandchildren.

To my religious and priest-friends, who struggle in their ministry, to combine personal qualityprayer with their publicly-exposed community ritualistic prayers.

To all my lay friends, who, though busy in irksome chores of earthly life, long to understand and experience a qualityprayerlife and reap the benefits from it.

ACKNOWLEDGMENTS

A PROFOUND RESPECT and deep indebtedness to many senior Jesuits, particularly my spiritual fathers, at my birthplace as well as in my seminary life, who taught me how to uphold the spirit of prayer as a tool for union with God and in the footsteps of St. Ignatius, to fulfill all prayer duties *'for the greater glory of God.'*

Loving thanks to my Charismatic friends in the diocese of Tulsa, who ignited the fire of prayer in me, whenever I felt discouraged in my prayer efforts.

There are many Christian prayerwarriors who have been following me throughout my prayer journey, especially the Spirit-filled parishioners with whom I have served the Lord in USA specifically in the parishes I have been performing my pastoral ministry. I wholeheartedly thank them for their practical help, friendship, and encouragement.

My sincere gratitude and appreciation to Mrs. Paula Green, who, in the midst of her daily duties at home and in her job, helped me in typing, proofing, and sometimes correcting my thoughts with deeper discussions on prayer.

I am indebted to Larry Montanye, Skiatook, OK, who has been one of the angels helping me in my personal and pastoral life, in particular encouraging me in bringing out this book as I dreamt of. I gratefully acknowledge his contribution of the pictures he took exclusively for this book's cover.

INTRODUCTION
A Prey of Prayer

Yes, I am a victim of prayer habit like most of you. Even though people say every human heart is created to crave for God no human being gets into the habit of prayer instantly or automatically. It is true I crave for my security, my safety, my prosperity, my health, my love-affairs, my sex, my popularity, my food, my drink, my dress, my home, my promotion and prestige but not for praying. As many sociologists and researchers prove, prayer is not one of my basic needs.

Yet since I was born in an orthodox Catholic family and to a dad who was a man of prayer I was thrust into the habit of prayer. As my dad was once brainwashed in a way by his elders, especially by his priests, so was he pushing me harder and harder, even sometimes with the penalty of denial of tasty homemade cookies. From my childhood I had been taught by catechists, by priests and nuns and surely by the words and deeds of my dad how to pray, what to pray, when to pray and why to pray. Still prayer was not my priority in my daily schedule. I was made to memorize some Catholic formal prayers and whenever I prayed those prayers I was just lisping them, only my lips were moving but in the bottom of my heart I lodged bitterness against my prayer time including daily masses, and other devotions like Rosary recitation.

At my teen age I began reading secretly some authors who condemn this kind of religious practices. This led me to hate not only prayer but also the religion itself and slowly directed me to ignore even my belief in God. In order to be earthly and successful and practical in my handling of life I became purely materialist and totally secular. Becoming adolescent I began asking terrible questions about myself, about life, about humanity and even about God. I felt by this kind of questioning and analyzing I could show myself and my worth that I was unique, I was individual. Physically I was growing rapidly and intellectually as well. I began rereading my life. All this time, I felt, I had been controlled by my peer group, my parents, my religion, my books and my whims and fancies. However, I pretended myself individually standing by myself as Liberty Statue. I was escorted to both positive and negative performances. I grew to be very smart in influencing others, very practical in managing my life and finance, and very skillful in applying my talents. I was very productive.

As an adult I chose my profession as my life partner and gradually building up a family of my own. I desired to include as many friends and relatives as possible; I dreamed of overflowing with milk and honey all the days of my life; I desired to hold as much wealth as possible, to possess as much property and popularity as possible so that I can keep others begging me, saluting me, keeping me not just in their hearts but being enthroned over their shoulders as slaves. Still I was purely secular and natural. I was managing my life successfully. I got what I dreamed of. Everything was there at my reach.

But one thing was all the time missing. Peace! Inner Joy! Heart-felt contentment! At the end every accomplishment and acquirement of what I longed for, when I was alone I was restless. I was feeling alone even though my friends and relatives were around me. I constructed a wonderful house of my own with all its decorations though not as much as the 'Never Land.' But I furnished my home with all available and modern furniture, with a good collection of antiques, with beautiful China cupboard, and with a closet filled with suits and variety of seasonal dresses. Yet when I was left alone at my home I felt empty, a vacuum and a loner.

One day at my regular visit to my doctor for physicals I was told I had developed some chronic disease. I was put under daily medication of swallowing five pills a day; one day I met with a mobile accident in which I broke my leg and hand. I was laid up in bed for three months after a hard surgery; once I went to Casino to try my luck but lost a big amount. Slowly

I was getting nervous. Very sadly some days later my dearmost friend disowned me and in a way cheated me. I felt I was gradually losing my grip on life. Though I was by right conscience behaving well in my business and services applying my natural straightforwardness, my enthusiasm for total perfection in performance and duty-consciousness, I was thoroughly misunderstood by my friends and relatives; I had to undergo hurts and pains because of their slanders and gossips.

One of the early days of summer some of my close friends floated some bad news about my performing my priestly duties. That was the climax of all my individual loss of grip and balance. I suddenly went into deep depression. I was truly descending into hell. Underline this date. That was the day when I got into the real territory of prayer. I felt myself the need of prayer. I became once again a prey to the prayer habit, but this time not compelled or thrusted from outside but purely from within. I began praying intensively as the Psalmist would pray: *"Save me, God, for the waters have reached my neck. I have sunk into the mire of the deep, where there is no foothold. I have gone down to the watery depths; the flood overwhelms me."* (Ps. 69: 2-3)

When I started, of my own accord, becoming a victim of prayer I thought I was entering into a minefield of all that I could grab instantly. My main focus in my prayer life was both being liberated from all kinds of harms, perils, evils and being led into a life of prosperity, health, popularity and all kinds of blessings from God so that my earthly life as well as my life after death could be in happiness and peaceful settlement.

With this attitude I read the Scriptures all that I need as proofs for the efficacy of prayer. I read the Lord saying: *"Ask and it will be given to you; seek and you will find; knock and the door will be opened to you. For everyone who asks, receives; and the one who seeks, finds; and to the one who knocks, the door will be opened. Which one of you would hand his son a stone when he asks for a loaf of bread, or a snake when he asks for a fish? If you then, who are wicked, know how to give good gifts to your children, how much more will your heavenly Father give good things to those who ask him."* (Mt. 7: 7-11) *"Therefore I tell you, all that you ask for in prayer, believe that you will receive it and it shall be yours."* (Mk. 11: 24) *"And whatever you ask in my name, I will do, so that the*

Father may be glorified in the Son. If you ask anything of me in my name, I will do it." (Jn. 14: 13-14)

After reading what Jesus has said of the efficacy of prayer, I began browsing the Old Testament Books. There I found so many references and examples for the magic power of prayer. One of the prophets who stands number one in using this instrument of prayer is Elijah. Through the power of prayer he could bring down draught and rain as well. James quotes about him in his letter: *"The fervent prayer of a righteous person is very powerful. Elijah was a human being like us; yet he prayed earnestly that it might not rain, and for three years and six months it did not rain upon the land. Then he prayed again, and the sky gave rain and the earth produced its fruit"*. (Jas. 5: 16-18)

In psalms there are hundreds of references pointing out the key-role of prayer in the Psalmist's relationship with God. His main argument for trusting God despite of all the troubles and pains he undergoes is based on the experience of the power of prayer. *"When the poor man called the Lord answered him." "The Lord is worthy of all praise: when I call I am saved from my foes." "In my distress I called out: LORD! I cried out to my God. From his temple he heard my voice; my cry to him reached his ears." "O LORD, my God, I cried out to you and you healed me." "The Lord listened and had pity. The Lord came to my help. For me you have changed my mourning into dancing."*

Very interestingly in the same OT I found two striking parallel passages that equally highlight the power of both the 'Word of God' and 'prayer of the human'. In the Book of Sirach 35:17-18 I read: *"The prayer of the lowly pierces the clouds; it does not rest till it reaches its goal, nor will it withdraw till the most high responds, judges justly and affirms the right"*. In a similar tone the Prophet Isaiah speaks about the power of the Word of God (55:11): *"So shall my Word be that goes forth from my mouth; it shall not return to me void, but shall do my will, achieving the end for which I sent it"*. What a wonderful parallelism. In both passages I noticed a strong enforcement on the power of both the prayer of the humans and the Word of the Divine. Both will not return void but they will achieve the end for which they are sent! So naturally and more biblically I thought I should make use of my prayer and prayers to adorn myself first with all the blessings from heaven.

This is what majority of us consider our prayer efforts. Recently I had discussion with some of my parishioners about their handling of prayer. One said: 'Before I go for interview I pray that I should get a dumb interviewer;' another one remarked: 'As I am about to move from one place to another for a new job I pray that God may change the whole new environment to be the best it could be; a third parishioner very frankly portrayed her prayer habit: 'One day I went to a McDonald's to buy a hamburger. I forgot to bring cash. This happened many years back when McDonald's did not take credit cards. So before I entered there, I prayed spontaneously for some good soul ready to give me a free burger; whenever I go for playful gambling. I am compelled to pray before I touch the slot machine that I might get atleast 10 dollars more than the amount I plan to spend; I pray daily for the increase of my pay; I pray for everyone around me do and say as I want; I pray for my Lady Luck always accompanying me wherever I go for my green pastures.'

Exactly the same kind of habit I got into in my life of prayer and expected too many results out of it. I can go on and on listing my appeals, petitions, requests, applications and demands I submitted to the Lord over the years. All were in the time and name of prayer. I was making all these prayers with one and only thought that prayer is after all a magic key to open the door of heaven, to open the treasures of God, to lock the gates of misfortunes and unfair games of human life. But all that I demanded from God in prayer were not granted by Him. I was thoroughly disappointed. I thought God once again failed me or the Scriptures and the Church had cheated me. I felt that, by having recourse to prayer of my own accord, I cheated myself and burying my individuality and self image into a pit. I was actually descending into hell again.

From the depths of despair and depression I cried: "Are you there my God? If so, where are your promises about prayer and its efficacy? I have been asking and asking thousand and one times some help from you. But it had not been granted. Why? What is wrong with you? Or is there something wrong in my way of prayer? Tell me Lord. I listen to you."

Very astonishingly during this agony of being disappointed in prayer I was hearing at the back of my head, as if a recorded BGM audio, a lamenting voice: *'My God my God! Why have you forsaken me?'* I interpreted it as some sort of brainwashed condition of a prey of prayer. So, as much as possible I tried to ignore this BGM. I could in no way silence it. The more I tried to quash it, the greater was its volume. One day I sat in the church and gave a keen listening to the same voice. The voice stopped its mourning. It was Jesus who spoke to me in a loving tone: "My friend! You should read me in the Scriptures little more carefully. All the Scriptural passages that promise wonderful effects of prayer are really true. There is no doubt about it. But you should have read them in connection with other words I have uttered and with my prayer-behavior and the way I dealt with earthly life and my relationship with God."

And therefore when I began enlightening myself on the issue of prayer as demanded by Jesus I found out the first thing I had to do was to relate myself to my God who is always 'the beyond'. I too discovered God wants me as a Christian to be always in search of his 'beyondness.' My next quest was: What role my prayer was performing in this God-searching journey. In my reflections of the Scriptural words I began defining my act of prayer as an act of exercising all my bodily and spiritual resources to get closer a bit more daily to that Dream of my life and show this element of my closeness and nearness through my daily actions, performances and interactions with my fellow-human beings. If I dream of my God as the greatest Lover in the universe I too must try to be the greatest lover ever lived in my territory. If I think of Him as an all-joyful and ever-peaceful One, I too should aim at keeping my face always smiling like the sunshine and become a jolly-good fellow and a peace-maker in my family, ministry and in any involvement with community.

This does not mean I have possessed God completely and owned him totally. It is presumptuous to contend that I have no tension and struggle in my life. In the midst of these struggles and challenges of life I go consistently to my inner altar of my God and I close all its doors and windows; browse my dreams in my personal computer of heart and mind; take enough time to read all the emails of God of the Beyond available in the Books I hold as sacred and authentic, in the testimonies shared by committed religious people, and in the arguments that are presented by modern scientists and philanthropists. Every day I resolve in my own sanctuary what is God to me and the universe and how to appropriate his character in my life and what should I accomplish today as God of my dreams proposes to me.

After double conversion this is my current act of prayer. This helps me a lot, especially these days when I have to deal with very earth-bound issues: Some fellowhumans still judge me color-blindly as a stranger and foreigner; some others having their personal agendas at the back of their minds and carry heavy burden of troubled conscience blame me for not attending our church. Besides, there are many unfulfilled dreams in my present life, for an example, I wish that my parishioners whom I serve turn out to be the 'people on fire', becoming committed and dedicated stewards of our Leader Jesus alive and fully involved in church growth, church fellowship and church prosperity. In this bitter situation what better act of praying would be other than re-stabilizing myself by listening to the Almighty God, reflecting over my fellowhumans' godly experiences and dreaming more dreams of God and resolving to walk the walk of innumerable saints toward the God of my Dreams, a God of the Beyond?

As a matter of fact my journey to God in prayer has not yet reached its fullness. It has got its own uphills and downhills. Still I approach prayer sometimes with pleasure at which time I feel an exuberated sensation and a pleasant experience (not much during prayer that happens very rare) before I begin my prayer. Some other times I go to prayer out of needs of the hour. I sense I am incapable of performing certain life's hardest roles or I feel let down by my friends and even God abandoning me with unresolved, unexpected life's turnings.

Many times I perform prayer as duty or as means of avoiding any scandal to my near and dear ones. But most of the time prayer becomes spontaneous. I may call it: Instinct, mannerism, habit, culture, or a part of life-game! This means I cannot anymore get out of this habit of prayer. In a way it has entered into me as one of the constituents of my personality. Thus lately I have discovered that there is an intrinsic connection between religion, personality and prayer. What I believe as God and religion formed my prayer habit and mutually my prayer-exercises shaped my view of religion and God. In the same vein, my holdings about religion and prayer developed my personality.

However, at this phase of my journey to a God of 'the Beyond' and during a period of inner search for Him in Spirit and in Truth I hate to see myself entangled by these mixed feelings about prayer. I want to be freed of such false, fake, slavish and selfish acts of praying. I try to connect my act of prayer to the little truth I know about God the beyond. I wish I could find the genuine meaning of prayer as my Teacher taught. I long for an experiential prayer more than theological prayer, dogmatic prayer, traditional prayer, bookish and sheepish prayer.

Often I question myself whether my personality influences my prayer this way or vice versa. As age grows I am informed well about myself, about life, about the universe and about values. I have outgrown many habits, many bad-manners, many uncouth ways of dealing with other people; I have matured in holding my relationship with others; I have been well-qualified to play my social roles in the community; I am aware where I come from, where I stand now and where I am heading to. This is literally a growth of my personality. In this personal development process my religion and prayer too had undergone lots of change. Many of our saints have testified to the important and effective role played by prayer in this process of changing and growing of personality in their lives.

Human life is a bundle of experiences. Each human develops one's personality through those experiences. This is simply the creative process of humanity. This does not need any adherence to religion or prayer. As the seed of a tree opens itself for its natural development and growth so does the human DNA. Experiences in life, like water and manure to a tree, nourish and shape up the personality of human beings.

While in this natural process of human development prayer is not a resource and support, it is by all means an indispensable source and basis for developing a matured 'Christian personality'. Christian personality is well-described by Jesus' life and sayings which are echoed in Paul's writings. Paul prays for Christians: *"That God may grant you in accord with the riches of his glory to be strengthened with power through his Spirit in the inner self, and that Christ may dwell in your hearts through faith; that you, rooted and grounded in love, may have strength to comprehend with all the holy ones what is the breadth and length and height and depth, and to know the love of Christ that surpasses knowledge, so that you may be filled with all the fullness of God."* (Eph. 3: 14-19)

However, mere formal or traditional prayer would do no good in this regard. It would help us to keep up our status quo. That is all. It will never contribute to our growth of Christian personality. Even the prayer of the intellect, namely prayerful meditation or reflection would not do that much help, as it should. This kind of prayer would meet its immature death as I had gone through sometime back. Once the intellect gets more truths and facts about life, God, religion and universe it would surely put a full stop to prayer. But if the same prayer is experiential and personal, if it is intensively connecting the soul to its God, the Ground of being, the Beyond of everything, if it accelerates the process of intimacy between the human and the Divine, then surely prayer becomes the primary source of change, growth and development in human personality and through him/her influences the entire universe. This is what happened in Jesus and so in His disciples and godly people of today. I dare to name this kind of prayer **"QualityPrayer"**.

I am fully aware of the unsavory prayersituation of many of my fellow-Christians like that of mine in the past. Because of continued doubts and complaints they are led to pray as merely some routine, religious and devotional exercises, rituals and practices that are not concerned with obtaining proper results. Consciously or unconsciously many are convinced that prayer is not very important to everyday life and that it does not apply to the real world. Prayer is not an instrument of support to their burdensome life. Prayer is not a priority for the majority of people. Other activities are more exciting, fruitful and necessary. Some people use prayer as an 'out-sourcing' scheme in their life or crisis management. Very sadly many have turned out to be atheists or constant doubters about God and His Presence.

From my past experiences and reflections as a 'prey of prayer' I have come to a conclusion that all those negative views against prayer rise out of lack of understanding about the real meaning and nature of qualityprayer. Jesus our Master and Savior taught us how to pray not just any prayer; he disclosed the nature and method of 'QualityPrayer'. All that we use-time, energy, talent, power, space and other life's resources—must be quality-oriented, leading to achieve the purpose for which prayer is intended. Qualityprayer is the result of our 'fear of God'. It is our solitude going with Jesus to rest. And as Tertullian well said, it is *an offering that belongs to God.*

Some months back in one of my retreats I had sufficient time for counting the hours of my past as well as the hours left for me in stipulated possible future life. As of today for example, I am 65 years old. From my birth up to this day God has gifted me with 569400 hours; and if God permits me to live probably 20 years more the hours left to me are: 175200. God in Jesus has advised us: "Give to God what is God's." My Christian conscience pesters me asking, 'how many hours have you given to God in the past from those 569400 God's hours; and how many are you going to offer to Him from the probable future hours?' I am sure my friends who possess a genuine Christian conscience would feel the same.

However many of us may justify ourselves saying 'I need not worry about such questions because I am giving my whole life to my God.' That sounds like cheating ourselves. Actually if we deeply study and reflect God's words in our Scriptures we hear the demands of God from us for certain specifics about our giving hours to Him: He expects us to give Him one full day a week as Sabbath; specific days as holy and consecrated for Him. We read also in the Bible God delights in meeting us personally on daily basis. During His meeting with us he prescribes certain specs about time, location, mode and style, physical and mental position, specific gestures and rituals but always 'in spirit and in truth.'

In one of parish bulletin letters I wrote about the common but unwanted approach of prayer discovered among many Christians. The letter was entitled *"Our Prayer Time: Is it just a Show Time?"* During our prayer times, many request the Lord to show Himself to them. "Otherwise, Lord," they warn Him, "I would make my own god, and even make myself a god! I would speak to myself, and I would listen and obey myself. This means I would be creating a monster like a little Hitler out of myself." Therefore, they even command the Lord to show Himself to them and to speak to them as early as possible. Many catholic friends, considering their Holy Communion time as an appropriate occasion to catch their Eucharistic Lord and ask him to make them conscious of his presence. The Qualityprayer, I am proposing to my readers, is not a kind of showoff as a magical Rod; it is not to get even with God; not to instruct God; not to prevail on God; not to get his attention toward us; and not to give any direction to God.

My readers should never think I am introducing in this book one more new style of praying among many already expounded and proposed by traditional, conservative and modern pray-ers. I love all their spiritually-committed efforts in teaching us different patterns of prayer like 'centering prayer', contemplative prayer', listening prayer, breath prayer, prayer of the heart, ejaculatory prayer', prophetic prayer, charismatic prayer, sozo prayer, and soaking prayer and many others. My purpose here is to direct the users of those different praying styles to take advantage of them as fruitful 'QualityPrayer'.

In this publication I share some thought-provoking ideas about the reality of Christian QualityPrayer. I expose descriptively but succinctly Christian QualityPrayer's character, its foundation-what source from which it flows, its upshots-its goal and aim, its components with which it is fashioned. My great desire in my priestly life is always to help all my friends who are truly struggling as 'the preys to prayer' like me. That is my reason for bringing out this book. Through reading this book I envisage that they will discover the current status of their prayerlife and surely they will plan to apply in their prayer all the principles of qualityprayer deliberated here and thus giving to God very generously their God-given hours as He is all-lavishing.

As Paul portrays, all of us as the disciples of the risen Lord, are bestowed with specific roles to perform in this world. Some of us are apostles, others prophets, some others pastors and preachers, many others teachers and guides and good many of us parents and elders of the family and community. Every role we carry out, in Jesus' eyes, is a life-ministry for God's glory and our salvation as well. For a successful execution of those roles the act of 'qualityprayer' has been included by Jesus and his followers as an intrinsic component. Therefore we can very well say that praying qualityprayer is a ministry, not one among many, but essential ingredient in any ministry we handle in God's kingdom.

My one and only aim of publishing this book on 'qualityprayer' is nothing but Paul's own wish and prayer: *"To equip the holy ones for the work of ministry, for building up the body of Christ, until we all attain to the unity of faith and knowledge of the Son of God, to mature manhood, to the extent of the full stature of Christ, so that we may no longer be infants, tossed by waves and swept along by every wind of teaching arising from human trickery, from their cunning in the interests of deceitful scheming. Rather, living the truth in love, we should grow in every way into him who is the head, Christ, from whom the whole body, joined and held together by every supporting ligament, with the proper functioning of each part, brings about the body's growth and builds itself up in love."* (Eph. 4: 12-16)

My deliberations regarding 'QualityPrayer' are meant for those Christians who recognize the importance of prayer in their lives. They fully believe what Pope Benedict XVI said in one of his Lenten messages: *"Prayer is not something accessory, it is not "optional," but rather a question of life or death. Only one who prays, that is, who entrusts himself to God with filial love, can enter into eternal life, which is God himself."* These are the disciples who want to pray like Jesus; they long for not only dwelling in the House of the Lord but also seeing His Face even while they are walking in this valley of darkness. If my book assists them in all possible ways, surely with the grace of the Almighty, in realizing their yearnings I will surely hear from my Master saying to me at the end of my race as a Christian, much more as a priest: "Well done, my good and faithful servant. Since you were faithful in small matters, I will give you great responsibilities. Come, share your master's joy." (Matt. 25: 21)

Prayerfully Yours,

Benjamin A. Vima

CHAPTER 1
What Is Quality Prayer?

A. Prayer in general

Meaning of the word 'Prayer'

THE WORD 'PRAYER' comes from the Latin *precare* (late) and *precari* (classical) meaning "to entreat, pray." The word *precor* is also used in Latin meaning "to wish well or ill to anyone," "to hail, salute," or "address one with a wish." The Latin word *orare* "to speak" later took over the role of *precari* to mean "pray." In this etymological understanding and usage of the word 'prayer', traditionally 'prayer' has been considered as a term to be used for formal acts of prayer such as: Giving exclusive time and place for God; reciting formal prayers either memorized or spontaneous; sacramental prayers; devotions; and sometimes meditative prayers.

This makes sense why the Webster's 1828 Dictionary, as quoted in cbt.ministries.org, defines "Prayer" as *"in worship, a solemn address to the Supreme Being, consisting of adoration, or an expression of our sense of God's glorious perfections, confession of our sins, supplication for mercy and forgiveness, intercession for blessings on others, and thanksgiving, or an expression of gratitude to God for his mercies and benefits."*

> *'Nothing is equal to prayer; for what is impossible it makes possible, what is difficult, easy.'* (St. John Chrysostom) *'Prayer is the expression of humanity's desire for God'.* (St. Thomas Aquinas)

In Christianity there were efforts of introducing different new forms of prayers and different holdings and interpretations—both conservatively and liberally, about them. But never have we seen any wrong attempts to adulterate the august nature of prayer. All uphold the same identity and importance of prayer as John Chrysostom's: *'Nothing is equal to prayer; for what is impossible it makes possible, what is difficult, easy . . . For it is impossible, utterly impossible, for the man who prays eagerly and invokes God ceaselessly ever to sin.'* Even to this day every religious person would agree with St. Thomas Aquinas, one of the greatest theologians of history who defined prayer as: 'The expression of humanity's desire for God'.

Development of Prayer Practice

With this traditional view on prayer almost all religions around the globe have been making use of prayer. Though it does not belong to any one religion it is at the heart of them all. It knows no boundaries of color, creed, class, or country. It is a universal language and a way of invoking energy so that the motivating force of prayer, referred to as spiritual or love energy, can be sent from us to its target.

> As the human culture grew so did the style of prayer.

However prayer has found its expression in many forms and styles throughout the world. Over the centuries every culture, race, and religion has perfected its own particular style of prayer. It all started through symbols and signs, went through bodily gestures of devotional dances according to the beats of drums and natural music, and culminated in the forms of liturgy, rituals, rubrics, chanting and classical music. As the human culture grew so did the style of prayer.

Community-based Prayer

Practice of prayer in Abramic religions like Christianity has become more impressive and popular in its august form of congregational liturgy which is performed in the church where all the elements of cultural signs, symbols, music, gestures and poetic hymns, beautiful vestments, flowery, decorative and ornamental environments of the House of Prayer, as Jesus called it, are found.

Personal Prayer

While this collective prayer is embraced by the majority of religious people as their favorite, there has been a slack approach to personal and private prayer; hence efforts were taken to immortalize personal prayer's importance and existence, especially in Christianity. This is well-supported in all sacred Books of those religions. According to the Mazkeret Shem ha-Gedolim (a Jewish text book of prayer), Jewish people are urged to pray with every fiber of their being, mind, soul, and spirit. *"In prayer he roared like a lion until the hearts of all who heard him would break and melt like water."* In private mystic contemplative prayer, this minority group of pray-ers seek communion with God, one's Higher Self.

In the history of the church we notice many attempts have been pursued to resurrect the personal and private form of prayer. Prayer movements as shoots of private prayer-efforts have mushroomed recent years in different facets such as: prophetic prayer, prophetic intercession, soaking prayer, sozo prayer, and so on. Sadly many of them are not based on Biblical or traditional teachings of the Church. However one among those movements is 'contemplative prayer' which is founded on both the Bible and Christian Tradition.

Contemplative Prayer

The verb "to contemplate" is defined in the Webster's 1828 Dictionary as "to view or consider with continued attention; to study; to meditate on." Contemplative Prayer is also known as centering prayer, listening prayer, breath prayer, and prayer of the heart. In this process of praying one attempts to offer sufficient room for the Supreme Being to enter into oneself so that one can listen to God's voice clearly and beg Him personally for all the graces to be filled. About this prayer form Abbot Thomas Keating writes: *"Contemplative Prayer is a prayer of silence, an experience of God's presence."* He also adds: "[Contemplative Prayer] ... *is a process of inner transformation, a conversation initiated by God and leading, if we consent, to divine union. One's way of seeing reality changes in the process. A restructuring of consciousness takes place which empowers one to perceive, relate and respond with increasing sensitivity to the divine presence in, through, and beyond everything that exists."*

Ejaculatory Prayer

There is, in the history of the Church, another form of private prayer uninterruptedly proposed and practiced. It is labeled as 'ejaculatory prayer.' They are short prayers labeled also as 'Invocations' and 'aspirations'. They are meant to be memorized and repeated throughout the day in order to uninterruptedly turn devotees' thoughts toward God. Christians esteem this 'ejaculatory prayer'-form a secret and sudden lifting up of their souls' desires to God, upon any emergency that may occur in earthly life. It helps them to maintain fellowship with God, without any interruption of their lawful undertakings. It may also be an ammunition to fend off temptations and to marshal their hearts for a more committed and intensive participation in regular duties of prayer, labor and witnessing to the Kingdom.

> Christians esteem this 'ejaculatory prayer'-form
> a secret and sudden lifting up of their souls' desires to God,
> upon any emergency that may occur in earthly life.

From the early days of Christianity, Christians came to the understanding of the great power of the very name of Jesus and the recitation of his Name was itself a form of individual prayer. They strongly believed the words of Paul who proclaimed that *"God greatly exalted him and bestowed on him the name that is above every name, that at the name of Jesus every knee should bend, of those in heaven and on earth and under the earth."* (Phi. 2: 9-10)

According to their conviction, if they fill the otherwise wasted moments of their day with the Holy Name of Jesus they would keep their thoughts focused on Him and grow in His grace. In modern times still Christians, especially those belonging to Greek Orthodox Church, use the same technique in their prayers as a powerful form of prayer. It is customarily called "The Jesus Prayer," which in middle ages the Greek Saints had perfected as a formula of simple repetition: *"O Lord Jesus Christ, Son of the living God, have mercy on me, a sinner."*

This continuous interior Prayer of Jesus, as described in Meditation and Spiritual Life by Swami Yatiswarannanda, is a constant uninterrupted calling upon the Divine name of Jesus with the lips, in the spirit, in the heart; while forming a mental picture of His constant presence and imploring His grace, during every occupation, at all times, in all places, even during sleep.

In his writing on Spiritual exercises St Alphonsus de Liguori writes: *"Cultivate the habit of often using the name "Jesus," in silent prayer. When you get up in the morning and retire at night, invoke His Holy Name. And during the day, learn to associate whatever you are doing with a moment's prayerful aspiration, pronouncing the word "Jesus." If you do this, you will not only grow in your belief that Jesus is indeed God who became man, you will experience the spiritual power that is available to those who call upon Him in faith."*

Pope John Paul II, in one of his addresses about the psalms, has said that ancient monks used parts of the psalms as brief prayers "to release a special 'energy' of the Holy Spirit." He also described that this use of the psalms was known as *'ejaculatory prayer'*—from the Latin word *'iaculum'* that is 'a dart'—to indicate concise phrases from the psalms which they could 'let fly' almost like flaming arrows, for example, against temptations.

The same ejaculatory prayer in single word or a phrase or a sentence is also recommended in the act of contemplative prayer to clear one's mind from outer distractions and anxieties and to focus one's attention and discipline one's concentration toward the 'Grand Self' within oneself. *"Choose a sacred word or phrase. Consistently use the same word throughout the prayer. Begin silently to repeat your sacred word or phrase."*—Mark Yaconelli, Youth Specialties, National Pastor's Convention.

In some world religions of the East this ejaculatory prayerstyle is a popular and centuries-old practice: In Islam, for example, the Sufi mystics have for centuries employed the repetition of Allah or Ali as a means of getting spiritual illumination.

In Hinduism the most common invocation is *'Sri Rama Jayam'*, which may mean to some 'Victory to Rama' that their god Rama should live always; he should always stay in their hearts and show them the right paths; in addition, he should survive in the hearts of believers forever. To many this invocation may indicate a 'victory by Rama', that every success they encounter in daily endeavors and achievements is being bestowed by their god Rama. They are convinced Rama will bring to them nothing but victory as upshot of their every act. Therefore many Hindus take a vow to write this ejaculatory prayer for some millions of times or to chant it every day atleast for 108 times whenever possible or before starting a work and do so religiously and sincerely hoping to get blessings of Lord Rama whom the Hindus adore as the seventh avatar (incarnation) of God. Many devotees want get some 'presence' of Rama in them or their environs before they start a work; some others pray this short prayer whenever their minds are in turmoil; and in crises if they pray with this invocation magically their worries and burdens lessened. It is said that whenever Gandhi became ill he would refuse his medication and tell his aides to leave him alone. He would repeat the mantra, a name of a Hindu god 'RAM', and he would emerge in good health. He called this practice "the poor man's medicine."

Primary factor of Prayer

As we notice in the world of religions there are many forms of prayer according to its aim and content: There are prayers of petition; prayers of mourning; prayers of complaining; prayers of thanking; prayers of wonderings; prayers of worshipping; prayers of fighting; prayers of surrendering and intercessory and contemplative prayers.

> Generally people begin their prayer from one of those dimensions and end it with another; sometimes they keep both integrated together in the whole process of prayer.

Despite the fact the style and method of prayer has been changed and enhanced, its nature and identity remains the same. All those forms of prayer, used by religions for centuries, are designed to be used to raise oneself closer to the Divine and to help others (intercession). In using any form of prayer the 'pray-ers' try to include their dual dimension of humanity-body and soul, plus their personal and social characteristics. Generally people begin their prayer from one of those dimensions and end it with another; sometimes they keep both integrated together in the whole process of prayer; for example, in liturgical prayer they become part of the congregation as social beings but hold on to their personal and interior involvement during the rituals. The same way their first step in private contemplative prayer is physical effort of lisping prayers and exercise of the mind in meditation but as their final focus they reach all the way to the most deeper stage of the soul: standing in front of God and many times seeing His Face in supernatural manner.

B. The Concept of QualityPrayer

Saul Bellow, a Nobel Prizewinner, when he was interviewed by Antonio Monda for the book *'Do You Believe?' is quoted saying: "I pray, but I don't believe in petition prayers; my requirements are trivial. I don't bug God. I consider prayer above all an act of gratitude for existence. Personally I see prayer as an intimate checkup with the headquarters of the universe."*

In this post-modern Age while so many have drifted away from the religious practice of praying, there are millions who still continue to have the recourse to prayer according to their convictions and views as Saul Bellow holds. Here our quest is to find out the effective and pragmatic use of any form of prayer. As Christians we have to hold the views of God-in-Jesus regarding our prayerstyle. That is truly the 'qualityprayer'.

Before I chalk out my deliberations about qualityprayer I would like to quote the words of Pope Benedict XVI on prayer and acknowledge them gratefully as the summary of all my explanations about qualityprayer: *"Prayer is an inner attitude before being a series of practices or formulas; it is a manner of being in God's presence before the carrying out of acts of worship or speaking words. Prayer has its center and sinks its roots in the depth of the* person. *That is why it is not easily decipherable and, for the same reason, why it can be the object of misunderstanding and manipulation . . . The experience of prayer is a challenge for all, a 'grace' that must be invoked, a gift of the One to whom we address ourselves."*

Most probably since the 1970s the term 'quality' is commonly used as noun to denote excellence or eminence or worth of some person or something and also to mean their feature or characteristic or attribute. In informal dialogue or even sometimes in formal writings we come across the word 'quality' being placed as an adjective, to qualify nouns like time, product and so on.

> *"Prayer is an inner attitude before being a series of practices or formulas; it is a manner of being in God's presence before the carrying out of acts of worship or speaking words."* (Pope Benedict XVI)

'Quality time' informally refers to time spent with loved ones such as, lifepartners and children or close relatives and friends. It is a time which is well spent exclusively paying full and undivided attention to the person in their interest. Thus this time becomes special, productive and profitable. 'Quality Product' signifies the 'standardness' of a something created, produced or manufactured. It means that particular product is guaranteed for its results for which it has been produced.

In the same vein when authors and preachers use 'Quality' as an adjective to prayer they mean 'a time appropriately-spent with God to enhance our relationship with Him'; in qualityprayer God's devotees give to Him qualitytime and not merely quantitytime of their undivided attention; and if a prayer aims at quality-results as it is intended by the Almighty then it is considered as qualityprayer. Qualityprayer is a balanced plan designed to cultivate inner strength and guidance, as well as to radiate power outward to help, heal, and transform our world.

QualityPrayer is a prayer of 'Intimacy'

Generally prayer, especially praying in solitude, is misused by many as a time of brooding over our past hurts; some others waste that moment simply selfpitying; a few consider this hour as a time of taking pleasure in patting ourselves and making some plans for our worldly affairs as the rich man in Jesus' parable does: *"There was a rich man whose land produced a bountiful harvest. He asked himself, 'What shall I do, for I do not have space to store my harvest?' And he said, 'this is what I shall do: I shall tear down my barns and build larger ones. There I shall store all my grain and other goods and I shall say to myself, "Now as for you, you have so many good things stored up for many years, rest, eat, drink, be merry!"* (Lk. 12: 16-19)

Prayer and its quality depend on its endresult-experience which largely flows out of our attitudes about God and our relationship to Him in religion: Some pray a *'prayer of conspiracy'* in which they seek their own gratification; they esteem their personal contribution and human effort greater than God's intervention; they cheat others as if they pray; they participate in prayer for the sake of pleasing others. There is also the *'prayer of begging'* through which people seek from God all support possible for their lives. They want him to clear their doubts about him. To them He must do lots of magic and instant miracles through his 'super-power.' He must forgive them immediately when they beg forgiveness. He also should accept their intercessory prayers for others and perform miracles in their lives too.

In some others' prayer, we can label it the *'prayer of Demands'* we observe the use of their rights of being the children of God and of being good Christians. As spoiled brats they demand all that they need but not doing their duties as God expects them to do. Many pray the *'prayer of Negotiations'* in which they make a contract with God telling him if he does what they ask they would do what he wants. In other words they put the Lord to the test as the devil tempted Jesus in the desert.

There is also another kind of prayer used by many religious people. It is called the *'prayer of morality.'* In this prayer they concentrate only on themselves how to be good; they do not want anyone to see them doing wrong; they always judge themselves and others by the criterion of morals.

Legalism is their code of conduct. They forget God and His love as the core and center of their life. Their priority in prayer is to see what they are before God and others.

Another unqualified and unprofitable prayer most of the religious people hold on to is the *'prayer of supremacy.'* In this people play a game with God using their labels as trump cards—'chosen', 'elected', 'called' and 'predestined'. While they pray they feel great and therefore they recite some prayers of pity and mercy for all others whom they consider as 'pagans', 'cursed', 'going to hell', and 'not redeemed.' This sense of supremacy largely comes out of the religion of morality and good behavior.

Qualityprayer which I am exposing here does not belong to the list of the above-mentioned prayers. Qualityprayer is a *'prayer of intimacy'* in which as saints did, we seek God, knowing He also seeks us; we long for God as He longs for us; we pray incessantly; we feel every minute of the day that God and ourselves are one; living for each other. In this prayer we get an experience which is called 'Ecstasy', in Greek *'ekstasis'*. This word usually is used by Church Fathers to describe God's love within the Trinity.

The main identity of qualityprayer is a dialogue or intimate conversation between two loving persons: God and me. During this prayer time while God keeps silent but actively and intensely present due to his love that is so deep and ineffably so intimate, the human person is involved so intimately that his intimacy with God supersedes fear and falseness in God's presence. In OT we notice this element of intimacy in the prayer-deals of Biblical heroes like Abraham, Isaac, Joseph, Moses, Gideon, David, Esther and many others.

> Qualityprayer is a *'prayer of intimacy'* in which as saints did, we seek God, knowing He also seeks us; we long for God as He longs for us; we pray incessantly; we feel every minute of the day that God and ourselves are one; living for each other.

There was a wonderful relationship found between Abraham and God; Abraham was at all times persevering in his deals with God and both conversed with each other with so much intimacy and confidence; there was a give-and-take policy, and a friendly but personal negotiation going on in their conversation. This is literally called interpersonal communication where we find emotions; rationality and intimacy meet together, where two persons enjoy a spiritual intercourse.

The same experience is also found in Moses' life. In the book of Exodus: 17: 8-13, we read how Moses was praying on the mountain and "as long as Moses kept his hands raised up, Israel had the better of the fight, but when he let his hands rest, Amalek had the better of the fight." This expresses the intense relationship found between God and Moses; it is also a sign that tells us how in prayer both God and human can control each other.

Also, in the book of Genesis 32: 25-31, we find Jacob really fighting with the divine person from heaven. Even if the other wants to leave, Jacob is so persistent in not letting him go until he blessed Jacob. Therefore the Divine relents to Jacob and names him as Israel which means *'one who has contended with divine and has prevailed'*. There are many more examples, found in the Bible, which narrate many incidents in which God and men conversed as intimate as possible.

QualityPrayer is Lifeline, Loveline and Hotline between God and humans

In Qualityprayer two lifepartners 'God and me' are in intensive, intimate and surely very active communication and communion: God speaks and we listen; we speak and God listens. God extends his hands and we take hold of them; we lift up our hands and God grabs them. God manifests himself to us exclusively and we feel his presence intimately; we show our nakedness, sinfulness, limitation and weakness to God and he cleanses us, clothes us and brightens us with his shining light. In order to confirm this reality of prayer, God brings to us in the Bible many rolemodels of such qualityprayer. For example:

Abram: In the Scriptures we observe Abram was always a man of prayer. Both in his time of troubles and joys he connected himself to his Creator through qualityprayer. At one stage of his life, as we read in Gen. 15: 1-3, he was in agony facing two bitter lifesituations. First he felt himself fish out of water in his life because in accordance with the Lord's will he had journeyed from his native land to a place of foreigners; secondly he was very much upset for not having a child from Sarah his beloved wife even after many years of married life.

We are told God took the first initiative to communicate to Abram. God says to him: *"Fear not, Abram! I am your shield; I will make your reward very great."* But Abram with all his mourning and groaning responded very disparagingly, *"O Lord GOD, what good will your gifts be, if I keep on being childless and have as my heir the steward of my house, Eliezer?"* Abram continued, *"See, you have given me no offspring, and so one of my servants will be my heir."* Despite his complaints, God listened to him because, as the Scripture says, he found God's favor due to his faith and love toward his Creator. Abram's encountering and covenant-making with God proved to be a life-altering moment for him. No longer being a wandering Aramean, Abraham would become the father of a people whose faith, like his, continues to transform lives and change the world for the better.

David: Almost in all David's Psalms we hear his qualityprayer. His approach to prayer is found in his Psalms among which I have chosen Psalms 23 and 27 as the summarized pattern for his prayerstyle. His qualityprayer consists of:

> Strong conviction about who God is to him: *The LORD is my light and my salvation; The LORD is my life's refuge."* (Ps. 27: 1-2) *"The LORD is my shepherd; there is nothing I lack. In green pastures he makes me lie down; to still waters he leads me; he restores my soul. He guides me along right paths for the sake of his name."* (Ps. 23: 1-3)

> His one and only motivation for his act of praying: *"One thing I ask of the LORD; this I seek: To dwell in the LORD's house all the days of my life, to gaze on the LORD's beauty, to visit his temple."* (Ps. 27: 4)

> Faith, hope and trust imbedded in his spirit: *"Whom should I fear? When evildoers come at me to devour my flesh, these my enemies and*

foes themselves stumble and fall. Though an army encamp against me, my heart does not fear; though war be waged against me, even then do I trust." "For God will hide me in his shelter in time of trouble. He will conceal me in the cover of his tent; and set me high upon a rock." (27: 4-5) "Even though I walk through the valley of the shadow of death, I will fear no evil, for you are with me; your rod and your staff comfort me." (23: 4)

A spiritual joy of contentment: "Even now my head is held high above my enemies on every side! I will offer in his tent sacrifices with shouts of joy; I will sing and chant praise to the LORD. (27: 6)

A torrent of petitions: "Hear my voice, LORD, when I call; have mercy on me and answer me . . . Do not hide your face from me; do not repel your servant in anger. You are my salvation; do not cast me off; do not forsake me, God my savior! LORD, show me your way; lead me on a level path because of my enemies. Do not abandon me to the desire of my foes; malicious and lying witnesses have risen against me." (27:7-12)

Sweet agony of waiting: "I believe I shall see the LORD's goodness in the land of the living. Wait for the LORD, take courage; be stouthearted, wait for the LORD!" (27: 13-14) "Indeed, goodness and mercy will pursue me all the days of my life; I will dwell in the house of the LORD for endless days." (23: 6)

Jesus: In the Gospel we hear about Jesus who was constantly praying to his Father not just weekly or a few times daily but ceaselessly. Surely he prayed daily at specified places and specified hours. *In those days he departed to the mountain to pray, and he spent the night in prayer to God.* (Lk. 6: 12) *Rising very early before dawn, he left and went off to a deserted place, where he prayed.* (Mk. 1: 35)

Jesus faced many bitter situations and he never drifted away from qualityprayer. In the Gospel of Luke one such qualityprayertime of Jesus is portrayed. It happened in a very critical moment of his life. As he was at the brink of his passion and death and at the premonition of his Father he already started predicting his final shameful end to his disciples, he was feeling troubled as human he was; in addition he was so much frustrated noticing his own disciples not relishing what he was predicting about his ignominious death and many of them were preventing him to choose his end that way. Hence he needed his inner strength and trust in his Father to be enlivened; with this specific purpose in mind he climbed up a mountain to be alone with his Father. He too brought with him his three special friends, not for his own safety or consolation but he wanted them to be convinced that the death he was about to face was according to his Father's will.

During this prayer-moment two lifepartners God and Jesus communed with each other in lifeline and hotline as well. God offered Jesus a heavenly bliss and beauty which He usually gives to his lovers as it is traditionally called 'mystic experience.' In addition the Father sent two of his men, Moses and Elijah from heaven who appeared in glory and spoke of Jesus' exodus that he was going to accomplish in Jerusalem. God dispatched these two men to Jesus so that he could be more convinced of the greatness and importance of his own death by hearing from the mouths of his rolemodels.

Truly Jesus was strengthened and got the release of his spiritual power. His growing awareness of himself and his role as God's Word of love for the world was becoming evident in him. His deepening commitment to the mission he had been sent to accomplish made Jesus transparent. He glowed with passion and purpose that would enable him to continue his journey to Jerusalem, to the cross and to death.

Paul: We hear Paul say in many of his letters that he was like Jesus; "imitate me' he said to his Christians; he made his entire life as a ceaseless prayer and living sacrifice to God; in prayer he was taken to third heaven; in tears he was interceding for the followers of Jesus; in prayer Jesus visited him and God directly talked to him. In his Letters we hear him advising them to be imitators of God and imitators of Jesus Christ. He was so much imitating Jesus in his prayer-life that his spiritual power had been released from within and therefore he could feel 'I live not I but Christ lives in me.' Therefore as he must have been in the intensive hotline-prayer habit in prison Paul could daringly order the Christians of Philippi to imitate him. As he was high-spirited and filled with the joy of the Spirit due to his qualityprayer while he was undergoing sufferings in prison he could suggest to his Christians 'Rejoice, I say it again, rejoice.'

> During this prayer-moment two lifepartners God and Jesus communed with each other in lifeline and hotline as well. God offered Jesus a heavenly bliss and beauty which He usually gives to his lovers as it is traditionally called 'mystic experience.'

From all the prayer-experiences of Biblical rolemodels we conclude that qualityprayer is not one of many mechanisms and strategies we employ to reap our life's quests. Rather it is a lifeline activity between Creator and Creature; it is a hotline sharing between two lovers the Divine and the human; it is a pipeline of healing graces and living waters from the Life-Source and the little lives. If such interactions are genuinely found in prayer, the persons who benefit the most is none other than us. The greatest result that comes out of true prayer is the release of God's Presence from within.

By nature we are endowed with God's presence and His shared Gifts, because as the Bible says, 'we are made in the likeness and image of God.' These heavenly treasures stay within us as hidden power and perhaps as sleeping beauty, unless and until we become fully aware of them and begin to release them. It's like the gas and oil lying inert in the depths of the earth waiting for its release. As there is the possibility of a natural leak of oil and gas and the natural springs of water are found on the surface of the earth, we can encounter numerous cases of marvelous deeds and events that leach from the Throne of God occurring in human lives without human efforts of prayer.

However in the revelation of God in Jesus we are advised to pray for marvelous deeds to be experienced in our lives. Among those miraculous deeds the main event that demands prayer from us is the change and renewal of humans. It is largely about our spiritual dimension that is hidden in every individual born human. It is exactly like a well buried inside of every person. Jesus points out in the Gospel: *"Whoever believes in me, as scripture says: 'Rivers of living water will flow from within him."* (John 7: 38)

I love to compare the inner well Jesus indicates to the oil and gas wells as my personal and a post-modern metaphor. Interestingly, in the 7th century petroleum was known in Japan as 'burning water.' We are aware of the uses of oil and gas in our daily lives.

The earliest oil wells were drilled percussively by hammering a cable tool into the earth. Soon after, cable tools were replaced with rotary drilling, which could drill boreholes to much greater depths and in less time. Until the 1970s, most oil wells were vertical; in this new age of science modern directional drilling technologies allow for strongly deviated wells which can, given sufficient depth and with the proper tools, actually become horizontal.

In many wells the natural pressure of the subsurface reservoir is high enough for the oil or gas to flow to the surface. In some lower pressure sites common solutions like downhole pumps, gas lift, or surface pump jacks are installed to the flow of the oil and gas. Once the petroleum springs out of the well it is connected to a distribution network of pipelines and tanks to supply the product to refineries, natural gas compressor stations or oil export terminals.

In the same way Godliness and all the powers that flow from it are hidden as the heavenly treasure within every human. It's a divinely-revealed and humanly-experienced truth that these spiritual resources are released by the tool of qualityprayer. During such spiritual release we feel physically and emotionally being liberated from sinful burdens, from guilty consciousness, from fear, from anxiety and surely healed from sicknesses. As an immediate result we become elated with joy. We also notice the spiritual power within us being released from us; we see visions of God, saints and all heavenly bliss and thus being led into spiritual ecstasy. In addition, this release of spiritual power within us performs certain unfathomable deeds in the form of miracles, not for ourselves but always for the benefit of others. At that moment, so many of our intercessory prayers for others are answered.

Sometime back I read in one of the church signboards, *'prayer is the Stop that keeps you going.'* That's hundred percent true! A qualityprayer strengthens us in our convictions that our citizenship is in heaven and that God walks with us in our onward journey to that home sweet home of heaven; thus it keeps us going in the midst of drudgeries; in troubles; in fears; in battles; in the valley of tears and darkness and at the brink of death. Through the qualityprayer the greatest miracle we can experience in this earthly life is that we turn out to be one day an intimate partner with the Lord in prayer.

> Godliness and all the powers that flow from it are hidden as the heavenly treasure within every human. It's a divinely-revealed and humanly-experienced truth that these spiritual resources are released by the tool of qualityprayer.

Our external transformations like our physical appearance, our physical strength, our portfolio, our accomplishment in worldly affairs, are natural effects and results of our birth as the seasons change and are transformed. But our inner transformation, namely changing the inner soul into the sanctuary of God, turning our stony heart into a loving and melted one, becoming fully groomed in the likeness of Christ, is a precious gift from God. That can happen only by the qualityprayer. Unless and until we make some specific stops at specific times, at specific places and with specific purposes for qualityprayer and stay with the Lord as much time as possible we can never become transformed as needed. If we don't persevere in such stops and pullovers as our daily habit, we will miss a lot in life. Even if we get some gifts from God at some prayer times, we may lose them and the backlashes will be horrible.

N.T. Wright aptly hints at a wonderful truth about qualityprayer: *'The intimate closeness of God and His powerful and real love we encounter in those prayer moments are resourceful oases; they aren't for nothing. Rather, these* moments of transformative joy and glory are given us so that we can be better servants of God in the world.'

QualityPrayer is our Life in God

QualityPrayer is not just an activity, a ritual, or an obligation. QualityPrayer is not prayers. It is not one among many activities we perform. QualityPrayer is a state of body, mind and soul in union with God the Supreme spiritual. There is no specific time, place or any physical dimension to this union because God is totally spiritual. It is a conscious and unconscious wheel rolling itself with no stop but journeying toward the beyond.

QualityPrayer is as extensive as life itself. It is indeed a habit of being. This can be possible only when we give special time and place consciously to be present in God. When we specify daily certain holy intervals exclusively for communing with God, we uninterruptedly continue to live life in God. Those specific acts of prayer can be performed either being alone in solitude or in group worship. Thus regular moments of praying lead us to qualityprayerlife which is nothing but life in God. It connects and reconnects us to God. It rectifies disintegration and builds up integration between our two forms of life: bodily and spiritual. It's a place and time where and when an integration of word and action, faith and practice occurs. It recharges our spiritual battery to run our wheel of spirituality. It is our daily time to be seduced by God who is an aggressive lover.

In qualityprayer our life is consecrated totally to the Lord, consciously being present, moving and having our being in him, through him and with him. This is what Paul refers to when he writes: *"Pray without ceasing."* (1 Thess. 5:17) *"We and everydayness belongs to Him,"* said Karl Rahner. The entire life of the disciples, committed to Jesus, becomes prayer as they abide in Jesus like the vine and branch. A summation of Christian life is described by Jesus this way: *"Remain in me, as I remain in you. Just as a branch cannot bear fruit on its own unless it remains on the vine, so neither can you unless you remain in me. I am the vine, you are the branches. Whoever remains in me and I in him will bear much fruit, because without me you can do nothing."* (Jn. 15: 4-8.)

A saint was playing chess with a friend, while a group of elders were chatting nearby. The subject of their discussion turned to what each would do if told he had to die within that very hour. One said, 'I would hurry home to join with my family; another one told, 'I would go quickly to confirm that my property is in order; the third one remarked, 'I would immediately confess my sins; the fourth proudly said, 'I would fall to my knees and pray devoutly.' Finally they turned to the saint for his reply. He said quite simply that he would continue his game of chess. It was a shock for all. Again the saint broke the silence and explained: "I have built into my life moments when I play chess with great pleasure and gratitude to God for the leisure time. And therefore I cannot imagine anything better than being called away to God in the midst of something God Himself has so graciously provided." This is the wisdom of very high order that characterizes qualityprayer.

Qualityprayer is a 'searching Prayer'

QualityPrayer can also be defined as a precious and exclusive time in our life to be engaged in search of God the Beyond. As God has created us in His likeness and image we hunger and thirst for possessing Him and His Gifts as well. There are so many gifts in God's list to share with us. They can be categorized under three headings: Wisdom, Power and Joy. All of them in a creaturely way are enjoyed by us either temporarily or incompletely. However our hearts crave for their totality.

They are esteemed by Christ as precious pearls. Jesus wanted us to be in search of those fine pearls: "*The kingdom of heaven is like a merchant searching for fine pearls. When he finds a pearl of great price, he goes and sells all that he has and buys it.*" (Matt. 13: 45-46) From his saying we understand these gifts of God are hoarded already in the kingdom of heaven. They are like treasure hidden somewhere. "*The kingdom of heaven is like a treasure buried in a field, which a person finds and hides again, and out of joy goes and sells all that he has and buys that field.*" (Matt. 13: 44) Now where is this treasure-filled kingdom? When we connect the previous sayings of Jesus about the 'Treasure Land' to his proclamation of the presence of this kingdom we can get an answer: He declares, *"The kingdom of heaven is within you,-in the midst of you and at hand."* This means the kingdom of heaven which is a 'treasure land' is hidden within us and the heavenly pearls of God are stockpiled in us.

As the Book of Wisdom advises, we can never find and possess the gifts of God unless otherwise we strenuously search for them as gifts. *"My son, if you receive my words and treasure my commands, turning your ear to wisdom, inclining your heart to understanding; yes, if you call for intelligence, and to understanding raise your voice; if you seek her like silver, and like hidden treasures search her out, then will you understand the fear of the LORD; the knowledge of God you will find; for the LORD gives wisdom, from his mouth come knowledge and understanding."* (Wis. 2: 1-6)

Those heavenly pearls are not found anywhere, outside, not even in religions, gurus or philosophers they are truly and wholistically present within us. There may be many labels given to this inner chamber of ours: Soul, Inner sanctuary, the Temple of the Holy Spirit, etc. The best name among all these is what Jesus dictated to us: 'The Kingdom of God.' The one and only valid and effective means to find those hidden pearls of heaven is to enter deeply into that interior place of God's kingdom within us. Many sages call this effort as meditative prayer of entering into our consciousness. I name it *'the InTravel prayer.'* It is a qualityprayer in its totality, in its wholeness and at its best. About his I will discuss in the chapter on the method of qualityprayer.

The problem we find is that we do not want to search for God in different ways. Once we get a way, we are stuck there. We love to go on with our old pattern of searching Him. We are satisfied with conventional and traditional ways of seeing and hearing Him. We read an event of prayer in the life of the Prophet Elijah whom the Lord wanted to search for Him in new ways. Yahweh had been revealing Himself in the time past through the earthquake, storm, fire and so on. The prophet thought he could find the Lord in those conventional situations. But God's ways are not human ways. On that particular day God revealed Himself to the

Prophet in the gentle breeze, which means, in the stillness and silence of life situation.

> Those heavenly pearls are not found anywhere, outside, not even in religions, gurus or philosophers they are truly and wholistically present within us. The best name for it is what Jesus dictated to us: 'The Kingdom of God.'

Searching God does not mean just to recite prayers, to attend mass, or receive sacraments. It is simply and fervently holding on to our faith in God and through and with Jesus we continue our ordinary duties in the situations that God has placed us. We go on telling Him, "I will not let you go, nor let me go.

QualityPrayer is our presence in God's absence

Many times we feel discouraged at the absence, coldness, silence and distance of God to our prayers. Yet we can start loving his silence in this following way: While 99.99% he is absent and imperceptible, that .01% of His coming and going in the midst of our clouds, hubbubs, and even in stormy winds, gives us great energy to move on through those dark days of our life. That dream about God, that vision about His Glory and that hope and faith in His ever-loving presence takes us through that major portion of our life in His absence. Prayer is not something we do, but it is a time we spend in His absence. While we spend .01% of our lifetime in His absence through prayer, we become His presence in the world for the rest of our days.

We read in many holy people's lives, that they had intimate vision and intense conversation with God in solitude of prayer. Even recently, an author became an instant bestseller as he wrote three volumes on *'his conversation with God'*. Humans love to converse with God, debate and argue with Him. Jesus too wanted man and women to converse that way with His Father, calling Him 'Abba Father'. However, one thing we should know that all these human acts-praying, conversing and imploring before God, are performed at a spiritual level and not in a physical and tangible way. It's all done in the impressive absence of God. This means God is, though absent to our physical dimension, present spiritually. Because all-knowing God knows our limitation at spiritual level, he takes full charge of that period of prayer. He is fully engaged in us. As we come out of prayertime and begin to go through our physical and material engagements, He begins to be present fully through our physicality. He runs the whole show. Outside of their prayer circle, 'prayer-persons' do not themselves move and have their being; it's the Lord who is actively present.

QualityPrayer to us therefore is our conscious presence in God's absence; and all the rest we do is our conscious absence in God's presence. We perform all our duties; we play the roles we have to play in this world as if God does. Paul very well said: *"Yet I live, no longer I, but Christ lives in me; insofar as I now live in the flesh, I live by faith in the Son of God who has loved me and given himself up for me".* (Gal. 2: 20) Jesus is quoted saying: *"When you have done all you have been commanded, say 'we are unprofitable servants; we have done what we were obliged to do."* (Lk.17: 10) This is the way we should integrate God in our life: To pray in His absence but to act in His presence.

QualityPrayer is Communication toward communing

QualityPrayer is not communication, but communion with God. Prayer in our life is an environment wherein, a communication process goes on between us and God. It is indeed an interpersonal communication of two genuine persons communicating heart-to-heart, one-to-one intimately. This is performed at spiritual level of two beings. It surely starts with communication by words, actions, symbols and various modes but the endresult is both communicator and receiver communing with each other, two becoming one by sharing each other's self.

We must be very clear about a truth on prayer. We pray not for God's sake, but for our own. In one of the Prefaces at weekday masses the priest reads: *Father, you have no need of our praise, yet our desire to thank you is itself your gift. Our prayer of thanksgiving adds nothing to your greatness but makes us grow in your grace.* This prayer underlines the truth that we pray because, voicing our praise, expressing our need and offering our thanks and prayers, helps us to know who we are before God and all others. We pray not to inform God of anything but to sensitize our own hearts and minds and souls to the many propositions of God, be they large or small. In sum the ultimate goal of prayer is a mechanism to integrate our will with God's will, our life-view with his view and our plan with his.

A QualityPrayer is a dialogue or intimate conversation between two loving persons: *God and me.* During this prayer time while God keeps silent but actively and intensely present due to his love that is so deep and ineffably so intimate, the human person is involved so intimately that his intimacy with God supersedes fear and falseness in God's presence.

QualityPrayer is 'dating with' the Lord

There is a primal desire in every human not only to enter into communication with another spirit-being, to share ideas and ideals, but, above all, to enter into the deepest communion, a union with. Our lives are boring, empty and meaningless until we enter into an oneness with another. This is why we date with persons who we think and esteem one day would be the partners of this oneness. Dating is an act of two persons who intensively tend to exchange their desire to love and to be loved, their personal longing to live with another spirit-being and their need to be loved and cared. Qualityprayer is a similar event of dating that happens between God and the human person. Dating with the Lord means being with the Lord; living with the Lord; sharing with the Lord; and rejoicing with the Lord.

What is usually happening at the time of lovers' dating? If one of them is late or both of them had done something to hurt each other, they ask pardon from each other. They spend their time and energy intensively and intimately for each other. Their whole attention is focused on each other, not even their close relations or any other commitments distract them. They choose a place separating them from the crowd. Though they plan out the dating date, time and location most of the time they do not know well in advance how things will turn out to be in their dating. They let loose their individual whims and fancies and surrender to the other and each one abides by the other's convenience and pleasure. They share their ambitions and dreams, their expectations of life, their likes and dislikes. One speaks while the other listens. They exchange sometimes their love by physical intimacy. They promise each other to continue their relationship that would one day lead to marriage to form a family. Even after getting married if the couples do not continue their dating periodically, researchers say, their marriage would fail.

All the above-mentioned and even more happen in the time of qualityprayer as a human person makes an effort to pray truly and fruitfully. Even our 'other Partner' takes His lead in this regard at times when we do not know how to relate ourselves to Him. That is what Paul points out when he writes: *"In the same way, the Spirit too comes to the aid of our weakness; for we do not know how to pray as we ought, but the Spirit itself intercedes with inexpressible groanings."* (Rom. 8: 26)

If God is love and we have been made by God for Him, then we have been made for love. But love is a call to intimacy. God, being Love, longs to be intimately related to Him and in the OT He wants His people to choose atleast certain days of their lives as special to Him: *This is the day the LORD has made; let us rejoice in it and be glad.* (Ps. 118: 24) The Lord's Day for example has been chosen by God as exclusive day for himself; He blessed it and commanded it to be observed as our date with him. *"Remember to keep holy the Sabbath day. Six days you may labor and do all your work, but the seventh day is a Sabbath of the LORD your God. You shall not do any work, either you, your son or your daughter, your male or female slave, your work animal, or the resident alien within your gates."* (Ex. 20: 8-10)

> Our entire human life is totally a dating with God; we were created only for this purpose to stay with Him forever. This is why deep down in our soul we feel a strong craving for spiritual intimacy.

But Jesus proclaimed that every day is a date with the Lord. He wanted us to be one with him as he is with his Father. *"That they may all be one, as you, Father, are in me and I in you, that they also may be in us, that the world may believe that you sent me. And I have given them the glory you gave me, so that they may be one, as we are one, I in them and you in me, that they may be brought to perfection as one, that the world may know that you sent me, and that you loved them even as you loved me."* (Jn. 17: 21-23) Jesus, emphasizing his longing for dating with his followers, called them, 'no more servants, but friends;' we hear in the Gospels he chose his disciples not just to learn his teachings and go out to witness but mainly 'to be with him.' (Mk. 3: 13-15) During his qualityprayer of agony in the Garden of Gesthemane he very sorrowfully and disappointedly remarked: 'Can you not stay with me even an hour?'

Our entire human life is totally a dating with God; we were created only for this purpose to stay with Him forever. This is why deep down in our soul we feel a strong craving for spiritual intimacy. As the followers of Jesus, who is the Face of God, our Christian life, starting from Baptism, is a dating with the Lord Jesus. Paul insists this mystical dating: *For I am jealous of you with the jealousy of God, since I betrothed you to one husband to present you as a chaste virgin to Christ. But I am afraid that, as the serpent deceived Eve by his cunning, your thoughts may be corrupted from a sincere (and pure) commitment to Christ.* (2 Cor. 11: 2-3)

In qualityprayer we esteem the Lord as our true lover. What we do in dating with the Lord is "just being with Him.' We spend our time, place and energy exclusively for him and with him. We stay with him. We abide with him. We commune with him. We are silently listening to him. We too speak a lot with him sharing all our likes and dislikes, ambitions and dreams. Prayer time is the dating time with the Lord. When we love God in Jesus we enter into the very heart of God. This is called qualityprayer. Loving God is prayer. Living with God is prayer. Being with God is prayer. Being present to each other is the one and only element in any 'dating'. All other activities follow it. St. Augustine very well said: *"True, whole prayer is nothing but love."*

St. John Vianney was a village pastor in France. He was renowned as a holy and wise counselor and hundreds of people used to come to his church for confession. Each afternoon as he entered the church, he would see an elderly man sitting in a pew before the tabernacle. When he left the church several hours later, the man would still be there. One day, St. John went up to the man and asked, "What do you do sitting here all afternoon, day after day?" "I don't do anything," he replied, "I just look at God and God looks at me."

QualityPrayer is Sweet Agony of Waiting

Will Rogers used to say: *"In Oklahoma if you don't like the current weather; just wait for 10 minutes; the weather will be transformed".* We cannot assert this way about the results of prayer. However as the Book of Habakkuk we hope one day we will be gifted with what we desire: *"If it seems slow, wait for it; it will surely come, it will not delay"* (Hab. 2:3). Ours is a culture unwilling to wait. In our impatience, we too quickly conclude that if the promise is not fulfilled now, it will not be fulfilled. But the future cannot be forced; it lies in the hands of God. Abraham's belief in this truth empowered his whole life. Surely we can similarly entrust ourselves and our future to God.

Qualityprayer can be defined as a sweet agony of waiting. In history, prayer becomes so intensive when people are in a critical socio-cultural situation, as those Jews in OT time being tossed around by foreign invasions. They were praying continuously for liberation and freedom. Their prayer was: *"Why do you let us wander, O LORD, from your ways, and harden our hearts so that we fear you not? Return for the sake of your servants, the tribes of your heritage".* After the time of the Lord Jesus, when Christians were persecuted both by the Jews and the pagans as well, their prayer was a sweet agony of waiting.

Even today the same waiting-factor remains alive in millions of people toward the countdown of Christ's coming in their day-today lives. There are too many people among us who are terminally ill; people who wander about from one country to another as refugees for safety and security; people whose national economy is in downfall; people who are hungering and thirsting for spiritual strength; people who are recently separated, divorced or deserted from family relationship; people who are in the midst of gun-smoke and warcries; people who are fighting against all kinds of diseases and plagues. It is keeping them in his mind Jesus has said: *"Beware that your hearts do not become drowsy from carousing and drunkenness and the anxieties of daily life, and that day catch you by surprise like a trap. For that day will assault everyone who lives on the face of the earth. Be vigilant at all times and pray that you have the strength to escape the tribulations that are imminent and to stand before the Son of Man."* (Lk. 21: 34-36)

To all those waiting people, the gospel-countdown of Jesus' arrival is something heart-filling and encouraging and most significant. In no way is this countdown message of Jesus going to be momentous for those people who are content with their lives. It is not a meaningful message for those who are satisfied with what they are and with what they are accomplishing. It is rather an enlivening message only to those who feel they are empty (poor in spirit), and dissatisfied despite all their human possessions, endeavors and enterprises. To them qualityprayer is the backbone and source of energy either to fight against the evils or for surrendering to the will of God saying, 'Lord let this chalice pass away from me; however not my will but your will be done.'

> Qualityprayer is an anticipated hope-filled waiting state of the mind toward the peace, joy, harmony, and glory that are going to be experienced on the day of the Lord's coming.

'Waiting' is always a sweet-agony. Truly we hate to wait. Worse than ever before, at this age of laser speed, we want everything 'micro and macro-waved.' We are terribly irritated to wait at the red traffic signal. We are very much impatient while we wait for our 'physical' test lab results. We prefer priority mail to regular mail. We like to transact our business with the bank via e-mail, instead of standing in cue before the teller desk. We would rather buy a lottery ticket than earning money by slow and steady saving and budgeting. We even dream of a New World order where we could wipe out the onerous act of waiting as our forbearers eliminated slavery, castecism and feudalism out of our society. Yes. We hate to wait!

The amazing fact is that the same burdensome 'waiting' which generates bitterness and irritation in our emotional realm, simultaneously increases the pleasure of anticipated fulfillment.

It was my boyhood experience that when my mom cooked homemade cakes and cookies, the entire house was fully aromatic with the sweet smell coming out of the kitchen. By the time the cookies were out of the oven, I would have traded my birthright for one of them. There is an excitement in waiting for something or somebody that we long to see. There is some sweetness and joy in waiting. This is exactly the feelings we get while we pray, even when we don't get what we asked for. Qualityprayer is an anticipated hope-filled waiting state of the mind toward the peace, joy, harmony, and glory that are going to be experienced on the day of the Lord's coming.

Qualityprayer is the sign and gesture of God's people to express our waiting for His coming in glory and power to bring in us and among us 'the new heavens and new earth.' In all those prayertimes we must first remember God's marvelous deeds done in the past: *"The loving deeds of the LORD I will recall, the glorious acts of the LORD, Because of all the LORD has done for us, the immense goodness to the house of Israel, Which he has granted according to his mercy and his many loving deeds."* (Is. 63: 7) And consequently hold a strong hope and belief that the same God would perform such unbelievable deeds only to those who wait in sincerity and unscrupulous perseverance: *"While you worked awesome deeds we could not hope for, such as had not been heard of from of old. No ear has ever heard, no eye ever seen, any God but you working such deeds for those who wait for him."* (Is. 64: 2-3)

QualityPrayer is a Decision-making Moment

We should consider our daily prayer time is one of decision-making moment. It is the norm of qualityprayer. While we pray, if we are truly in the Lord's presence, the first question that is inspired by the Spirit in our hearts is: "Do you also go away?" When we entered into the redemptive project of God in Jesus through Baptism we made many promises to God either through some proxies (parents, godparents) or personally. There was a long list of our promises and beliefs. But very sadly we notice ourselves having sidetracked in our journey toward our destiny forgetting or ignoring or even rejecting many of our beliefs and promises; many times we have compromised them putting the blame on the influence of the philosophical, cultural and social changes occurring in the society.

> Most of us think drifting away from religion or Church is some sort business deal or shopping around for better purchase. Rather, it is simply getting out of our Center, losing grip of oneself and being disintegrated. This drifting away process either will lead us to depression, to exaggerated hate or even to kill oneself.

We too observe many of our friends have drifted away. Some are gone for good; others are still fluctuating, they are regularly in and out. Only when we are in prayer situation we can see through all these mishaps. We observe many of our own relatives and friends, religious leaders and preachers having closed their door to the Lord and gone far away from their own religious, spiritual and Christian convictions and promises. We begin to doubt the integrity and relevance of our own holdings regarding our religious adherences. Consequently we are agitated, indecisive and hold on to a double-hearted and double-minded life. This is why in qualityprayer time the Lord questions us: "Do you also plan to go away?"

We know well it is not that easy to go away from the Supreme Truth, Supreme Love and Supreme Life. It won't be like that of moving away from our lifelong friends, partners and spouses. Most of us think drifting away from religion or Church is some sort business deal or shopping around for better purchase. Rather, it is simply getting out of our Center, losing grip of oneself and being disintegrated. This drifting away process either will lead us to depression, to exaggerated hate or even to kill oneself. When some of us make wrong decision about our spiritual, religious holdings, naturally we will be prone to make wrong choices regarding our marriage, family, business, ministry and other day-today enterprises.

In qualityprayertime our God in Jesus demands us to answer the question: "Do you also go away?" Should our answer be as that of Peter:

"Where shall we go Lord? Thou hast the Word of Eternal Life"? Or as Israelites answered to Joshua who demanded from them to decide either to serve the Lord or not, *"Far be it from me to forsake the Lord for the service of other gods . . . I will serve the Lord, for he is my Go."*?

The matter of decisionmaking for the Lord is a very risky business. May be, this is why many of us do not want to pray the qualityprayer alone daily in the Lord. Qualityprayertime is a demanding time, questioning time and straightening time. But if only we make prayer of remaining before the Lord as our daily schedule, we will be offered our true 'daily bread from heaven.'

To sum up the nature and identity of QualityPrayer:

Qualityprayer is not communication but communion with God. It connects and reconnects us to God. It rectifies disintegration and builds up integration between our two forms of life: bodily and spiritual. It's a place and time where and when an integration of word and action, faith and practice occurs. It recharges our spiritual battery to run our wheel of spirituality. It is a daily time to be seduced by God who is an aggressive lover.

Qualityprayer is also a decision-making process. It is a time of waiting and hoping. It is a time of transfiguration. It becomes an empty tomb from where we rise to life. It is an immersion into the unknown; a regular exercise of renewing our personal commitment to God; the result of our fear of God; and our solitude going with Jesus to rest. It is for God to be glorified in us and us to be glorified by Him as well.

As one spiritual author puts it, any qualityprayer is 'moving inward; moving upward; moving outward. This is what God will compel us to do when we begin to live with him. Our God is a jealous God. As Jeremiah cries out, He will sometimes dupe us, entice us and corner us but always for moving inward, upward and outward. We must wait patiently for God's time in their life and avoid the mad rush to acquire wealth and money through dubious and ungodly means. *"It is only when things are done at God's time and leading, will one enjoy such blessings."* (Habakkuk 2: 2-3)

C. Foundation of Christian Qualityprayer

Before entering into the discussion of the goal and results of 'QualityPrayer' it is good to know about the Jewish approach to prayer which has been the initial and basic concept of prayer that Jesus and his disciples themselves followed and taught to us. Christianity is the offshoot of Jewish religion. Jesus as well as many of his disciples as the disciples of John the Baptist and probably belonging to the sect of Essenes who were at Jesus' time the guardians of Jewish prayer-system intact. They literally and meticulously followed the prayerstyle of Judaism. When Jesus began his school of thought and reformation of human approach to religion as the kingdom of God he profiled himself as the pioneer of new style of prayer, not destroying the Jewish system of prayer, rather enhancing it with his revelation he brought from his Father. Hence what we handle today as Christian prayerstyle is based on Jewish religion's view and use of prayer.

Jewish faith in Prayer

From both our Scriptures and Jewish Literatures, we observe Jews possessed a very dynamic and never-dying faith in the power of prayer. Prayer, for any Jew of Jesus' time was an integral part of their daily experience and customary practice. Their Jewish belief in prayer emerges from the faith in God's power, His intervention in human history and in their own day today life. According to the Hebrews a human person is a body-soul. He is viewed, unlike the Greek thinking, as a unity, an indivisible whole. In Hebraic tradition, human beings live as souls; they do not have souls.

To a Jew, to know the Lord was not an intellectual assent to Him or His Truths. But it was to experience His power existentially through His creative acts of grace and love. The whole life of a person becomes a part of divine life. From this concept of God and man relationship, we can deduct clearly how the prayer in Jewish life is esteemed not as mere communication but as participation. There was no difference between the sacred and the secular areas of life, and so, between prayer and life. Prayer is relational and not creedal.

This is why they had a belief that we do not pray alone but God prays with us. Paul, a faithful Pharisee, and a well-read Jewish theologian, contends in his letter to Romans 8:26-27: '*In the same way, the Spirit too comes to the aid of our weakness; for we do not know how to pray as we ought, but the Spirit itself interceded with inexpressible groanings. And the one who searches hearts knows what the intention of the Spirit is, because it intercedes for the holy ones according to God's will*".

> To a Jew, to know the Lord was not an intellectual assent to Him or His Truths. But it was to experience His power existentially through His creative acts of grace and love. The whole life of a person becomes a part of divine life.

P.T. Forsyth writes: '*When we speak to God it is really the God who lives in us speaking through us to Himself*'. He also adds, '*The dialogue of grace is really the monologue of the divine nature in self-communing love*'. In prayer we pray, and yet it is not we who pray, but a 'Greater' who prays in us. This is how those Jewish disciples of Jesus thought about prayer.

Besides this, when we look into the Hebrew mind, portrayed in the Bible, we can see that to the Jews everything was theological. Prayer in their life was an integral part from birth to death. In Jewish tradition, prayer and life was one unit. The Psalms speak about a non-stop meditation and prayer. "*Rather, the law of the LORD is his joy; and on his law he meditates day and night.*" (Ps.1: 2). In Old Testament times the Hebrew farmer recited a special prayer in order to remind himself that the occupation of tilling the soil is sacred.

"*Then you shall declare in the presence of the LORD, your God, "My father was a refugee Aramean who went down to Egypt with a small household and lived there as a resident alien. But there he became a nation great, strong and numerous. When the Egyptians maltreated and oppressed us, imposing harsh servitude upon us, we cried to the LORD, the God of our ancestors, and the LORD heard our cry and saw our affliction, our toil and our oppression. Then the LORD brought us out of Egypt with a strong hand and outstretched arm, with terrifying power, with signs and wonders, and brought us to this place, and gave us this land, a land flowing with milk and honey. Now, therefore, I have brought the first fruits of the products of the soil which you, LORD, have given me." You shall set them before the LORD, your God, and you shall bow down before the LORD, your God."* (Deut.26:5-10a)

Reflecting his strong Jewish background, Paul writes, *'so, whether you eat or drink, or whatever you do, do it all for the glory of God'* (1Cor.10:31). He also advises Thessalonians, *'Pray without ceasing'* (1Thess.5:17).

The main feature of Jewish prayer at the time of Jesus was its pervasiveness. There were more than one hundred of those (*berakhot*) 'blessings', which were recited by the Jews throughout the day. A Jew offered prayer in the presence of thunder, lightening, and so on. Prayer was recited before, in, and after every meal. A Jew even was instructed to offer prayer (several times each day) to bless God that one is able to go bathroom and toilet. In addition to these individualistic customs, there are other communal and liturgical prayers which were recited and performed in public, in synagogue and in the temple. There are numerous references to this participatory style of prayer found both in OT and NT Scriptures. Starting from Cain and Abel (Gen.4:3-5), going through the lives of Abraham (Gen.15:1-21), Moses (Ex.33:11-23), Judges, Kings, prophets, Judith (jud.4:13-45), Esther and Maccabees (2Mac.1:23-36), we can trace out how Jewish people were approaching prayer in their lives.

Revival of Jewish view of prayer in Jesus' time and by Jesus

By the prevalent spiritual revolution that was taking place at the time of Jesus, a revivalistic enthusiasm was being sparkled among the Israelites, especially the disciples of Jesus. This is why whenever they noticed Jesus being wrapped up in prayer they tried to ask him some valuable tips for such 'QualityPrayer'(Luke11:1-4).

As we know from the archeological and historical studies undertaken for the past many years, there were three important different schools of thought existing and dominating the ideology and religious value systems of Judaism in the Second Temple Period. While Sadducees who were conservative and belonging to the priestly clan, were keen on observing the Torah to its letters, Pharisees who were named by Sadducees as 'separated ones', were progressive in the sense that they accepted besides written law, the oral interpretation in accordance with the signs of the time. However, the Essenes, who were the third group, stamped as 'pious ones', lived in Qumran Valley, were very charismatic and spiritual in their approach to religion. It was also discovered from the Dead Sea scrolls that these Essenes were influencing very much the Jewish religious values and practices in their lives.

> By the prevalent spiritual revolution that was taking place at the time of Jesus, a revivalistic enthusiasm was being sparkled among the Israelites, especially the disciples of Jesus.

The Qumran community widely is recognized as that of Essenes by Biblical scholars. The Dead Sea Scrolls (QH) offers us lot of prayers and instructions in the form of hymns. Those documents speak about the founder of the community or the author of those hymns as 'the Righteous Teacher'. This is supposed to be referred or prophesied in Habakkuk 2:4. Perhaps this teacher would have died in 135-104 BC. He had his followers who were waiting for the Messiah to come. Many times those Qumran settlements were destroyed by different people. At the time of Jesus, probably these followers of 'Righteous Teacher' would have fled away from those settlements and scattered in and around Palestine and would have been living in hiding places and yet influencing many Jews by their teachings.

Jesus' disciples and his other followers who would have heard about this Righteous Teacher and his teachings through his followers and about John the Baptizer teaching his own disciples. So unhesitently they wanted their Teacher to instruct them on prayer, besides other interested issues of that time. They esteemed Him as the 'Righteous Teacher'. Jesus referred himself as 'teacher'. He was in the eyes of the disciples one such teacher in the scribal traditions (Mt.13:52). The Gospels refer to Jesus as *didaskalos* 'teacher' forty one times and as 'rabbi' sixteen times. He taught like a scribe in synagogues (Mk.1:21), sat to teach (Lk.5:3); expounded Scripture (Lk.4:16-21). Jesus was esteemed as a prophet and wise men by the Jews of His time. He was greater than Solomon (Lk.11:31; 1Cor.1:30). He was an itinerant teacher who was fully engaged in spontaneous teaching which has been one of the forms of learning in Jewish tradition different from scheduled study.

Plus they were attracted and bewildered towards the manner and state in which their teacher was wrapped up in prayer. They were with him all the time. They watched him closely a number of times, especially at the time of his prayer. He has been praying day and night as his routine schedule (Mk.1:35; 6:46; Mt.14:23; Lk.5:16; 6:12; 9:28; 11:1). He too in special occasion (after Baptism) spent forty days and forty nights in the desert (Lk.4:1-2).

They were astounded as they noticed in his prayertimes how his face became so radiant and glowed with divine light; how he was serene and silent for hours together; how he could afford to spend so much time in prayer despite his tight schedule with people, the sick, the suffering and the dying. They also were noticing his Jewish way of combining and integrating both, the secular and the sacred, world and heaven, service and prayer, humanity and divinity. They knew well that that was their Jewish heritage received orally and through Torah from their parents, priests and the prophets.

In their Master they saw a Jewish person, of their own blood and flesh, but living and enjoying in reality this blessed heritage of integration and participation of human and divine in prayer. They encountered face to face something unique in his dealings with their Yahweh. There was something unique in his approach to prayer. They therefore wanted their prayer view should be revived and revitalized as that of Jesus. Consequently they approached Jesus, their Teacher to instruct them about prayer. Thanks to Jesus' love and concern for and his followers and thanks to disciples' humility and faith got what disciples requested of. It was the disciples' prayer which became the standardized pattern and model of all Christian prayers (Lk.11:2-4).

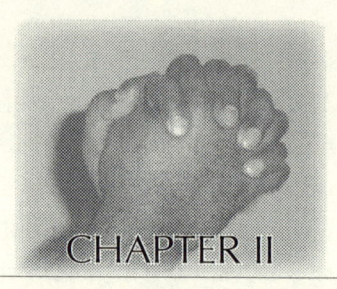

CHAPTER II
The Upshot of QualityPrayer

A. The Ultimate Goal in QualityPrayer

From Biblical times to this day, as we find in both Christian, Jewish sacred Books and in most of the Church teachings, the primary goal of prayer for God's people seems to be to directly appeal to God to grant their requests. We can consider it as a social approach to prayer but in many ways it is the simplest form of prayer. What we discover in this prayer is that people who are involved seriously in this sort of 'requesting prayer' directly enter into God's rest and ask for their needs to be fulfilled. In fact God listens to them but may or may not answer in accordance to the quality of their prayer.

The underlying beliefs in the various forms and uses of prayer in different cultures over the centuries are: That the finite can actually communicate with the infinite; and that the infinite is interested in communicating with the finite. There exits a long catalog of results of prayer around the world such as: to inculcate certain attitudes in the one who prays, rather than to influence the recipient; that prayer is intended to train a person to focus on the recipient through philosophy and intellectual contemplation; that prayer is intended to enable a person to gain a direct experience of the recipient; that prayer is intended to affect the very fabric of reality as we perceive it; that prayer is a catalyst for change in one's self and/or one's circumstances, or likewise those of third party beneficiaries; and that the recipient desires and appreciates prayer, or any combination of these.

> If God is the 'whole' we are spots or small bits in it. The whole of our finite and limited life's deeds and accomplishments are part of His glory and mutually the glory of the Whole fills us, the bits, with needed benefits. We expound in this book, is to achieve what we intend to reach in our life, namely to *be with, in, for and like God.*

Exponents of the goal of common prayer differ in their views. Some contend that it is to instill certain positive and balanced attitudes in us and not to influence; others, highlighting the importance of human rationality propose the ultimate goal of prayer as training a person to focus on divinity through philosophy and intellectual meditation. Ordinarily many users of prayer perform the act of praying in order to affect the very fabric of reality as they perceive it; they prefer their prayer to be a means for change in themselves or their lifesituations. Many others maintain that the purpose of prayer is to enable the person praying to gain a direct experience of the Supreme Spiritual Being.

Undoubtedly the ultimate goal of our qualityprayer, as like everything we say and do in our Christian life is twofold: Primarily for God's glory and secondarily for our benefits. Anything that God does, allows and ordains, is in the supreme sense for His glory. Certainly when God is glorified humans benefit. In the same vein when we pray to glorify God we also receive abundant benefits from His hands. Even in the light of the fact that God knows the upshot of our prayer from its beginning, our prayer is for our benefit. If God is the 'whole' we are spots or small bits in it. The whole of our finite and limited life's deeds and accomplishments are part of His glory and mutually the glory of the Whole fills us, the bits, with needed benefits. we expound in this book, is to achieve what we intend to reach in our life, namely to *be with, in, for and like God.* Every prayer-move should aim at this target. But we should never forget that this is not just the post-effect of prayer that occurs after we get out of the prayer environment but that is encountered within prayer.

The Ecstatic Experience

The driving force behind our act of qualityprayer is the pining heartbeats for encountering God's true Face. The peak of qualityprayer is ecstasy, as from early days of the church Greek Fathers named, which is an element of God's love that describes His movement out of Himself. It is a habitual "standing outside" of one's controlled and self-possessed being. It is a burning, driving force toward someone else to be gift to the other. It is a coming home and a finding of one's identity as a unique person in the loving surrender to another. This climatic goal realization would happen like the hilltop experience the Apostles had in their lives. Before reaching the high mountain we have to go through different stages of our Goal-trip.

This is the climatic *ecstatic environment* which many sages call '*the mystic moment*', where we encounter God, hug him, listen to him, speak with him and stay there as long as the Lord wills. In this period of prayer sometimes we withdraw from our own physical body and senses. This will not need our efforts but God would take care of this. Other times we receive certain god-guaranteed revelations and inspirations that can be executed later in life. A. Lalande, in his book 'Vocubulaire de la philosophie' offers us a preferential definition for 'mysticism': "*Mysticism is belief in the possibility of an intimate and direct union of the human spirit with the fundamental principle of being, a union which constitutes at once a mode of existence and a mode of knowledge different from superior to normal existence and knowledge.*"

Such a breathtaking experience with God can be only a split second, simply a sparkle like that of a lightning strike. The supreme Divine meets with the earthly human spirit in timeless time. This is called 'hilltop' experience. The fact of getting such encounters with God is possible only in spiritual realm, which is higher and deeper than the physical or even human-spirit's (intellectual) dimensions.

During this moment of qualityprayer we become fully aware of our Triune God invading our inner sanctuary. At that time we feel an inexplicable light—a spiritual electric power, if I am permitted to use a colloquial term, striking our interiority. We get into a status of exuberant joy, pervading all of our spiritual and physical dimensions. It is nothing but an awareness of our original status of humanity as God created us in His likeness and image; it is a deep sensitiveness toward the presence of the kingdom of God redeemed in Baptism.

> Such a breathtaking experience with God can be only a split second, simply a sparkle like that of a lightning strike. The supreme Divine meets with the earthly human spirit in timeless time. This is called 'hilltop' experience.

Look at Jesus at his time of Qualityprayer. Luke picturizes the Lord's exterior appearance while he was praying, *"his face changed in appearance and his clothing became dazzling white."* (9: 29) This change in the external look of Jesus indicated all that was going on in his interior castle. It has been the regular experience in the prayer-lives of Jesus' disciples and saints.

QualityPrayer is Transfiguration Time

Qualityprayer is a time of transfiguration. It becomes an empty tomb from where we rise to life. It is a time of waiting and hoping. It also is an immersion into the unknown. It is a regular exercise of renewing our personal commitment to God.

In the event of transfiguration as narrated in the Gospel. Both Jesus and his disciples encountered such an experience on the Mount Tabor. Similar events we read in the Bible plus in the biographies of saints and sages. At the Tabor event we notice was a spiritual encounter of the Apostles with the Supreme Being. When such hilltop experience occurs in qualityprayer we perceive in the praying persons the human spirit is elevated, connected, related and intimately present with their Creator, the heavenly Father. God speaks and the human spirit listens. During this experience humans lose themselves but gain God. They become nobody but everybody; they are nowhere but everywhere; they see not one thing but everything; they lose something of them but gain everything of them; they don't care about themselves, rather they focus only on God.

> To walk in the valley of darkness *this spiritual lightening* from the sky to the earth helps the humans and strengthens them to go a long way to reach their Promised Land. Every child from Adam to the newly born baby this day is entitled to this experience.

Like Peter in the Transfiguration event these lucky persons would say that it is good that they are there; and they would be bothered about the august presence of God, the heavenly scene, in front of them, praying as Peter did, to make *three tents, one for Jesus, one for Moses, and one for Elijah,* forgetting completely about himself and his friends. While a human spirit comes across such heavenly experience it feels it is trapped and intoxicated, as Peter felt and did not know what he was talking about. Abraham on the other hand, as we read in OT, was trembling whenever he encountered God. Everybody who enters into this hilltop experience withdraws from the self-holding and completely possessed by the Divine. This is what Jeremiah did at one of his qualityprayertime. He cried out to God 'You duped me Lord, you duped me.'

Our life in this world after all is a journey, a pilgrimage. It seems most of the time a desert full of temptations as it was for Jesus; it is an exile filled with rejections, humiliations, loneliness, fear and hopelessness; many a time it is a vale of tears crowded with sufferings, pains and passions. Such a life surely demands a beyond-vision to go through it hopefully and successfully. Those who walk in the light of faith are often strengthened and revived by spiritual experiences God bestows on them. These 'mountaintop experiences' come upon them at their qualityprayertime.

Peter maintains it and proclaims that such visionary encounters with the Lord Jesus, especially the Transfiguration experience on Mount Tabor, strengthened him and his companions in believing, following and proclaiming Jesus as the Lord and Savior. *"We did not follow cleverly devised myths,"* he says, *"when we made known to you the power and coming of our Lord Jesus Christ, but we had been eyewitnesses of his majesty."* And he too adds, *"For he received honor and glory from God the Father when that unique declaration came to him from the majestic glory, "This is my Son, my beloved, with whom I* am well pleased." *We ourselves heard this voice come from heaven while we were with him on the holy mountain. Moreover, we possess the prophetic message that is altogether reliable. You will do well to be attentive to it, as to a lamp shining in a dark place, until day dawns and the morning star rises in your hearts."* (2 Peter 1: 16-19)

To walk in the valley of darkness this spiritual lightening from the sky to the earth helps the humans and strengthens them to go a long way to reach their Promised Land. Every child from Adam to the newly born baby this day is entitled to this experience. Many people in human history have been benefiting by it. Jesus' main purpose of coming down from heaven is just to show the way for his disciples to encounter the Divine very often but fully in this world. In his own life of sufferings and pains he showed us an example of how to get these mountaintop experiences.

B. Shortterm Goals of QualityPrayer

Discovery of the true God

If we consider the hilltop experience as the longterm goal of qualityprayer there exist many shortterm goals to be realized. There are countless counterfeit faces of various gods and goddesses man-made, discovered and preached about. We ourselves carry on our shoulders and even in our hearts knowingly or unknowingly by our bringing up, formation and other social situations. We should worship one true God and Him wholeheartedly; therefore we must see only Him face to face. One of the shortterm goals in our qualityprayer is therefore to get rid of such phony gods' faces.

> Here let us be fully convinced of the truth that such shortterm goal-oriented prayers will not take us to the ultimate One. Our whole purpose even of such prayers inside our qualityprayertime should be, as Paul says, 'so that we may obtain the salvation to be found in Christ Jesus and with it eternal glory.'

The second shortterm goal is to listen clearly and distinctly God's true voice in the midst of too many disturbing and distorting voices around us. As third shortterm goal we aim at a 'grace-filling' Pentecostal experience of the Holy Spirit and His Power in our bodies and souls, in order to go to the streets and homes to live in peace and joy and to witness and proclaim that Jesus is the face of God, the Lord and Savior whom we saw, we touched, we heard and we encountered intimately.

Miraculous results

As one of the shortterm goals of qualityprayer we can surely beg God for His blessings. Prayer is sometimes used as a means of asking for something. Those people who adhere to this view contend they are very scriptural. A priest asked a little boy: "Do you say your prayers every night?" "No, Sir," replied the boy. "Some nights I don't want anything." Certainly to most children, prayer means asking God or the Absolute for various things, just as they would ask their parents. This concept of prayer is often carried over to adulthood. Many people look upon the Creator as a great benevolent figure like Santa who gives them things. They ask for this and that, and then, if their prayers aren't answered, they doubt God's very existence.

We deal with such petitioning dimension of qualityprayer in another chapter. Here let us be fully convinced of the truth that such shortterm goal-oriented prayers will not take us to the ultimate One. Our whole purpose even of such prayers inside our qualityprayertime should be, as Paul says, *'so that we may obtain the salvation to be found in Christ Jesus and with it eternal glory.'* In qualityprayer we pray for His blessings and for His healing. But when we get them—whether health, or wealth, power or talents—let us ask from Him, "No more blessings Lord, we want you yourself, not to accomplish things for You in this world but to be with You forever". The main and only aim for prayer is to come in the presence of the exalted Jesus, staying with him, interceding with him and integrating oneself with him with a totality of humanity.

Change of fake self to true Self

Another shortterm goal in our qualityprayer is to give ourselves away. The important point to understand this truth is that prayer is not so much to affect God, to change God, because God is already and always on our side; but rather prayer is to affect ourselves, to change ourselves, so that we are always on God's side. Therefore, the culmination of all prayer is: "Thy will be done, not mine." There's an interesting scene in the movie "Shadowlands," the story of C.S. Lewis' life. In the scene, Lewis, played by Anthony Hopkins, was praying fervently for his wife, who was dying of cancer. When he finished praying, one of Lewis' friends commented that surely God would hear his prayer and heal his sick wife. Lewis then offered a surprising reply. He said, "I don't pray to change God. I pray that God might change me." I recently read a commentary on this parable by Fr. Jude Winkler, who writes: *"Do we change God's mind when we pray? A better way of describing the power of our prayer is that God trusts us so much that he invites us to join him in the decision-making process. It is not that God decides everything—or that we do. It is a union of the two (for God has called us to be his friends who assist him in his work for recreating this world in his image)."*

> **"Pray as if it all depends on God and act as if it all depends on us."** This is an ageold axiom we should always remember in our begging prayer. Jesus shows us that qualityprayer consists precisely in uniting our will to the Father's.

In fact we pray the prayer of requesting not to move God, but to move ourselves—to move ourselves to equally persistent, persevering action. In other words, our action is God's response to our prayer because prayer without action is, in reality, no prayer at all. We cannot pray for forgiveness without forgiving; we cannot pray for peace without being peacemakers. Qualityprayer has to do with action, even action as concrete and worldly and secular as that. In a survey taken by the University of Chicago survey on married couples, 75 percent of the Americans who pray with their spouses reported that their marriages are "very happy" (compared to 57 percent of those who don't). Those who pray together are also more likely to say they respect each other and discuss their relationship together.

Jesus says that 'God will give justice to those who cry out for it day and night.' This is certainly so, because in qualityprayer, the very praying itself brings about justice within ourselves by making us witnesses of justice for others. *"Pray as if it all depends on God and act as if it all depends on us."* This is an ageold axiom we should always remember in our begging prayer. Jesus shows us that qualityprayer consists precisely in uniting our will to the Father's. A Christian to pray, as Pope Benedict XVI points out, *'is not to evade reality and the responsibilities it entails, but to assume them to the end, trusting in the faithful and inexhaustible love of the Lord.'*

Rest in God

Our qualityprayer can also be targeted to one more very important shortterm objective: to get rest in God. *'Peace is the center of the atom, the core; Of quiet within the storm . . . Peace is not placidity: peace is The power to endure the megatron of pain; With joy, the silent thunder of release, The ordering of Love. Peace is the atom's start, The primal image: God within the heart.'* (From the last collection of Madeleine L'Engle's poems, *The Ordering of Love*)

God in the Scriptures tells us the main reason for us to be restless and live a peaceless life is not abiding in Him and being careless in listening to Him. God is peace and therefore He is the source of peace. Jesus, His Face earthbound, whose birth was prophesied by the Prophets declared him as the Prince of peace: *"For unto us a Child is born, unto us a Son is given; and the government will be upon His shoulder. And His name will be called Wonderful, Counselor, Mighty God, Everlasting Father, Prince of Peace"*. (Isaiah 9:6). The same Prince is portrayed by Paul in his Letter to Ephesians as peace: *"For he himself is our peace . . . He came and preached peace to you who were afar off and to those who were near."* (Eph. 2:14, 17).

Our God of peace will surely keep us in peace and rest if we stay with Him: *"You will keep him in perfect peace, whose mind is stayed on You . . ."* (Isaiah 26:3, 4) He promises peace to those who seek Him and listen to

Him: *"For I know the thoughts that I think toward you, says the Lord, thoughts of peace and not of evil, to give you a future and a hope. Then you will call upon Me and go and pray to Me, and I will listen to you. And you will seek Me and find Me, when you search for Me with all your heart"* (Jeremiah 29:11-13).

The Prince of Peace offered his friendly promise of peace to his followers: "Peace I leave with you. My peace I give to you; not as the world gives do I give to you. Let not your heart be troubled, neither let it be afraid" (John 14:27). He gave them the legitimate way to attain this peace. If they don't follow his directions for true peace he can do only one thing—just weep over them. At one time when he saw how the future inhabitants of Jerusalem city would become desolate and peaceless he wept for the humans. *"As Jesus drew near Jerusalem, he saw the city and wept over it, saying, "If this day you only knew what makes for peace? But now it is hidden from your eyes."* (Lk. 19: 41-42) The Prince of peace wept not only for such future desolation of his kin in the city but also for their carelessness and ignorance of means to achieve the true peace.

Paul tells us in qualityprayer the God of peace will take care of our inner tranquility through Jesus: *"Be anxious for nothing, but in everything by prayer and supplication, with thanksgiving, let your requests be made known to God; and the peace of God, which surpasses all understanding, will guard your hearts and minds through Christ Jesus."* (Phi. 4:6, 7)

Very surprisingly the same God of peace warns us that we will never get His rest until we listen to Him: *"Do not harden your hearts as at Meribah, as on the day of Massah in the desert. There your ancestors tested me; they tried me though they had seen my works. Forty years I loathed that generation; I said: "This people's heart goes astray; they do not know my ways." Therefore I swore in my anger: "They shall never enter my rest."* (Ps. 95: 8-11) Though OT people thought the 'rest' God was speaking about referred only to the eternal rest after death. Very interestingly the author of the Letter to the Hebrews interprets it as the 'Sabbath Rest': *For we who believed enter into [that] rest, just as he has said: "As I swore in my wrath, 'They shall not enter into my rest,'" and yet his works were accomplished at the foundation of the world. For he has spoken somewhere about the seventh day in this manner, "And God rested* on the seventh day from all his works"; and again, in the previously mentioned place, "They shall not enter into my rest" . . . Now if Joshua had given them rest, he would not have spoken afterwards of another day. Therefore, a Sabbath rest still remains for the people of God. And whoever enters into God's rest rests from his own works as God did from his. Therefore, let us strive to enter into that rest, so that no one may fall after the same example of disobedience." (Heb. 4: 3-11)

Jesus, our Master, expected his followers to enjoy God's rest not only in life after death and not just on the Sabbath day, but as he did, every day of their lives, especially at the times of weariness and cramped workload. In Mark we read that after the disciples came from their hectic journey of preaching and healing around Palestine Jesus told them: "*Come away by yourselves to a deserted place and rest a while.*" (Mk. 6: 31) Jesus too made a general invitation to all his disciples who were and who would be for the same rest: "*Come to me, all you who labor and are burdened, and I will give you rest. Take my yoke upon you and learn from me, for I am meek and humble of heart; and you will find rest for yourselves.*" (Matt. 11: 28-30)

> *To be still* is 'to go deeper always with Jesus into ourselves-as I personally love to label it as 'in-traveling' into our inner sanctuary, where the kingdom of God has been already established.' This is exactly the 'qualityprayer.'

We should not misunderstand Jesus' invitation to rest. He is not offering a 20-minute power nap, but a spiritual pause and a place to rest and be refreshed so that we will be fortified in faith and energized in our service. The invitation to pause and rest was not unique to Jesus. It was deeply rooted in the spirituality of Israel. In Psalm 46 we hear God's Spirit's invitation: "*LORD, my heart is not proud; nor are my eyes haughty. I do not busy myself with great matters, with things too sublime for me. Rather, I have stilled my soul, hushed it like a weaned child. Like a weaned child on its mother's lap, so is my soul within me. Israel, hope in the LORD, now and forever.*" (Ps. 131: 1-3)

We always think to be still means to be silent. True, it is one dimension of being still; but even silence can be a signlanguage to show our restlessness out of hatred, aversion, opposition, jealousy and vengeance. In the Scriptures, the Hebrew imperative "Be still" has been variously translated as "Desist!"; "Give in!" and "Let be!" as in an authoritative order to a contentious person to "Shut up!" or "Stop it!" Rather than be overwhelmed by life's troubles, believers are to let go and let God act. Jesus' invitation is not simply to rest, as in "Take a load off" or "Put your feet up." To be still and take rest refers to more than all these: It is 'to go deeper always with Jesus into ourselves-as I personally love to label it as 'in-traveling' into our inner sanctuary, where the kingdom of God has been already established.' This is exactly the qualityprayer.'

Rest during qualityprayer

At that sacred space we get to know who God is; get to listen more clearly the true to voice of God and teachings; get to discover and be amazed of the marvelous pearls of God in Jesus. We will be very close to Jesus and we will listen more clearly what he teaches us. We will know and understand most of his heavenly secrets as his little ones. This is what we hear from Jesus in his prayer of praise: *"I give praise to you, Father, Lord of heaven and earth, for although you have hidden these things from the wise and the learned you have revealed them to little ones."* (Matt. 11: 25)

Those hidden heavenly secrets are 'meekness and humility.' *'Learn from me'*, he advises us, *'my meekness and humility.'* Meekness is the characteristic, Zechariah uses, to describe the promised Messiah. Etymologically, the word "meek" was always associated with the strength and courage that are expressed in gentleness toward God and all others. In Jesus' sight meekness means perfect trust, willing obedience and lived faith; in its posture toward others, meekness means force of character and inner strength that invite admiration and a desire to emulate such virtue. These are the lessons Jesus teaches to those who will pause, be still and come to rest in him.

To the post-modern age people such a pause for rest and renewal seems impractical, a waste of time. Many consider it a mark of laziness. Nevertheless, the disciples of Jesus are fully aware of the fact that these pauses are as necessary to our busy lives as breathing, for within those few moments of rest in the Lord, we grow and deepen and mature. St. Augustine's prayer was: "God! Our hearts are restless until they rest in thee."

There are millions in this world who are too anxious to bring peace and rest around their communities and nations. But in themselves they are too restless, despite their prosperity and material blessings; plus they know well all their attempts of peace are unproductive and not bringing solid fruits. In this frustrating world's restless situation we hear the words of God: *"I swore in my anger: "They shall never enter my rest."*

However there are so many disciples of Jesus, the little ones as Jesus calls them, who are fully aware of the need of 'qualityprayer' and the rest that flows out of it. Many years back I became acquainted with an elderly lady at a parish in Chicago where I was performing my pastoral duties as resident priest. She approached our parish priest and told him: "Father I have two requests from you. One, I need a church key so that I can continue to come and visit the Lord and pray before him. Second, kindly allow me to clean daily the tabernacle and the altar so that the Lord may find his living quarter spotless." The priest with no hesitation granted her request. Every day as I went for my regular visit to the Eucharistic Lord I noticed this lady doing that job perfectly and sitting in front of the sanctuary for many hours. One day out of curiosity I approached her and asked,'Grandma, what makes you to come daily here and do this kind of job?" She responded: "My son, I see Jesus here. I get complete peace and rest in him." This little one's spirit of qualityprayer increased my own commitment to my qualityprayer leading to the 'priestly qualitylife.'

C. Qualitylife: the Endresult of Qualityprayer

We share God's abundant life

All the earlier-mentioned shortterm goals and the ultimate goal of qualityprayer result in energizing the praying person to lead a 'qualitylife'. All the experiences we receive during prayertime in any form or style, especially the climatic ecstasy, bring us to a changed and renewed lifesituation where only goodness and holiness prevail. In John 10: 10 Jesus as a Good Shepherd declares that he gave his very life for us for bestowing qualitylife: *I came so that they might have life and have it more abundantly.* (New American Bible) These words read in other versions: *"My purpose is to give life in all its fullness."* (Living Bible) *"I came, so that they might have life—to the fullest!"* (Simple English Version) *"I have come so that they may have life and have it to the full."* (New Jerusalem Bible)

We enjoy a resurrected life

Undoubtedly our God in Jesus is the God of the living and not of the dead. *"As for the dead being raised, have you not read in the Book of Moses, in the passage about the bush, how God told him, 'I am the God of Abraham, [the] God of Isaac, and [the] God of Jacob'? He is not God of the dead but of the living."* (Mk. 12: 26-27) He, as Creator, is the bestower of every kind of life in the universe: *"I charge [you] before God, who gives life to all things."* (1 Tim. 6:13) The same power of giving and restoring life was imparted to Jesus by his Father: *"For just as the Father raises the dead and gives life, so also does the Son give life to whomever he wishes."* (John 5:21)

> In qualityprayer, if it is sincerely and strenuously performed, the inner experiences we encounter during those qualitytimes will bring us new qualitylife to us who feel like dry bones.

Therefore we, the disciples of the resurrected Jesus firmly believe like Paul that Christ is the bestower of resurrection life: *"So, too, it is written, "The first man, Adam, became a living being," the last Adam a life-giving spirit."* (1 Cor. 15:45) He possesses the capacity to change, fashion, mould, shape and renew our fragile and vulnerable human life into the qualitylife that will never see death or any annihilation at all: *"If the Spirit of the one who raised Jesus from the dead dwells in you, the one who raised Christ from the dead will give life to your mortal bodies also, through his Spirit that dwells in you."* (Rom. 8:1)

In qualityprayer, if it is sincerely and strenuously performed, the inner experiences we encounter during those qualitytimes will bring us new qualitylife to us who feel like dry bones. Ordinary earthly life will be changed into God's qualitylife as we read in the Book of Ezekiel: *"Dry bone! Hear the word of the LORD! Thus says the Lord GOD to these bones: Listen! I will make breath enter you so you may come to life. I will put sinews on you, make flesh grow over you, cover you with skin, and put breath into you so you may come to life. Then you shall know that I am the LORD."* (Ezek. 37: 4b-6) We may feel we are clay; we can low-esteem ourselves as mere dust.

We live a life in the Spirit

However through the same qualityprayer an unthinkable re-creation will occur; our entire life will be a life in the Holy Spirit and not of the flesh; a life with purified divine ordinances, leveled—out grievances and revived dying zeal. Our attitude will be changed into the likeness of Jesus who is meek and humble of heart. We begin to live always in the Spirit. As Paul writes, *"You are not in the flesh; on the contrary, you are in the spirit, if only the Spirit of God dwells in you. Whoever does not have the Spirit of Christ does not belong to him. But if Christ is in you, although the body is dead because of sin, the spirit is alive because of righteousness."* (Rom. 8: 9-10) We will be no more in the flesh; we will not be debtors or slaves to the flesh, to live according to the flesh; but by the Spirit we will put to death the deeds of the body and thereby we will live a qualitylife, an eternal godly life.

We are gifted with life of satisfaction

Qualitylife in Christ is inclusive of all good, and stands in opposition to the death threatened. The Qualitylife God bestows us through Jesus' Spirit is abundant, full and overflowing; it's not only living, but living comfortably, living plentifully and living joyfully and peacefully. The same qualitylife of abundance can also indicate its eternal dimension, a life without death or fear of death, life and much more.

As the Psalmist expresses his status of daily living a qualitylife in the Psalm 23, our qualityprayer brings about qualitylife where we taste the goodness of God in all our enjoyments, though we have but little of the world it seems always a green pasture; we enjoy quiet and contentment in the mind, whatever the lot is; and we will be filled with the consolations of the Holy Spirit like the still waters by which we take permanent rest. In welcoming the gift of His Spirit, we will drink from His spring, source of that living water which 'gushes up to eternal life'". In our qualitylife our yoke of commitment becomes easy and our burden of duties turns out to be light and pleasant; any work of righteousness is performed in peace.

In qualitylife we will never feel anything missing because as Jesus promises our life is full and abundant. There is no fear or anxiety altogether about our precarious lifesituation because we become fully conscious of God's presence within us and a tranquil certainty settles in our hearts that we are guided and protected and sheltered by Him from all dangers.

We begin living in indomitable faith and hope

In qualitylife we won't be agitated even if we land in the darkest valley or any deserted place. Because where our praying hearts beat there is our God who will take us to the oasis, its whereabouts our all-knowing Shepherd is fully aware of. If the front door closes He will open the back one; if both doors shut, He will open a window. There is certainty in our mind in those of his oases all things are abundant. The continuous hilltop experiences of communing with the Almighty in qualityprayer establish in our inner shrine a radical experience of faith, namely the mystical, not mere ritual. The closeness of God transforms the entire human natural reality in such a way that all the evils that happen, be they social, spiritual, natural, as in the grimmest canyon, lose all their perilous holds".

> We begin blessing His name every moment of our lives Our heartbeats and lips every moment thank and praise Him for all his marvelous works; all his kindness and mercy; all his goodness; all his faithfulness; all his holiness in his works and dealings; all his magnanimity of lifting up all who are falling; and of raising up all who are bowed down.

We carry life's burden with heavenly Yokemate

After qualityprayer we begin to feel all life's burdens easy and light. Jesus' promise of an easy or well-fitting yoke does not mean that his followers would be freed of all challenges of unfairness of life or burdens of human roles and duties; rather, He did not bring a Gospel of prosperity, or that of comfort. His compassion led him to take an entirely different approach. He promised to help the burdened to bear whatever load they had to carry through life. Usually, as any farm laborers know, yokes are often built for two oxen. In life's yokes, according to Jesus' promise, a 'qualityprayer person' is not alone to carry them; rather Jesus joins with that 'qualityprayer person' to be the yokemate. All those burdens, carried in the spirit of divine love and certainly shared by a loving yokemate such as Jesus, as one rabbi put it, *"My burden is become my song."*

We lead a 'Magnificat'-life

There is one more result happening after qualityprayer. We begin singing the song of rejoicing as the Psalmist would sing: *"I will extol you, my God and king; I will bless your name forever and ever. Every day I will bless you; I will praise your name forever and ever. Great is the LORD and worthy of much praise, whose grandeur is beyond understanding."* (Ps. 145: 1-3) We begin blessing His name every moment of our lives Our heartbeats and lips every moment thank and praise Him for all his marvelous works; all his kindness and mercy; all his goodness; all his faithfulness; all his holiness in his works and dealings; all his magnanimity of lifting up all who are falling; and of raising up all who are bowed down. Does it not sound like our beloved Mother Mary's song: *My soul proclaims the greatness of the Lord; my spirit rejoices in God my Savior. For he has looked upon his handmaid's lowliness; behold, from now on will all ages call me blessed. The Mighty One has done great things for me, and holy is his name.* (Lk. 1: 46-49)

The qualitylife which will be the ultimate gift of God to us who sincerely take efforts to pray in a qualitative way is to be lived and possessed by us not only in this earthly situation but also in eternity. Jesus always connected these two situations our human lifesituation-earthly and heavenly, life before our death and that life after death, in his promise of qualitylife for all of us, *"Amen, I say to you, there is no one who has given up house or wife or brothers or parents or children for the sake of the kingdom of God who will not receive [back]* **an overabundant return in this present age and eternal life in the age to come."**

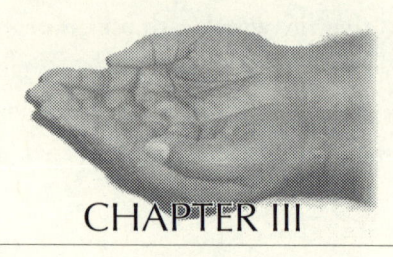

CHAPTER III
Ingredients of Quality Prayer

A. According to Jesus' formula: "The Lord's Prayer"

ARE WE PRAYING to ourselves? Is the prayer simply giving directions to ourselves for spending this particular day or even our entire life? Are we sure we are reflecting and meditating during the time of prayer to gather some notes for our next Sunday Bible class or homily? If we are truly praying to God, what kind of God are we praying to? We believe and worship a God who is one in three: Father, Son and Holy Spirit. If so, to which Person of the Three are we praying? Is that person He or She or It? In our prayer what should we pray? How should we pray?

Similar and more other questions arise in the minds of beginners in qualityprayer if they are sincere about their praying efforts. Most of us got use to setting aside these analytic questions in our prayertimes because we are in a hurry or in full attention to submit our needy petitions or fill our prayertime with formal prayers. This kind of prayer can be qualityprayer when humans are infants, as Paul indicates, who need only milk for their strength or when people are worn out and lost all their physical and emotional stamina due to chronic or terminal illness or even old age. However we are discussing here the qualityprayer of adults—energetic, vibrant, committed disciples of Jesus who need and long for 'meat' for their spiritual journey with their Master.

> Prayer in our lives is the most vital project in our building up a relationship with God and that should be properly implemented.

If we are such authentic disciples of Jesus our qualityprayer should always start with a creed which is nothing but our statement before God on our personal perspective/view about God and surely about ourselves and about the right attitude on qualityprayer. To get the right answers to all of our brainy but practical questions regarding qualityprayer we should better follow the advice of Paul who writes: *"Bringing into captivity every thought to the obedience of Christ."* (2 Cor. 10:5) In other words Paul tried to take every one of his life-projects prisoner to make it obey Christ. We should not perform anything for God at the instigation of our own human nature which has not been spiritualized by determined discipline. Instead we must bring every thought and deed into captivity for Christ.

Prayer in our lives is the most vital project in our building up a relationship with God and that should be properly implemented. This human project of praying can also be performed as a project of our mere emotions and feelings and consequently being influenced by our own personal views about God and other spiritual matters. As Jesus' disciples we are supposed to be fully committed to Jesus' view of God, of the world, of religion and all that we handle especially in our spiritual realm.

As we described in an earlier chapter on the quest of Jesus' disciples to renew their prayer efforts while He was with them we must also go to Jesus to get his advice on our qualityprayer. Though in many other times Jesus spoke about his view on qualityprayer at one time at the explicit request of his disciples he gave them a list of the elements contained in any qualityprayer. *"Jesus was praying in a certain place, and when he had finished, one of his disciples said to him, "Lord, teach us to pray just as John taught his disciples." He said to them, "When you pray, say . . .".* (Lk. 11: 1-2) The disciples asked Jesus to teach them not exactly the technique of praying. Even if they had meant it, the Lord in fact taught us through them 'what to pray', namely the contents of our prayer. As for the method and technique of prayer, which we will discuss in the next chapter, he showed it through his own prayerlife.

> As most of the Biblical scholars would agree, Jesus was not interested so much in giving us a prayer to recite as in sharing with us a blueprint of qualityprayer and showing us the way in which to pray. He provided us with an outline of priorities or important ingredients that must be contained in our praying.

While Luke offers us the situation in which Jesus gave us the qualityprayer formula, Matthew 6: 9-13 informs us about the intention of Jesus in presenting us his qualityprayer. According to Matthew Jesus says, *"This is how you are to pray"*, meaning 'pray this way', and not 'pray this prayer' or 'pray these words.' As most of the Biblical scholars would agree, Jesus was not interested so much in giving us a prayer to recite as in sharing with us a blueprint of qualityprayer and showing us the way in which to pray. He provided us with an outline of priorities or important ingredients that must be contained in our praying.

In his prayer formula Jesus included eight features, as found in the Gospel of Matthew, that constitute any genuine prayer. If all those contents Jesus proposed are found in any prayer that prayer is to be named as 'qualityprayer.' In all those constituents the Lord infused the spirit and attitude with which we should enter into qualityprayer:

1. *Our Father in heaven*
2. *Hallowed be your name*
3. *Your kingdom come*
4. *Your will be done on earth as in heaven*
5. *Give us today our daily bread*
6. *Forgive us our debts as we forgive our debtors*
8. *Do not subject us to the final test, but deliver us from the evil one.*

Feature-1: Praying with proper perspective of God

In *The Institutes of the Christian Religion* John Calvin writes: "It is very much in our interests that we be constantly supplicating Him, first that our heart might always be inflamed with the serious and ardent desire of seeking, loving, and serving Him as the sacred anchor in every necessity. Secondly, that no desire, no longing whatever that we are ashamed to make Him the witness, enter our minds while we learn to place all of our wishes in His sight, and thus pour out our heart before Him. Lastly that we might be prepared to receive all of His benefits with true gratitude and thanksgiving, while our prayers remind us that they proceed from His hand." (Book 3, Chapter 20, section 3) All Christians, committed sincerely to qualityprayer, like John Calvin, center their entire prayertime on God the Supreme Being from its start till its end. It is the will of our Master Jesus who asks us to begin, to proceed and end our qualityprayer in, with and for God: *"Our Father in heaven."*

> Almost all religious leaders publicize these days about the existence of *a god of secularism, materialism, licentiousness, worldliness and immorality* in the lives of post-modern Christians. We can observe this fact as the attendance of Sunday services is shrinking and the longing for the Scriptural teachings of the true God and religious practices of true religion are disappearing.

Breaking away from fake, false gods

However, we humans have a tendency to create our own gods, as the molten calf, fabricated by the Israelites in the desert, which are the gods of death, violence, hatred, and vengeance. In this new era of Science and Technology we create and worship: *A god of fanaticism of any kind*. It can be religious, social, and racial. Paul confesses all the atrocities he performed against Christians came out of his ignorance in unbelief. But the modern terrorists have been doing their malicious acts out of sheer ignorance of their own belief. Our human history, including the church history, tells us that from the past till this day many of those atrocities we have been inflicting on others may be out of our ignorance or belief.

There is also *a god of terrorism, violence, and injustice*. This god is very subtle and pleasant in his intrusion into the human lives through some modern Media such as TV, Movies, radio, Music. Whenever we wage war against evil forces, surely the true God approves it and even He continues to join with us in the battle. If we are not very careful in planning our strategies and purifying our motivations in this battle, we will end up worshipping *a god of hatred, retaliation, and vengeance.* Almost all religious leaders publicize these days about the existence of *a god of secularism, materialism, licentiousness, worldliness and immorality* in the lives of post-modern Christians. We can observe this fact as the attendance of Sunday services is shrinking and the longing for the Scriptural teachings of the true God and religious practices of true religion are disappearing.

As we start our qualityprayer we must recognize and accept the God Jesus has revealed as the true Triune God, a God of love. Let us pledge allegiance to God of Jesus. Let us destroy all those idols of molten calves the modern generation creates as its god.

Professing our recognition and acceptance of 'who God is'

We should first know well to whom we are praying. We can never perform a genuine qualityprayer for qualitylife without right perspective about the One whom we deal with in prayer. This is why the Church never ceases to advise us to start every prayer effort with the creed we learned in our childhood. In order to make our prayer a genuine communication process first we must know who stands there on the other end of communication track. In prayer both God and ourselves communicate to each other. Sometimes God expects us to listen to him, other times we expect God to pay heed to us. This prayer becomes complete, total and successful only when the wishes of both communication partners are satisfied. According to the revelation we have received from the Scriptures, in our qualityprayer God's primary expectation from His praying partners is a wise understanding of who He is.

We are so glad to know from our faith that God is himself an embodiment of communication. In a tripod style one communication is going on between the three persons: Father, Son and Spirit. Having communication as his inner nature we have little doubt that he would deny or ignore our personal communication and feedback sent to him through our available media.

In most Christians' lives, especially if we are cradle Christians, we can discover that the God, whom we believe firmly and worship faithfully, is the One whom our parents and religion introduced to us in our early childhood as the Triune God. We heard about God's deeds to humanity and in nature both as bedtime stories from our parents and as subjects to be memorized for our catechism and Bible classes. This religious formation made us esteem God as a Global Warrior who attacks evil persons and destroys them; also as a ever-vigilant Policeman who acts like an owl looking over us round the clock when we make any mistake so that we can be punished; we were also thinking of Him as a magician who works millions of miracles through His angels and the sacramental resources our religion provides. Later days when we completed our college studies we began to consider Him as our beginning, namely He is the Creator of us and the entire universe; He is surely the end of everything, especially to the humans He is their destiny.

Charles Colson once wrote: *"It's true that most Americans profess to believe in God, but this God is a far cry from the God of Scripture. More than a century of naturalism has eroded our belief that God is providential—that is, in charge of all events."* Mr. Colson has a point. Many of us profess to be Christians, but we are actually deists. We have a tendency to believe God created the universe and then left it on its own. After creating the world, He apparently went on vacation and left no forwarding address.

The true God whom we worship, and so in all the religions, is a God of love, compassion, forgiveness, goodness, justice and peace. He is a God of life. As Pope John Paul II said, when God gives life, He creates it for eternity. *"The Lord relented in the punishment he had threatened to inflict on his people."* *"The grace of our Lord has been abundant, along with the faith and love that are in Christ Jesus. Christ Jesus came into the world to save sinners."* *"I tell you, there will be more joy in heaven over one sinner who repents than over ninety-nine righteous people who have no need of repentance."*

Praying to a God of intimacy

As the first ingredient in our qualityprayer Jesus advises us to uphold a total, right and sincere view of the God to whom we commune with. The first content of his prayer formula is: *'Our Father in heaven'*: In using a Hebrew term *'Abba'*, which is an intimate term used by a loving child to call his Father, surely he expects us to begin our prayer with an intimate feeling of God's immanent presence and His nearness within us. We too should dig into Jesus' usage of the word 'Father'. When He wants us to address God 'Father' he actually points out to us the right view we should hold about Him who is the Triune God, Father, Son and the Spirit. Being His Son, Jesus demands from all of us to call God in that filial affection and trust 'Abba Father.' This is because he was the one who bought us back from the Devil and brought us into the realm of the Triune God as adopted sons and daughters; through his efforts of redemption we were filled with the Holy Spirit.

> When Jesus wants us to address God 'Father' he actually points out to us the right view we should hold about Him who is the Triune God, Father, Son and the Spirit.

St. Cyprian emphasizes this amazing fact in his writing about the Lord's Prayer: *"The new man, re-born and brought back to God by his grace, says Father at the very beginning, for he has just begun to be God's son. He came to his own, and his own did not accept him. But to those who did accept him he gave power to become children of God, to those who believe in his name. Whoever believes in God's name and has become his Son, should start here so that he can give thanks and profess himself to be God's son, by calling God as his Father."* (St. Cyprian)

We have been praying and prattling at our prayertimes in different ways: personally or in community; in silence or in words; through symbols or signs. And what is the result of them all? In many cases it is only very negative. It is because we never made the hour of prayer as a time of interpersonal communication with God; we have not approached prayer with an attitude of intimate relationship with Him; we always think of God or make God appear to us as a judge, and face Him at His court rather than at His private chamber. On the contrary remembering and using always Jesus' words 'our Father', we should recognize we are dealing in qualityprayer with a person and not with a power or energy or an idol or a sleeping beauty.

Praying to a God of Abundance

The God we relate to in qualityprayer is a God of abundance. God applies eternally an astounding principle in all His deeds of creation and redemption, namely 'the law of abundance.' According to this law He creates something from nothing; more from less; and greater good from lesser evil. He redeems every human creature with no discrimination; He does His redeeming acts unconditionally; He stands knocking at humans' inner doors continuously and inviting them to receive His redeeming grace freely. Thus He proves His abundance of power and love.

In His accomplishments God manages to use his creatures, both animate and inanimate beings to bring about his creative abundance. He uses them as they are and with what they have. With the available resources and talents, found in those beings, he creates abundantly. With limited quantity or even restricted and perverted quality presented to him by his creatures, especially human beings, God is abundantly blessing his universe.

In God we observe the abundance in love, justice and generosity, abundance in blessings, resources and gifts. We hear frequently about this from God's own mouth in Scriptures. We too read in them all about His marvelous deeds of love and blessings. People of God in the OT discovered this truth in God's creation and redemptive works. The Lord says: *"All you who are thirsty, come to the water! You, who have no money, come, receive grain and eat. Come, without paying and without cost, drink wine and milk!"* (Is. 55: 1)

About the abundance of God's love Paul describes his own experience and conviction even in his own deprivation and sufferings: *"In all these things we conquer overwhelmingly through him who loved us. For I am convinced that neither death, nor life, nor angels, nor principalities, nor present things, nor future things, for powers, nor height, nor depth, nor any other creature will be able to separate us from the love of God in Christ Jesus our Lord."* (Rom. 8: 37-39) In Psalm 145, the Psalmist sings: *The hand of the Lord feeds us; he answers all our needs. You give them their food in due season; you open your hand and satisfy the desire of every living thing.*

> With the available resources and talents, found in those beings, he creates abundantly. With limited quantity or even restricted and perverted quality presented to him by his creatures, especially human beings, God is abundantly blessing his universe.

In the Scriptures the God of Jesus reveals Himself as the God of abundance. He is abounding in everything that is good, in all that you and I need for our lives. In Genesis He reveals this first in His breathtaking superfluous creation, look at Animal planet and the Discovery Channel. And later to all His faithful servants by providing them all they need for life, materially, physically, intellectually, and spiritually. Name any one of the heroes in the Bible. Every one of them enjoyed God's protection, gifts, blessings and love abundantly. When Moses asked Him to reveal Himself to him more intimately, God cried, *The Lord, the Lord God, merciful and gracious, longsuffering, and abounding in goodness and truth.* (Ex.34/6) Throughout the Bible God exposes His abundance by sharing His gifts as a Father, Master, Creator, Redeemer, Lover and so on. The God of the Bible has been a God in abundance.

When Jesus came, he revealed the same kind of God who is generous and bountiful in all aspects of life. He is neither stingy nor tight and this is why as Jesus said, *'He does not ration his gift of the Spirit.'* (Jn.3/34) Jesus set as his life goal to offer abundant life to us. In John he says, *'I came so that they may have life and have it more abundantly.'* (10/10b) He too promises abundant rewards to all his followers. *'Everyone who has given up houses or brothers or sisters or father or mother or children or lands for the sake of my name will receive a hundred times more.'* (Mt.19/29)

When Jesus spoke of His gift of the Holy Spirit, he referred to him as the living water. It meant the Spirit's abundance, His ever-flowing nature and not a stagnant one. Jesus revealed a God in himself as a God of fullness. He made his life's aim to make his followers' joy complete, life full, peace eternal. In the Gospel we come to understand about Jesus' vision and dream of futuristic abundance in God's kingdom when he asked his disciples to pray to God for more laborers to reap the harvest. *"Then he said to his disciples, "The harvest is abundant but the laborers are few; so ask the master of the harvest to send out laborers for his harvest."* (Matt. 9: 37-38)

God therefore is abundant in every element of life: joy, peace, justice, love and mercy. He possesses full life which He longs to share with us and make us abundant too in enjoying His qualitylife: *"You have brought them abundant joy"* (Is. 9: 2) *"I have told you this so that my joy may be in you and your joy may be complete."* (Jn. 15: 11) When Jesus answered a question which was in Peter's mind, namely 'we have given up our possessions and followed you, what would we gain?', he pointed out how abundant the Lord's gifts are going to be for all his followers saying: *"Amen, I say to you, there is no one who has given up house or wife or brothers or parents or children for the sake of the kingdom of God who will not receive [back] an overabundant return in this present age and eternal life in the age to come."* (Lk. 18: 28-30)

The world needs this God of abundance. It's this God we should introduce to our world which is deprived of fullness and abundance. We are surrounded by a society that is costing its lot for abundance in different harmful ways. The world is truly in search of a God of abundance. It has not seen him or felt him. We are to be blamed for it, because Jesus entrusted that task to us, his disciples, to go and introduce the God of abundance to the world.

I love to say very frequently to my congregation that *'the Abundance belongs to the Divine; but its Sharing belongs to the human.'* Whatever be the abundance of God's gifts in this world, we know very well they are not possessed or enjoyed by all the humans equally. We find there is no distributive justice in sharing the goods of God's creation. Why? Who is to be blamed? God? That is what many humans of the modern world feel. But

God's Word instructs us that while the abundance of everything is on His side, its distribution or sharing is entirely depending on the humans.

> The Abundance belongs to the Divine;
> but its Sharing belongs to the human.

God as we read in Scriptures created and produced all his earthly goods and entrusted them into the hands of humans. *"God created man in his image; in the divine image he created him; male and female he created them. God blessed them, saying: "Be fertile and multiply; fill the earth and subdue it. Have dominion over the fish of the sea, the birds of the air, and all the living things that move on the earth." God also said: "See, I give you every seed-bearing plant all over the earth and every tree that has seed-bearing fruit on it to be your food; and to all the animals of the land, all the birds of the air, and all the living creatures that crawl on the ground, I give all the green plants for food." And so it happened. God looked at everything he had made, and he found it very good".* (Gen. 1: 27-31)

In the parable of the sower Jesus proclaims that God is a generous sower. When we look at living beings in nature, plants, and animals of all kinds, we see how much seed is generously sown. There is plenty of it, and yet few spring up and reproduce fruit. The same gardener; the same sower; the same natural ground or field; yet at the harvest time the world reaps different results and fruits. Yet the Lord of generosity himself keeps on sowing the seeds abundantly. (Matt. 13: 1-9)

Most of us unconsciously feel that it is we only who are after God for his abundance. We are accustomed to think we are the only people who are in search of God. On the other hand we forget that it is God who is seeking us and pursuing us like a hound as we read in the well-known poem of Francis Thompson 'The Hound of Heaven.' What does He want from us? Brilliant things? Beautiful things? Or even good things? No. God wants us to be just who we are and hand over to him just what we are already blessed with. Even it may be too little, nothing in comparison with the richness found around us.

This is what persons like Elisha's friend in the OT and the apostles in the Gospel were afraid of. When Elisha asked his servant to give the available little food to his people he said, "How can I set these twenty barley loaves before a hundred people?" (2 Kings 4: 43a) When the Lord asked his Apostles to feed the crowd of his hearers in the desert they responded to Him "What good of these five loaves and two fishes for so many?" (Jn. 6: 1-15) According to the Scriptures in both incidents when the beneficiaries had eaten, there was much left over.

When the Prophet asked his disciple and Jesus demanded his disciples to give the hungry something to eat, they were not asked to perform miracles. They were told to do what they could; to place in common and share what each one has. In arithmetic, multiplication and division are two opposite operations, but in the case of the application of God's principle of abundance they are the same. There is no "multiplication" without "partition" (or sharing). God in Jesus makes us abundantly fructifying in our undertakings only with those little and limited things, talents, and treasures we possess but always at his disposal. As Fred Rogers in his famous children's show once said, "God loves you just the way you are, but God never leaves you the way you are, because God loves you."

Keeping a friendly relationship with Jesus

The term 'Father' used in Jesus' and our qualityprayer implies that we should go into our prayerchamber with great reverence and awe and love toward all the three persons in one Godhead. God is like mother, even more than a mother: *"As a mother comforts her child, so I will comfort you; in Jerusalem you shall find your comfort. You will see and your heart shall exult, and your bodies shall flourish like the grass."* (Is. 66: 13-14)

At the same time we also must keep in mind at the entrance of our qualityprayer chamber that God also is a powerful person, a just Judge and always in fire: *"The LORD's power shall be revealed to his servants, but to his enemies, his wrath. For see, the LORD will come in fire, his chariots like the stormwind; to wreak his anger in burning rage and his rebuke in fiery flames.*

For with fire the LORD shall enter into judgment, and, with his sword, against all flesh; those slain by the LORD shall be many." (Is. 66: 14-16)

The same is true in our adhering to the resurrected Jesus, God's Son. He stated that we are his friends; he did die for our sakes as he promised. *"No one has greater love than this, to lay down one's life for one's friends. You are my friends if you do what I command you. I no longer call you slaves, because a slave does not know what his master is doing. I have called you friends, because I have told you everything I have heard from my Father."* (Jn. 15: 13-15)

Qualityprayer must be generated from the intimate connection with Jesus who is the vine and we are his branches. Our connection with Jesus is so ontological and spiritual that we cannot do anything without him: *"Remain in me, as I remain in you. Just as a branch cannot bear fruit on its own unless it remains on the vine, so neither can you unless you remain in me. I am the vine, you are the branches. Whoever remains in me and I in him will bear much fruit, because without me you can do nothing."* (Jn. 15: 4-5)

Praying in the Spirit

Jesus willed our qualityprayer, whatever may be its form, to be performed in Spirit and Truth. Referring to the presence and support of the Holy Spirit, third Person of Trinity, in our qualityprayer Jesus and his disciples had many things to say. As the form of worship qualityprayer is to be done in the Spirit: *"The hour is coming, and is now here, when true worshipers will worship the Father in Spirit and truth; and indeed the Father seeks such people to worship him. God is Spirit and those who worship him must worship in Spirit and truth."* (Jn. 4: 23-24)

Jesus too predicted that in all our interactions with God, the Spirit would guide us as an advocate: *"When the Advocate comes whom I will send you from the Father, the Spirit of truth that proceeds from the Father, he will testify to me."* (Jn. 15: 26)

Paul emphasizes that the Spirit of God always assists us in our prayer endeavors. *"The Spirit too comes to the aid of our weakness; for we do not know how to pray as we ought, but the Spirit itself intercedes with inexpressible groanings. And the one who searches hearts knows what is the intention of the*

Spirit, because it intercedes for the holy ones according to God's will." (Rom. 8: 26-27) Those who committed to qualityprayer would testify to this statement of Paul. There are so many times we discover our difficulty to pray as God wants us; it is simply the grace of God's Spirit that we have to rely on, not only the times we find it hard to perfectly pray, but also at every time we enter into prayer since we, the humans, are very weak and unholy to comply with the Lord's expectation of praying genuinely.

Christian teachings have for long held that prayer involves the action of the Holy Spirit, In Catechism of the Catholic Church (P. 2670) we are taught about the Catholic belief that the Holy Spirit, as the "master of prayer", both inspires and guides prayer. In the Catholic encyclopedia we read that prior to prayer, an act of adoration to God should be performed and a petition made for the prayer to be directed by the Holy Spirit. As St. Augustine would say, 'there is then within us a kind of instructed ignorance, instructed, that is, by the Spirit of God who helps our weakness.'

> In Catechism of the Catholic Church (P. 2670) we are taught about the Catholic belief that the Holy Spirit, as the "master of prayer", both inspires and guides prayer.

To conclude our discussion on Jesus' use of the term 'Father', this is what we should remember always. When we pray and have recourse the three persons of God separately we should in no way misunderstand that we approach one Person stealthily not permitting other Persons know about it, as we humans do in our contacts among humans, rather all Three as One God do everything we ask even if it is directed to One Person.

For example, when we hear that *Holy Spirit pleads for the saints*, we should in no way understand that the Holy Spirit of God pleads for the saints as if he were someone different from what God is: in the Trinity the Spirit is the unchangeable God and one God with the Father and the Son. The Words, *He pleads for the saints* because he moves the saints to plead, bear the same meaning as the Words of Scriptures: *The Lord your God tests you, to know if you love him*. This denotes that the Spirit moves the saints to plead with sighs too deep for words by inspiring in them a desire for the 'greater things'.

Praying as a corporate (communal) person

Jesus in his prayer addresses God as *"our* Father." In a Christian prayer no individualistic attitude should be present. He always connects himself to his fellow human beings and prays as, for and with 'us, our' and not 'I, and my'. Whether I pray alone or in group or in community, I pray as one of God's family members. As I cannot divide the Unity found in the Triune God, my corporate dimension can never be ignored or sidestepped. I would like to share here my personal perception of the term 'Israel' as an appropriate metaphor to explain the corporate character of qualityprayer.

Jesus exhorted: *"If any man will come after me, let him deny himself."* (Matt. 16:24) Individuality is the shell of human personality. Individuality usually separates and isolates ourselves from others. It is sheer childish character; this husk of individuality is a natural covering offered by God to humanity for their survival; unfortunately in most people's lives individuality takes a predominant role of coveting the attention of humans and hides completely the true self's personality. Individuality forges personality as lust fakes love. Thus individuality degrades human nature. It creates a fake self of its own and goes against God and consequently the gift of qualitylife is lost. This is why Jesus advised us to deny that fake self of individuality.

> When Jesus wanted us to call God 'our' Father, his main thrust was that we should never come out of our intrinsic connection with the humanity which is nothing but the family of God.

In OT books every individual was called by God as "Israel" which was the individual name of Jacob; then it was given to the whole People of God; later God uses it to call each individual Jew as 'Israel' insisting the corporate dimension of individuals. The same way Jesus does, but goes little further to call each one of the 'Humanity'. When he wanted us to call God 'our' Father, his main thrust was that we should never come out of our intrinsic connection with the humanity which is nothing but the family of God; if I weep the whole humanity weeps; if the other is suffering, I suffer as part of his humanity; if I pray individually I pray not as a loner, rather as a portion of the humanity. Only with this attitude we should enter into our act of prayer which then will be very well called 'qualityprayer.'

As St. Cyprian used to say, 'our Father is not my Father alone.' He writes: *"The Teacher of peace and Master of unity did not want prayer to be made singly and privately, so that whoever prayed would pray for himself alone. We do not say My Father, who art in heaven or Give me this day my daily bread; nor does each one ask that only his own debt should be forgiven him; nor does he request for himself alone that he may not be led into temptation but delivered from evil. Our prayer is public and common, and when we pray, we pray not for one person but for the whole people, since we, the whole people, are one."*

Our Master Jesus taught unity, willed that we should carry the whole humanity within us as he had done and pray for them. His final prayer with his disciples was that they all may be together as one family of his Father and member of his own mystical Body. He went to extreme, as he always did, to pray earnestly for us to be one as he and his Father are one. *"I pray not only for them, but also for those who will believe in me through their word, so that they may all be one, as you, Father, are in me and I in you, that they also may be in us, that the world may believe that you sent me."* (Jn. 17: 20-21)

Such a peaceful, sincere, and spiritual togetherness of brotherhood deserves merits from the Lord. In the Acts we notice this togetherness first among the Apostles and Mary and then the early Christians. *"They all continued with one accord in prayer, with the women and with Mary who was the mother of Jesus, and his brothers."* (Acts 1: 14) Their qualityprayer earned the 'empowerment of the Spirit.

Following the footsteps of Mary and the Apostles all new Christians lived, breathed and prayed in togetherness: *"The community of believers was of one heart and mind, and no one claimed that any of his possessions was his own, but they had everything in common . . . There was no needy person among them, for those who owned property or houses would sell them, bring the proceeds of the sale, and put them at the feet of the apostles, and they were distributed to each according to need."* (Acts 4: 32-35) What was the endresults of this Christian togetherness? *"They ate their meals with exultation and sincerity of heart, praising God and enjoying favor with all the people. And every day the Lord added to their number those who were being saved.* (Acts 2: 46-47)

Praying to the 'God of the beyond'

Jesus' qualityprayer starts addressing God 'our Father' adding to it *'in heaven'*. By this addition he portrays our Father's 'beyondness-dimension. The God, whom we are communing with in qualityprayer as our Father-identified as Triune, exists not in nowhere but everywhere. He is present invisibly far high that can be unreachable. Heaven signifies both our Father's all-presence and in a physically-unreachable realm. He therefore may seem to us humans to be physically absenting and distancing. However as Jesus claimed we can relate to Him in our spiritual dimension.

Whenever I am inspired during prayer time I get into the mood of writing my journals. Among many of my inspirational low-quality scribbling, I find one under the title *'In search of God'* in which I wrote about my discovery about four kinds of God in humanity as I read of them in one inspirational book:

i. The God of the Books. I call him a *God of the Desktop* who is kept in Treatises, Creeds and Dogmas of all religions. He is being torn between too many theological and Scriptural enunciations and interpretations of various religions and sects.

ii. The God of the Experiences: whom I name as the *God of the Laptop*. He is more personal to individuals. He is experienced by persons committed to His Name almost all time as a powerful Force and as an intimate Person, sometimes like a Dad, other times like Mom, but most of the time as a close friend to reach out to them with support and consolation whenever they need Him.

iii. The God of the Sciences: who can be named as a *God of the Lab*. He is thwarted and rejected by the modern scientific and technological inventions, researches, and findings.

iv. The God of the Beyond: whom I love to call as a *God of the Spaceship*. He is as He is in accordance with the available and achievable dreams of humans. He is the God of never-ending aspirations, dreams and fantasies of human beings. Human dreams are not just short-lived. They are eternal and interminable. There is no boundary to them. That human dream of eternity is the God of the Beyond.

It is this fourth kind of God I am directed by Jesus to believe, adore and obey and commune with. No humans can dare say they caught hold of that God. This God cannot be quarantined or restricted or glued to one or millions of ideas or versions. He is the God of the Beyond. This is the beauty and dignity of humanity. Until such God lives, the debate and struggle on his behalf will be continued with no single answer. Even the terms and descriptions I use here may not be the last one to answer about the identity of that God of Human Dreams.

> The God of the Beyond: whom I love to call as a *God of the Spaceship*. He is as He is in accordance with the available and achievable dreams of humans. He is the God of never-ending aspirations, dreams and fantasies of human beings.

Augmenting my perception on 'Father in heaven' as the God of the beyond, Sean Caulfield, a Trappist monk in his experiential discussion on prayer writes: *"I've come at last to know that God is not a "thing." He is not of the things and bits of his own creation, one more objective thing "out there," something amongst other things. He is not even the supreme thing, the first and the greatest in a series. He is not relative to anything. He is the altogether Other, the Mystery that cannot be contained or boxed in by any symbol or concept. Our response is awe, not understanding. If we find ourselves involved in a personal way with him the experience may well be one of being invaded with a sense of "no-thingness." All our self-protecting strengths and securities are swept from under our feet."*

If God were truly distant and uncaring, He never would have bothered with the defining aspect of Christianity: the Incarnation. If God were on a cosmic vacation, He never would have lowered Himself to be born in a stinky old stable. He certainly never would have offered up His life as an atoning sacrifice for our sins.

Feature-2: Praising and Glorifying God's Holiness

Jesus in our qualityprayer includes a formula of praising our Partner in qualityprayer: *"Hallowed be your name"*. St. Cyprian writes on this verse of Jesus: *This is not because we want God to be made holy by our prayers: what we are asking God is that his name should be hallowed within us. After all, how can anything be needed to sanctify God, who himself is the source of sanctity? But because he says be holy, as I am holy, we ask and beg of him that we, who have been sanctified in baptism, may continue in that which we have begun to be. And this we pray daily, for our need is for daily sanctification so that we who daily fall away may wash away our crimes by continual sanctification.*

As St. Cyprian says, God who is already holy doesn't need any of our petitioning for his holiness. Rather we praise and magnify his sanctity and in that praise we totally recognize God's wholistic and unreachable status of holiness; we long that *'sanctus, sanctus, sanctus'*-eminence of God be preserved safe and sound even in his dwelling among and within humans. Certainly we, as praying persons, express our sincere desire to encounter and possess that august personality of holiness in our lives; because we know our Master wanted us to *'be holy as our heavenly Father is holy'*.

Jesus taught us to include in our qualityprayer an element of filtering out all wrong and twisted purposes in our mind regarding prayer. We have to purify our intention of praying as we go into His presence. All that we are, all that we do and say in prayer is only for His great glory and that we start, proceed and end our prayer for His Name, in His Spirit's Name and through His Son's Name.

Feature-3: Praying with great longing for God's kingdom

Jesus insists to ignite our qualityprayer with the same vision for which he came down from heaven and lived, died and was buried;"The establishment of God's kingdom' in all human hearts and the whole universe. Making us to pray *'Your kingdom come'* Jesus wants us to hang on to his vision as our main goal in whatever we do, especially in the acts of praying. St. Augustine writes: *"As for our saying: Your kingdom come, it will surely come whether we will it or not. But we are stirring up our desires for the kingdom so that it can come to us and we can deserve to reign there."*

The Kingdom of God as theologians explain is not a physical and circumvented location, rather, it is the spiritual realm where the Supreme Spiritual Being exercises his Sovereignty. As it is believed by the disciples of Jesus and professed in the liturgy of the Church this kingdom of God is: *'a kingdom of truth and life, a kingdom of holiness and grace, and a kingdom of justice, love, and peace.'*

It is in this unique kingdom we long for personally becoming fullfledged faithful citizens of God; we too present our hopefilled heartbeats to Him, that we who started off as His subjects in this world may one day reign with Christ when he reigns according to his promise: *"Then the king will say to those on his right, 'Come, you who are blessed by my Father. Inherit the kingdom prepared for you from the foundation of the world."* (Matt. 25: 34)

There is also another way of looking at this insert of Jesus in his prayer formula. Let me quote here what St. Cyprian states: *"Christ himself is the kingdom of God, for whose coming we daily ask. For since he himself is our resurrection, since in him we rise again, so also the kingdom of God may be understood to be himself, since it is in him that we shall reign."*

Feature-4: Total surrendering to God's will

The terms like 'surrender' and 'obedience' are unknown and not well-received in the post-modern generation. Surprisingly Jesus demands this unusual 'surrender' in our qualityprayer, adding in his prayer formula:

'Your will be done, on earth as in heaven'. Freedom and dignity are our birthright; those are the endowments our Creator entrusted to us. He too is glorified when we respect those gifts. However we know His preference of how we should handle them. In the Bible He commanded all his human creatures, starting from Adam and Eve through kings and Prophets till this day all His faithful children, to choose to obey His Commandments and Laws and observe them in full freedom and with dignity.

Jesus was very clear in his vision and aim in his earthly life: *"I came down from heaven not to do my own will but the will of the one who sent me."* (Jn. 6: 38) *"My food is to do the will of the one who sent me and to finish his work."* (Jn. 4: 34) *"I do not seek my own will but the will of the one who sent me."* (Jn. 5: 30)

He not only spelt out his obedience and surrender to his Father's will in words but in his day today life as well. Jesus lived up to his Father's command from his conception till his last breath. *"For this reason, when he came into the world, he said: "Sacrifice and offering you did not desire, but a body you prepared for me; holocausts and sin offerings you took no delight in. Then I said, 'As is written of me in the scroll, Behold, I come to do your will, O God.'"* (Heb. 10: 5-7) Even during his life climatic situation of suffering ignominious agony he could tell God, *"Father, if you are willing, take this cup away from me; still, not my will but yours be done."* (Lk. 22: 42)

> According to Jesus' perception the only way to reach his life's victory was to surrender himself to his Father's will. This is why he demanded his followers to seek to fulfill God's will as an effective strategy for the ultimate victory in life.

Jesus owned in his heart and mind a perfect blueprint of his Father's will which he audibly declared to his disciples: *"This is the will of the one who sent me, that I should not lose anything of what he gave me, but that I should raise it [on] the last day. For this is the will of my Father, that everyone who sees the Son and believes in him may have eternal life, and I shall raise him [on] the last day."* (Jn. 6: 39-40)

According to his perception the only way to reach his life's victory was to surrender himself to his Father's will. This is why he demanded his followers to seek to fulfill God's will as an effective strategy for the ultimate victory in life. St. Augustine said: "When we say: *Your will be done on earth as it is in heaven*, we are asking God to make us obedient so that his will may be done in us as it is done in heaven by his angels".

As a matter of fact, no human can resist God in such a way as to prevent him from doing what he wills. But there is a reason behind Jesus adding 'thy will be done' to his qualityprayer formula. As a human he knew what stuff we are made of. When he saw his disciples sleeping in the Garden while he wanted them to pray with him, he said: *"Watch and pray that you may not undergo the test. The spirit is willing, but the flesh is weak."* (Matt. 26: 41) The devil, using our weak condition, hinders us from obeying God's holy will by thought and by deed. Therefore we wish and pray that God's will may be done in us.

God's will for us is, as we know from the Scriptures, to love Him with all our heart. In addition, fulfilling God's will means, as St. Cyprian writes, 'to be co-heirs with Christ in preferring nothing whatever to Christ; adhering inseparably to his love; standing faithfully and bravely by his cross; and being steadfast to meet any conflict in our witnessing to his name and honor.'

By including to this prayer 'as in heaven' Jesus willed that we should hold on to the belief on the existence of the abode of God where there are the host of angels and saints whose one and only aim in life was, is and will be forever to fulfill God's Will. In that crowd of obedient fulfillers of God's will many are still living in this world as—in the words of St. Augustine visible and invisible church members. Some of them may be around our lives standing before us as our rolemodels and inspirers. We long to join this holy crowd; we therefore carry this wish in our qualityprayer.

Feature-5: Praying with the attitude of 'daily-ness'

Another most important ingredient Jesus wants us to include into our qualityprayer is our awareness of today and its needs. *"Give us today our daily bread.*" It is true besides the spiritual elements Jesus expects us to stand on the earthly ground of today and not going on dreaming the 'beyondness'-dreams. St. Augustine quite rightly interprets the words 'this day' as 'in this world.' We are made of dual dimensions: spiritual as well as physical. In a way our human life can be explained as a sort of in-carnation of the likeness and image of God. We are 'little less than angels' as the Psalmist claims.

However we have a starving, thirsting, vulnerable, breakable and unpredictable body. Hence we need those basic needs to be fulfilled. During qualityprayer Jesus advises us to remember our physical reality-needs for which we should cling to God. The term 'Bread', as many Biblical scholars and church fathers interpret, means not just the human need of food but also all those human basic needs, namely sheltering, clothing, sexual fulfillment, fertility, self-esteem, love, self-actualization, and so on.

> Another most important ingredient Jesus wants us to include into our qualityprayer is our awareness of today and its needs. *"Give us today our daily bread."* It is true besides the spiritual elements Jesus expects us to stand on the earthly ground of today and not going on dreaming the 'beyondness'-dreams.

Besides these earthly human needs, Jesus pointed out the greatest need of his disciples, namely our spiritual life-giving Bread, Christ Himself. He identified himself as the Bread from heaven. *"I am the living bread that came down from heaven; whoever eats this bread will live forever; and the bread that I will give is my flesh for the life of the world."* (Jn. 6: 51) Hence he referred to this need and made us long for such 'Bread' daily to be received at our qualityprayer—private, communal or ritual.

By adding the terms 'this day' and 'daily' Jesus expected us holding a filial trust in our Father's providential care, we enter into the prayer chamber without any anxieties. First we should have no apprehension about our life's needs at all. *"Therefore I tell you, do not worry about your life, what you will eat [or drink], or about your body, what you will wear. Is not life more than food* and the body more than clothing?" (Matt. 6: 25); secondly we are to get rid of all our concerns about the past and the future. Jesus wished that we fully concentrate in qualityprayer on today's life. 'Now' is the only time to care about and the rest flow from it. *"Do not worry about tomorrow; tomorrow will take care of itself. Sufficient for a day is its own evil."* (Matt. 6: 34) Above all, we should keep the 'possessing' God's kingdom as primary and ultimate need in daily life. *"But seek first the kingdom (of God) and his righteousness, and all these things will be given you besides."* (Matt. 6: 33)

Feature-6: Entering the House of Prayer as 'Homecoming'

In our discussion on the identity of qualityprayer we said it's like a dating with our most romantic and loving Valentine. In a humans' dating, the demand of a girl is: 'I don't want you to date other girls, only me.' Unfortunately if her boy flirts around with different girls or dates another girl she will surely reject him and stop her dating with him. However when that same boy comes back to his senses and begs pardon from her and if his 'homecoming' is genuine and sincere the loving heart of her will be melted ready to go steady with him.

This is exactly what happens every time we date with the Lord in qualityprayer. We, the weak and fragile as we are, had been so distracted either by introversion or by extroversion, and completely distracted in our daily chores we forget the friendly and immanent presence of the Lord. When we come to His presence we truly come to our senses as the Prodigal son, convert ourselves to see what we are missing and get up and go back to our Valentine who is like a spouse, a parent, a friend and a master. *"How necessary, how provident, how salutary are we reminded that we are sinners, since we have to beg for forgiveness, and while we ask for God's pardon, we are reminded of our own consciousness of guilt!"* (St. Cyprian)

As the Prodigal son Jesus desires us to say to our Father: *"Father, I have sinned against heaven and against you; I no longer deserve to be called your son."* (Lk. 15: 21) this is what he meant when he asked us to incorporate into our qualityprayer the petition: *"Forgive us our trespasses"*. In this 'homecoming' we confess first the identity of our God as our Life, Love and Way. We confess His Sovereignty over us and the entire creation. "I am that I Am." Secondly we confess our own identity as His creation as a receiver of His Being. "I am that I am." I too confess to Him in what position I stand now. "I am what I am." I plead for mercy and His gratuitous grace for us being accepted by Him again into His Abode. *"If we say, 'We are without sin,' we deceive ourselves, and the truth is not in us. If we acknowledge our sins, he is faithful and just and will forgive our sins and cleanse us from every wrongdoing. If we say, 'We have not sinned,' we make him a liar, and his word is not in us."* (1 Jn. 1: 8-10)

> Christ insists on the spirit of forgiveness in our qualityprayer not as a condition for getting our own forgiveness from our merciful Father; rather it is for making ourselves worthy sons and daughters in front of Him so that He can stoop over us and bestow forgiveness.

Whatever we receive from God as gift in Jesus is gratuitous and unconditional. This is an eternal truth. However there are certain demands from God through his Prophets, especially through His Son and his disciples in order to please our Father and become worthy of His Gifts. For example we are told to uphold impudent faith in Him; He commanded us to obey His twofold command of love. In this formula of qualityprayer Jesus asks us to cherish in our mind that unless we forgive others' sins we will never be forgiven of our sins. *"If you forgive others their transgressions, your heavenly Father will forgive you. But if you do not forgive others, neither will your Father forgive your transgressions."* (Matt. 6: 14-15)

Therefore Jesus reminds us to place in '*as we forgive those who trespass against us*'. In continuation of this saying, Jesus went on explaining about this important spirit of forgiveness to be found in all our qualityprayer: *"When you stand to pray, forgive anyone against whom you have a grievance, so that your heavenly Father may in turn forgive you your transgressions."* (Mk. 11: 25)

St. Augustine clarifies this desire of Jesus writing: "when we say: *Forgive us our trespasses as we forgive those who trespass against us, we are reminding ourselves of what we must ask and what we must do in order to be worthy in turn to receive.*" He is correct in what he says about the forgiveness of others' sins. Christ insists on the spirit of forgiveness in our qualityprayer not as a condition for getting our own forgiveness from our merciful Father; rather it is for making ourselves worthy sons and daughters in front of Him so that He can stoop over us and bestow forgiveness. For Jesus remarked about our Father's smartness: *"Do not give what is holy to dogs, or throw your pearls before swine, lest they trample them underfoot, and turn and tear you to pieces."* (Matt. 7: 6)

Feature-7: Inclusion of praying in Tears

If our prayer is ranked as qualityprayer we would encounter certainly the holy and sacred presence of God during which time our eyes will be wet on two reasons: One, there comes a shaking and shattering moment in which we begin to tremble as Prophets like Isaiah and Jeremiah experienced discovering our nothingness, unholiness and unworthiness in God's tremendous presence. We observe our imprisonment by evils and strangled by temptations of the devil and other evil forces.

We begin to cry out and shed tears of sorrow, tears of helplessness and tears of captivity: *"Lead us not into temptation"* and *"deliver us from the evil."* Here I love to quote a wise interpretation of St. Augustine: *"In this final petition the Christian can utter his cries of sorrow, in it he can shed his tears, and through it he can begin, continue and conclude his prayer, whatever the distress in which he finds himself."* Luke in his Gospel brings to our notice very graphically how a praying person should pray in front of the divine with only bodily gesture and show one's love and penitential confession: *"Now there was a sinful woman in the city who learned that he was at table in the house of the Pharisee. Bringing an alabaster flask of ointment, she stood behind him at his feet weeping and began to bathe his feet with her tears. Then she wiped* them with her hair, kissed them, and anointed them with the ointment." (Lk. 7: 37-38)

Two, we also shed tears of joy perceiving the magnanimity of our God coming into my poverty-stricken abode, communicating and, more startlingly, communing with me in an ecstatic way. Hope enters in and fills the hearts to the brim. Tears would continue rolling down our cheeks when we remember the sad status of humanity; there are millions of our brethren who haven't had such an experience of God. They are victimized in imprisonment of the evil and succumbed to temptation. Tears still keep on running from our eyes in begging our Beloved to show consideration to them and grant the same spiritual gift that we have been blessed with.

B. Other Components of Qualityprayer

1. Unshaken faith

Besides giving many ingredients of qualityprayer through his Prayer formula, Jesus offered us some more of them through his sayings and parables. One of those components is 'Faith.' All Jesus' promises of the effects of prayer are centered on holding faith: *"Whatever you ask for in prayer with faith, you will receive."* (Matt. 21:22) *Therefore I tell you, all that you ask for in prayer, believe that you will receive it and it shall be yours."* (Mk. 11:24)

Jesus' disciples, after discovering their inability in casting out the evil spirit from people through qualityprayer, asked him, "Why could we not drive it out?" He said to them, *"Because of your little faith. Amen, I say to you, if you have faith the size of a mustard seed, you will say to this mountain, 'Move from here to there,' and it will move. Nothing will be impossible for you."* (Matt. 17: 14-20)

Faith in God is not a belief in a bulk of dogmas or practice of certain disciplines. The Church Fathers always considered faith in two kinds: One kind of faith concerns doctrines. It involves the soul's ascent to and acceptance of some particular matter. The other kind of faith is given by Christ by means of special grace. As Paul says, faith is a special gift of the Holy Spirit. While he enumerates the gifts of the Spirit to Jesus' disciples he includes *'to another, faith by the same Spirit'.* However he adds at the end of his exposition of gifts of the Spirit, *'But one and the same Spirit produces all of these, distributing them individually to each person as he wishes.'* (1 Cor. 12: 8-11) In other words the virtue of faith is nothing but the gratuitous gift from the Spirit of God.

> Faith is the gift of God, and through this virtue he enables us to call upon him in every circumstance, from desperation to joy, in tragedies and in blessings.

'To believe is to commit,' writes Oswald Chambers, in his book *'My utmost for His highest'*, a compilation of daily reflections. In his view Christian life is more personal relationship to Christ than anything else. He divides the meanings of faith in two ways: One is mental faith through which we commit ourselves, discarding all that is related to that commitment; two, he calls it 'personal belief' in which we morally bind ourselves to Jesus and his values and with no compromise whatsoever spiritually commit ourselves to him.

It's this qualityfaith, gratuitous gift from God and our personal commitment, which Jesus wanted us to include in our qualityprayer when he said: *'If you have faith, the size of a mustard seed.'*

Faith is the gift of God, and through this virtue he enables us to call upon him in every circumstance, from desperation to joy, in tragedies and in blessings. Cyril of Alexandria beautifully sums up the effective role of faith in our Christian life: "*It is of this kind of faith, moreover, that it is said: If you have faith like a grain of mustard seed. The mustard seed is small in size but it holds an explosive force; although it is sown in a small hole, it produces great ranches, and when it is grown birds can nest there. In the same way faith produces great effects in the soul instantaneously. Enlightened by faith, the soul pictures God and sees him as clearly as any soul can. It circles the earth; even before the end of this world it sees the judgment and the conferring of promised rewards.*"

Faith, applied in qualityprayer, never knows where it is being led, but it loves and knows the One who is leading. We hear from Scripture: *Faith is the substance of things hoped for, the evidence of things not seen.* (Heb. 11:1) The root of faith is the knowledge of a Person, who will certainly lead us to success.

In placing the 'faith' in our qualityprayer as its anchor in a right perspective and with sincerity we get all that we aim at through qualityprayer, especially the 'qualitylife' possible in this world and the fullness of it in heaven. Faith is like breathing; we don't think about; we just do it. We exercise faith everyday in life and don't even realize it. When, for example, we decide to sit down on a chair we go and do it holding faith that the chair will hold us.

Reasonable Faith

I agree with Periyar, EVR, an Indian rationalist, that *'reason is the life-blood of man. Among all creatures, only man possesses reason. The lower he is in the exercise of this faculty, comparably, the more of a barbarian he is. He attains maturity, consonant with the clarity he achieves through reason. Rationality is the capacity of thinking objectively.'* However I totally disagree with him in his statement that *'man should contemplate on anything, not by following the path of belief, but that of reason. He should see whether the object of his contemplation stands the test of inquiry. Only then he rises to human stature from a primitive state.'*

Like this great rationalist there are too many among us who deny the intrinsic connection between faith and reason. All balanced and matured Christians recognize the important role of human knowledge and reason in their faith-filled lives. Knowledge is God's, but ignorance is Satan's. Through ignorance we are led to so many destructive attitudes and deeds of hatred, discrimination, superstition, unjust social tradition, and so on. While God expects us to hold indomitable faith in Him, He demands from us to use our mind to know Him well and our heart to love Him totally. At my early childhood I was asked to memorize my Catholic 'penny catechism' consisting of questions and answers about God and religion. One question was: 'Why did God create man?' The answer to it was: "To know Him, to love Him, to serve Him and consequently reach heaven.'

The disciples of Jesus are fully aware of the truth that to know God is the highest and best form of knowledge. This spiritual knowledge is a source of strength to us. It strengthens our faith. In Scriptures all God's heroes and heroines are inevitably described as being persons who are enlightened and taught of the Lord. They are said to "have an unction from the Holy One." It is the Spirit's peculiar office to lead them into all truth, and all this for the increase and the fostering of their faith.

Certainly the Church acknowledges this intrinsic relation between reason and religion. In one of its Vatican Council's documents, highlighting the important role played by science and technology, the church says: "with the help of science and technology . . . , man has extended his mastery over almost the whole of nature", and thus "he now produces by his own enterprise benefits once looked for from heavenly powers" ("Gaudium et Spes," 33). Christianity totally denies any conflict between supernatural faith and scientific progress, rather it accepts that they mutually enhance each other. As Pope John Paul II, once observed: "Scientists, precisely because they 'know more', are called to 'serve more'. Since the freedom they enjoy in research gives them access to specialized knowledge, they have the responsibility of using that knowledge wisely for the benefit of the entire human family" (Address to the Pontifical Academy of Sciences, 11 November 2002).

The disciples of Jesus are fully aware of the truth that to know God is the highest and best form of knowledge. This spiritual knowledge is a source of strength to us. It strengthens our faith.

Expounding the correlation existing in the two abilities of humans, reasoning and believing, many noted philosophers and theologians have espoused the idea that faith is the basis of all knowledge. The idea of "faith seeking understanding" was set forth by St. Augustine of Hippo. He wrote: *"Crede, ut intelligas"* ("Believe in order that you may understand"). This statement extends beyond the sphere of religion to encompass the totality of knowledge. In essence, faith must be present in order to know anything.

In other words, one must assume, believe, or have faith in the credibility of a person, place, thing, or idea in order to have a basis for human knowledge. Faith therefore never knows where it is being led, but it loves and knows the One who is leading. It is a life of *Faith*, not of intellect and reason, but a life of knowing who makes us "go." The root of faith is the knowledge of a Person, who is faithful in His promises and surely will lead us to success.

Application of faith as 'yeast'

In one of Jesus' parables about God's Kingdom we hear him comparing it to the yeast. *"The kingdom of heaven is like yeast that a woman took and mixed with three measures of wheat flour until the whole batch was leavened."* (Matt. 13: 33) In the natural order of life 'yeast' is, as Jesus meant, a leavening agent in baking bread and bakery products, where it converts the fermentable; something that causes ferment, activity, or unrest. We can even call it a catalyst, which, though little in its measure, can bring very effective results in what it is mixed with. The same way the cardinal virtue of faith, though small like the size of mustard seed, can bring the expected results from qualityprayer.

There is also another side of the yeast effecting wrong and unwanted outcomes if it is not applied properly. In our prayer efforts if faith is not properly used as Jesus' wish we will end up in reaping evil fruits as the Pharisees and Sadducees did in Jesus' time. This is why Jesus warned his disciples about their view and handling of faith: *Jesus said to them, "Look out, and beware of the leaven of the Pharisees and Sadducees . . . Then they understood that he was not telling them to beware of the leaven of bread, but of the teaching of the Pharisees and Sadducees."* (Matt. 16: 6-12)

Faith as 'Chutzpah'

In order to find out the right meaning and use of qualityfaith in our qualityprayer we should go to Jesus himself. He used a Hebrew term 'Chutzpa' for 'faith'. It is a sort of supreme self-confidence or nerve that allows someone to do or say things that may seem shocking to others; we can even call it as 'nearly arrogant' courage; utter audacity, effrontery or impudence, persistence or relentlessness; it makes a person shameless in doing or speaking certain things which to others seem like crazy or freaky behavior.

> "I talked only to my boss, God," she said. "I didn't need any more humans."

At every time we come to prayer we should start 'from scratch': No question, no reason, no sight, no basis, no advice, no strings attached, no credibility and no needs at all. Simply we start from 'nowhere.' In other words: *from our faith and not by sight*. Ena Zizi, a 69-year-old ardent Roman Catholic, had been at a church meeting at the residence of Haiti's Roman Catholic archbishop when the Jan. 12 quake struck, trapping her in the debris. On Tuesday, that is a week after the earthquake, she was rescued by a Mexican disaster team. Zizi said after the quake, she spoke back and forth with a vicar who also was trapped. But he fell silent after a few days, and she spent the rest of the time praying and waiting. "I talked only to my boss, God," she said. "I didn't need any more humans." Doctors who examined Zizi on Tuesday said she was dehydrated and had a dislocated hip and a broken leg. Is she not crazy and impudent in her prayerful behavior? Our Master desires that our qualityprayer must be a prayer of qualityfaith as that of Ena Zizi's "faith-filled week of prayer under the rubble."

Jesus enriched us with his definition of qualityfaith to be found in qualityprayer through his life's incidents, parables and sayings. Jesus qualityfaith is a belief that contains peculiar but amazing characteristics of its own:

Unwavering consistency

The faith we hold in qualityprayer must have its consistency. To explain this truth and the fact of Jesus' worry about how his humans' faith would not be up to his expectation he narrated a parable: *"Then he told them a parable about the necessity for* **them to pray always without becoming weary.** *He said: "There was a judge in a certain town who neither feared God nor respected any human being. And a widow in that town used to come to him and* say, 'Render a just decision for me against my adversary.' For a long time the judge was unwilling, but eventually he thought, 'While it is true that I neither fear God nor respect any human being, because this widow keeps bothering me I shall deliver a just decision for her lest she finally come and strike me.'" The Lord said, "Pay attention to what the dishonest judge says. Will not God then secure the rights of his chosen ones who call out to him day and night? Will he be slow to answer them? I tell you, he will see to it that justice is done for them speedily. But when the Son of Man comes, **will he find faith** on earth?" (Lk. 18:1-8)

Jesus also told his followers to persevere in prayer. Perseverance is the condition or the most important quality of Jesus' prayer. Explaining through a small parable, he declares that even if the relationship between God and myself is not that good, he will get up to give me whatever I need because of my persistence. Rather, faith is simply persevering in our relationship, in our prayer, in our concentration toward God. Saints became saints by somehow hanging on to the stubborn conviction that things are not as they appear, and that the unseen world is as solid and trustworthy as the visible world around them and persist in praying to that invisible, unseen God.

Childlike Trust

As we have already expounded speaking about Jesus' formula of prayer, faith is a familial, an intimate feeling over the Supreme Being. It demands a behavior of a child from us. Prayer must start and continue in shameless faith and trust as children have toward their parents.

> We should hold the childlike trust and start and continue our qualityprayer because God is delighted in this familial relationship. He guarantees His trust and fidelity toward us and then He demands such attitude and behavior from us.

There is a beautiful lullaby of a mother, for her baby on her lap, bringing out the remarkable parental goodness: *"Hush, little baby, don't say a word, Mama's going to buy you a mockingbird. And if that mockingbird won't sing, Mama's going to buy you a diamond ring."* As it continues, this popular lullaby expresses the unquestioning willingness of parents to satisfy their child's every need and desire, whether these are as necessary as food and shelter or as frivolous as a mockingbird and diamond ring.

If parents with all of their imperfections are willing to provide for their own, how much more will God, who is the *embodiment of perfection?* (Lk. 11: 13) This is how Jesus argues with us when he highlights the importance of shameless faith to be included in our qualityprayer. In the Bible we notice Abraham during his prayertimes sounding like a crazy but bold child or friend of God and so were other Biblical persons like Jacob, Moses, David, Solomon, Isaiah and other Prophets.

We should hold the childlike trust and start and continue our qualityprayer because God is delighted in this familial relationship. He guarantees His trust and fidelity toward us and then He demands such attitude and behavior from us. *"But Zion said, 'The LORD has forsaken me; my Lord has forgotten me.' Can a mother forget her infant, be without tenderness for the child of her womb? Even should she forget, I will never forget you. See, upon the palms of my hands I have engraved you; your walls are ever before me."* (Is. 49: 14-16)

Blind Daring

There is one more thing Jesus wants his followers to put in to their prayer, namely boldness. We should be daring enough to ask God even if the situation seems one hundred percent hopeless, grim. Look at Abraham. Despite the fact that Sodom seemed a hopelessly lost cause, Abraham made his case to God boldly. Jesus instructed us in qualityprayer to: "Ask, seek, and knock." This means he asked us to ask first in an intimate way. If we have not received what we asked, then we should seek and find out why our Dad, our Papa is silent. If that too is failed, the only possible strategy is, we should knock and knock; we knock boldly even at midnight as we hear the needy friend's door-knocking in the parable of Jesus; and we must fight it out, if need be, as Jacob was struggling with the angel of God all night until he got back what he requested.

Why should we be bold in qualityprayer? If Abraham and all those prayer-warriors in the OT before Jesus had the guts to approach God with such boldness, why not we who have been cleansed by the blood of Jesus? In all his Letters Paul brings to our mind very convincingly the work of Jesus in us. *"He brought you to life along with him, having forgiven all our transgressions; obliterating the bond against us, with its legal claims, which was opposed to us, he also removed it from our midst, nailing it to the cross."* (Col. 2: 13-14)

In the Letter to the Hebrews we read, *"Therefore, since we have a great high priest who has passed through the heavens, Jesus, the Son of God, let us hold fast to our confession. For we do not have a high priest who is unable to sympathize with our weaknesses, but one who has similarly been tested in every way, yet without sin. So let us confidently approach the throne of grace to receive mercy and to find grace for timely help."* (Heb. 4: 14-16)

Besides, Jesus promised us, *'I am going to the Father. And whatever you ask in my name, I will do, so that the Father may be glorified in the Son. If you ask anything of me in my name, I will do it.'* (Jn.14: 12-14) In qualityprayer like Mary, sister of Lazarus, we sit at the feet of Jesus. We stay put in God's presence, remaining in a fixed or established position, persisting, unmoving and steady. Our whole preoccupation and concentration is on God. We persevere till the end at any cost.

In the Bible one of the heroes who portray the reality of qualityprayer is Abraham. Among many incidents in his prayer life, there is one which is very amusing but directly picturizes how impudent faith plays its role in qualityprayer. In Genesis 18: 20-33 we read about Abraham's chutzpah-filled conversation with God. Abraham's prayer sounds to most of us silly and childish. Yet in the Bible we are told God liked such ill-mannered daring of His children. Knocking at the door at midnight is some kind of shameful activity. Jesus demands such ill-mannered perseverance.

2. Authentic Humility

If we consider the unshaken faith in God as one side of the coin of qualityprayer, its other side is genuine humility. As faith is an intrinsic element to be found in qualityprayer's beginning, process and its end, so is humility. In the *Catechism of the Catholic Church* we are told that 'humility is the foundation of prayer.' (2559)

If we want our prayer to be effective and result oriented, it must have a spirit of humanness. Look at the tax collector in the parable of Jesus. (Lk. 18: 10-14) When he prays he brings up before God his entire humanity, a humanity that is vulnerable, sinful, weak, limited, needy and unworthy. Both his words and body language betrays this spirit. Jesus says, the tax collector stood off at a distance and would not even raise his eyes to heaven but beat his breast and prayed, 'O God, be merciful to me a sinner.' On the contrary the Pharisee points out his own divine quality, his goodness and his religious performances. Jesus says the tax collector's prayer was heard by God. In Sirach we read: *"The prayer of the lowly pierces the clouds; it will not rest till it reaches its goal."* (Sir. 35: 16)

> If we consider the unshaken faith in God as one side of the coin of qualityprayer, its other side is genuine humility. As faith is an intrinsic element to be found in qualityprayer's beginning, process and its end, so is humility.

From its root Latin word 'Humus' meaning 'earth' humility is to be understood as an awareness or consciousness of our origin, identity 'from the earth'. We are made out of clay. So we are very vulnerable, delicate, and breakable. There is an end to all we do. The body, we walk with; the life, we breathe in and out; and the earth, we possess; they are, though somewhat brownie-small supernatural creatures, limited and transient. Humility means also an awareness of our potential to be eternal. We possess within us the seed of eternity. As the Scriptures say, 'we have approached Mount Zion and the city of the living God, the heavenly Jerusalem'. (Heb.12/22) In other words, we are 'that close' to be superhuman.

A humble person therefore is one who sees one's own reality, accepts it fully and lives with it. Unfortunately we forget this 'humus' factor of us many times. We behave exactly like little children inside the flight. They run, play, sleep, dance in the plane, not being aware we are floating in the air.

Have you ever given a second to consider seriously the fact that we are just standing, walking, skiing, sleeping, dancing, running, jumping, just on the surface of a basketball-like planet which round the clock rotates, rolls like any other planets in the universe?

The real sense of humility makes us come out of our sleepy mood that may endanger our possible growth and sometimes may induce us to be hard on ourselves. It urges us very often to ask ourselves: 'who am I? What am I for? What about my relationships? My Profession? My Possessions?' This is the chemistry of humility. Such awareness will lead us to walk on the balanced and straight path toward our genuine growth. This also will help us to accept well the criticism and opinions of others about us. It would persuade us to feel happy about others' success, to appreciate their positive qualities and to forgive and tolerate others' defects and blunders.

Humility is the only way to be in the good book of God. Almost all holy people who have found favor with God and admitted in His kingdom of heaven are humble people. This is what He tells us through the Prophet Zephaniah: *"Seek the LORD, all you humble of the land, who have observed his law; Seek justice, seek humility; perhaps you will be sheltered on the day of the LORD's anger."* (Zeph. 2: 3); *"But I will leave as a remnant in your midst a people humble and lowly, who shall take refuge in the name of the LORD."* (Zeph. 3: 12)

Humility is the only virtue that makes human life joyful and content. A humble person takes the unfairness of life in his/her hands and moulds it into stepping stone for his success. Yoke of life turns to be sweet and the burden of 'humus' light. Jesus, the most honorable teacher of all teachers but the most humble one said: *"Learn from me. I am meek and humble of heart. My yoke is sweet and my burden light."* (Matt. 11: 29)

Humility is a virtue very unpopular and most misunderstood and therefore not practiced in life, especially in prayer. However in the Bible there are numerous references pointing out that humility is the virtue that paves way for human growth and development as well as enhances our prayer as qualityprayer. The book of Sirach says: *'Conduct your affairs with humility and you will be loved more than a giver of gifts. Humble yourself the more, the greater you are and you will find favor with God.'* Jesus' favorite statement was: *'Everyone who exalts himself will be humbled, but the one who humbles himself will be exalted."* (Lk.14/11)

> As children, depending on our parents and elders, we uphold some sort of humility; by the time we reach adolescence, nearly all of us see ourselves as the center of the universe; we live at the opposite pole from true humility. But as the hard knocks of life show us our actual position as only one of many, eventually the path toward humility begins.

All the saints turned out to be saints because of this virtue. Mary the queen of saints was a champion of humility. Her heart was always beating with the words: *'He looked upon his handmaid's lowliness; He lifted up the lowly.'* Who will inherit the earth? Jesus says: *"Blessed are the meek for they will inherit the earth."* From Scriptures we learn that if we want god's promises to be fulfilled in us, we have to possess the virtue of humility.

Humility therefore is the most essential quality for entering the sacred; it not only enables our prayer to be sincere and genuine, but also grows through the same. As children, depending on our parents and elders, we uphold some sort of humility; by the time we reach adolescence, nearly all of us see ourselves as the center of the universe; we live at the opposite pole from true humility. But as the hard knocks of life show us our actual position as only one of many, eventually the path toward humility begins. However most of us continue holding pride and arrogance as techniques of survival and success in life. We go too extreme-either low esteeming or high-esteeming, either going down with inferiority-complex or flying in the air with superiority complex.

In this unbalanced manner of living we don't enter into prayer with genuine humility and consequently lose its quality-results. When we straighten out this clumsy situation, we begin to be conscious of the presence of the Supreme Being and His greatness, plus our worth in reality, He being the Potter, we the clay. Our road toward humility accelerates, most of the time in qualityprayer, with an element of fear and trembling before our dim but growing intuition of the Greatness behind the universe. Thus, we become conscious of our nothingness before the Divine; at the same time reflecting on the words of Scriptures we feel our worth in the eyes of God in Jesus.

Understanding that utter humility is a precondition for contact with the Divine, we examine our own self-centeredness and search for ways to let go of our <u>egoism</u>. Finally, in moments of true emptiness, we drop our separateness from the Divine, with none of our self left to be afraid for, humility momentarily perfected. This is a part of mystery contained in qualityprayer.

Humility, as the first step in qualityprayer, is always difficult as a starting trouble. It needs some wisdom to understand where we are standing now in the eyes of God; it needs some humility to bow and accept 'yes' we are in an unfavorable state and we are in a wrong place with wrong attitudes; it needs certain guts to rise up and walk back to the Lord and say 'I am sorry' and 'I want to be received by you.' We then see pleasant surprises waiting from the side of God.

3. Tenacious Perseverance

Jesus instructed us through his sayings and parables and in a very special manner through his prayerlife, on the necessity of praying always and not losing heart. His parables, 'the widow and the judge', and 'the friend at the midnight', remind us how consistent and persistent we should be in our dealings with God. Our life journey consists of two parallel lines: One, our engagements with God and the other, our dealings with the earthly things and persons. In both dealings our success consists in persevering, not losing heart at any time and in performing our hard labor at our best.

It is true our secular studies and formation taught us that perseverance and hard labor are important tools for success in human efforts. Unfortunately the world and the age of Enlightenment have made us forget to use the same strategy in our successful dealings with God. As a matter of fact, the Scriptures remind us of the need of perseverance and hard work both in worldly and godly deeds as well.

In the OT Moses, the senior-most leader of the Israelites, asks his junior Joshua to go with his men to the battle field, while he himself kneels on the mountain top praying to God with his hands raised up. This tells us how we should put heart and soul and persevere in both human efforts and in relying on God. The story of Moses praying with raised hands is not some sort of ancient magic. It isn't recorded for us to read as a kind of mystical motion. Moses was acting out in a visible way his strong reliance on the power of God and the importance of persevering in prayer. Moses prayed for victory and he was persistent; he was uncompromising; he was aware that prayer alone was the key to victory and success; and he prayed without ceasing.

> If our prayermail is not stamped with our violent, impudent, persevering, persistent and consistent effort, that mail, however be it sacred to our eyes, will never be opened, rather it will be trashed by God. No wonder Jesus said, "When you pray: Ask, knock, and seek."

In Jesus' life too we see the same persistent prayer. He never ceased praying. He prayed day in, day out. He was praying alone, in group, with the crowd, in the temple, in synagogues, and finally on the cross too. He was praying that His Father's rule must come and reign the whole universe. During his hidden life in Nazareth we are told he obeyed his parents in everything, plus was growing in wisdom and the favor of God was upon him. This indicates, as we hear his going to the Temple for fulfilling his religious obligation at the age of twelve, he continued to pray according to every Jewish custom and tradition. Later in his public life he spent a large portion of his lifetime in prayer frequently, daily and ceaselessly.

I tell you, God considers most of our prayer efforts trash. Sometimes people, who are timid, mentally sick, or who have no backbone send us anonymous letters without signature or without a return address. What do we do with it if we are smart enough? We simply do not read them, rather trash them. The same way if our prayermail is not stamped with our violent, impudent, persevering, persistent and consistent effort, that mail, however be it sacred to our eyes, will never be opened, rather it will be trashed by God. No wonder Jesus said, "When you pray: Ask, knock, and seek."

He too emphasized the necessity of persistence in prayer through a parable of a man persisting in asking for help from his friend at midnight. "Suppose one of you has a friend to whom he goes at midnight and says, 'Friend, lend me three loaves of bread, for a friend of mine has arrived at my house from a journey and I have nothing to offer him,' and he says in reply from within, 'Do not bother me; the door has already been locked and my children and I are already in bed. I cannot get up to give you anything.' I tell you, if he does not get up to give him the loaves because of their friendship, he will get up to give him whatever he needs because of his persistence." (Matt. 11: 5-8)

Most of Jesus' sayings like this about prayer may sound like nagging, begging, badgering, pleading, and cajoling. But he knew what he was saying: The importance of perseverance is a necessary ingredient in qualityprayer.

Qualityprayer must have a spirit of steadfastness and consistency. Prayer must become a part of our system, our life's schedule. The Bible qualifies effective prayer with words like, 'cry of the oppressed', 'the wail of the orphan', and 'the widow's pouring out of her complaints'. Paul describes his life of prayer to one of the beloved disciples Timothy: It is a life of ceaseless offering to God; it is a sporty and combating life; it's a life of steadfast holding of his faith and of firmly hoping and longing and awaiting with a clear vision of his future of glory: "For I am already being poured out like a libation, and the time of my departure is at hand. I have competed well; I have finished the race; I have kept the faith. From now on the crown of righteousness awaits me, which the Lord, the just judge, will award to me on that day and not only to me, but to all who have longed for his appearance." (2Tim. 4: 6-8)

That is the way our qualityprayer should be. Never drop off from prayer even a single day. Once in a way you may hit a jackpot in and through prayer. Most of the time it takes time not necessarily for the Lord, but mostly for us in our complying to his demands in prayer and life, to enjoy all benefits from prayer. But we should never stop in praying. We should go on praying consistently and persistently and faithfully.

Madam Swetchine, a Russian Mystic says: *"There are two ways of attaining an important end—force and perseverance. Force falls to the lot of the privileged few, but austere and sustained perseverance can be practiced by the most insignificant. Its silent power grows irresistible with time."*

4. Human Chores

Our life journey consists of two parallel lines: One, our engagements with God and the other, our dealings with the earthly things and persons. In both dealings our success consists in persevering, not losing heart at any time and in performing our hard labor at our best. It is true our secular studies and formation taught us that perseverance and hard labor are important tools for success in human efforts. Unfortunately the world and the age of Enlightenment have made us forget or ignore to use the same strategy in our successful dealings with God. As a matter of fact, the Scriptures remind us of the need of perseverance and hard work both in worldly and godly deeds as well.

For example while Jesus was involved with His daily schedule of family and other works as a carpenter for thirty years, and later in his busy public life He was found moving through the street corners, the temple precincts, meadows, mountaintops, boats, and even on the cross, he continued to pray. On one line He was dealing with God intimately in a persevering prayer, and on another line He was performing all His daily works in sweat and blood.

As a matter of fact Jesus never divided this duality existing in humans' earthly life. As soul and body both prayer and action must go hand in hand. *"Not everyone who says to me, 'Lord, Lord,' will enter the kingdom of heaven, but only the one who does the will of my Father in heaven."* (Matt. 7: 21) In qualityprayertime we intend to spend much time in dialogical conversation with the Lord; many times deeply being silent in listening to Him; other times just reciting with our heartbeats certain ejaculatory prayers as 'Lord', 'Jesus', and so on. Undoubtedly that is one of the demands of qualityprayer. But there is also its intrinsic connection to our deeds outside our prayer. *"Everyone who listens to these words of mine and acts on them will be like a wise* man who built his house on rock. The rain fell, the floods came, and the winds blew and buffeted the house. But it did not collapse; it had been set solidly on rock. And everyone who listens to these words of mine but does not act on them will be like a fool who built his house on sand. The rain fell, the floods came, and the winds blew and buffeted the house. And it collapsed and was completely ruined." (Matt. 7: 24-27)

What God in Jesus advises us is that in prayer we should bring all our human endeavors, both accomplished and unfulfilled as well and hand them over to God as our sweet and thankful offerings. Also before we leave our prayer chamber we resolutely promise to the Lord all our future programs, plans, chores, of scheduled daily commitments according to our specific roles in our lifesituation and get His blessings for those deeds to be done. *"You are the light of the world. A city set on a mountain cannot be hidden. Nor do they light a lamp and then put it under a bushel basket; it is set on a lampstand, where it gives light to all in the house. Just so, your light must shine before others, that they may see your good deeds and glorify your heavenly Father."* (Matt. 5: 14-16)

> What God in Jesus advises us is that in prayer we should bring all our human endeavors, both accomplished and unfulfilled as well and hand them over to God as our sweet and thankful offerings.

Elaborating on the advice of Jesus as to how our Christian life should be permeated with the two essential elements of prayer and action, James writes: *"Be doers of the word and not hearers only, deluding yourselves. For, if anyone is a hearer of the word and not a doer, he is like a man who looks at his own face in a mirror. He sees himself, then goes off and promptly forgets what he looked like. But the one who peers into the perfect law of freedom and perseveres, and is not a hearer who forgets but a doer who acts, such a one shall be blessed in what he does."* (Js. 1: 22-25)

Whenever we are in qualityprayer, I personally feel, we are inside a Hall where God hosts His banquet of sumptuous food of life. I personally consider I am invited by the Host as his beloved guest. In most of the

Biblical events I observe God behaving both a Host and a guest as well in accordance with the root meaning of 'hostis' meaning dual role of being host and guest. While God in Jesus is being a person of banquet, whose only preoccupation in his life is to be a Host and a Guest, He naturally wants His children, the followers of Jesus to take this double role of being hosts and guests in our daily life. This is what Jesus is talking about at the dinner table in Martha's home. *"As they continued their journey he entered a village where a woman whose name was Martha welcomed him. She had a sister named Mary [who] sat beside the Lord at his feet listening to him speak. Martha, burdened with much serving, came to him and said, "Lord, do you not care that my sister has left me by myself to do the serving? Tell her to help me." The Lord said to her in reply, "Martha, Martha, you are anxious and worried about many things. There is need of only one thing. Mary has chosen the better part and it will not be taken from her."* (Lk. 10: 38-42)

Traditionally this gospel story has been interpreted to mean that a quiet life of contemplation and prayer, personified in Mary, is superior to a busy life of activity and action, personified in Martha. This is because Jesus says to the active Martha that Mary, seated at his feet and hearing his words, had chosen the better part. This is why for so many years we have erroneously thought that a monk who chooses the monastery and a nun who chooses the convent are by that very fact holier and better than those taken up with the activities of every-day life in the world. But this is not the case at all. Jesus did not intend to disparage Martha and her activity, but rather to show that hearing the word of God is the foundation of all action, that the word of God must permeate all other concerns.

While Martha was very busy in hosting a vagabond, traveler, Jesus, Mary her sister was being hosted by the Lord. This is what Jesus highlights when he compares both of them. He did not belittle or rebuke Martha's good hospitality to strangers or glorify Mary for her silent sitting near Jesus. Rather he wanted to emphasize both the hosting ministry of his disciples for their neighbors, as charitable works, business dealings, customers-services, or feeding and supporting our children, spouses, friends, even paying our tithes to the Church community must be blended and integrated with being committed guests to the Lord.

Jesus advises his followers to take the roles of both Martha and Mary. Unfortunately all of us want to behave either as Martha or Mary, and not both. Mary and Martha represent two different religions, or two different approaches to Godly life: While Mary represented the religion of hearers Martha symbolized the doers; Mary the religion of prayer but Martha that of action; one was more for giving, the other more for receiving; Mary leaned on silence and solitude while Martha on activism; Martha resembled people who enjoyed community or group works but Mary more for privacy and individualistic efforts. In sum, Martha loved to take only the role of host but Mary preferred the role of being guest.

If we are too busy like Martha in our daily life's chores, Jesus expects us to go and sit at his feet as Mary to listen, to learn, to pray, and to praise. On the other hand, if we are prone to spend our life's hours like Mary not concerned with our life's responsibilities, then, as we hear in other Gospel pages, Jesus wants us to get out of our ghettos to the street to help the needy, our neighbors, as Good Samaritans. Only those who have become the hearers of the word can truly become doers of the word. St. Teresa of Child Jesus said: *"To give the Lord a perfect hospitality, it is necessary that Mary and Martha must be joined as one."* So in our life let us take both roles of being God's guests and hosts: guests at qualityprayer and hosts in our working places.

We should be fully convinced of the truth that prayer is not better than action in the sense that they are contrary or contradictory realities, one to be preferred to the other; rather, prayer is primary in the sense of being like the source of a stream, while action is like being the flow of that same stream. They are continuous and complimentary and mutually dependent. Prayer without action is sterile, and action without prayer is empty.

Some months back, as I was browsing the internet blogs for my homily preparation, I came across a little poem. I think that it could very well be considered as the spirit of prayer and contemplation that is behind all the everyday action, which is the lot of the greatest majority of people in the world:

> *Lord of all pots and pans and things,*
> *Since I've no time to be*
> *A saint by doing holy things,*
> *Or contemplating thee,*
> *By praying in the dawn-light,*
> *Or storming heaven's gates,*
> *Make me a saint by getting meals,*
> *And washing up the plates.*

CHAPTER IV
The Method of Qualityprayer

Faking Prayer

A YOUNG ADULT who was attending a weekend retreat sponsored by a diocese tried his best to know as much as he could about genuine prayer. Being still a novice in his prayer life he had some doubts about his manner of praying. He went to the retreat preacher for guidance. His first question was, "Father, can I text or read the facebook or twitter while I pray?" The preacher said: "No. You cannot do all this and indulge yourself while you are speaking with the Lord". The young man came to his room sad and tried his best not to use any of his modern techs during his prayertime. However he could not stop texting. So next day he went to one of his colleagues, who was as amateur in praying as he was, and put this question: "Bob, tell me. Can I pray while I text or read my emails? His friend came out quickly: "Oh yes. You can and you should pray even while you text or anything you do in life".

Praying Hard or Praying Smart?

As this young man we are accustomed to justify our pattern of praying according to our whims and fancies and conveniences. There is an old saying: "Don't work hard but work smart." About quality prayer there are many of us who feel the same: It is not 'praying hard' but 'praying smart.' Most of us, in order to be more safe and undisturbed, continue the traditional way of praying as taught by elders in our childhood. Also good many of humanity crave for some new techniques and tips to change their old method of praying and fall victims to false religious and spiritual proponents of

New Age prayer models. Our Church warned us to be very cautious of such new efforts in prayer. Different warnings on differences and potential incompatibilities, between Christian prayer pattern and the various styles of prayer used in some non-Christian religions, were issued in the document of the congregation for the Doctrine of the Faith in 1989, formally known as 'Orationis Formas.'

Jesus our Grand Teacher never intended to propose to us any special method of praying, though he gave many tips for enhancing our prayer to the status of qualityprayer. He rather entrusted such responsibility to his Church. Undoubtedly, through his sayings and parables he taught us how our attitude and spirit should be during our qualityprayertime. Above all, he portrayed the genuine method of praying through his prayerlife.

When Jesus invited his hearers to follow him, some of them were curious to know of his whereabouts and whatabouts. He is quoted responding to them, "Come and see." (Jn. 1: 39) In Mark we read that the Master chose the Twelve *'that they might be with him and he might send them forth to preach.'* (Mk. 3: 14) His main intention was all his followers must stay closer to him and watch carefully his life-pattern, especially spiritual. As he noted at onetime about the relationship existing between the teacher and his disciple, he wanted all his disciples to learn from his life about qualityprayer and to try to follow him. *"No disciple is superior to the teacher; but when fully trained, every disciple will be like his teacher."* (Lk. 6: 40) Thus he taught them the method of praying by his exemplary qualityprayer. As we discussed in last chapter, even when his followers asked him to teach them how to pray, he didn't offer them a description of new technique of prayer, rather he enlisted the most important constituents to be infused into their qualityprayer.

> Qualityprayer is multidimensional. It needs full cooperation and involvement of our body, our emotionality, our intellect, our heart, our spirit, and above all spiritual dimension. God permits anything in prayer except human's evil-oriented or evil-led inclusions and practices.

Before entering into the discussion on the method of qualityprayer first we should understand that the so-called method, style, pattern, form of prayer may differ according to its settings, the praying person/s age, faith education, culture, status, and the environment where prayer is conducted, plus the time and need of the person/s lifesituations. Any suspicious question against qualityprayer arises from the mistaken understanding of prayer as one-dimensional. Rather, qualityprayer is multidimensional. It needs full cooperation and involvement of our body, our emotionality, our intellect, our heart, our spirit, and above all spiritual dimension. God permits anything in prayer except human's evil-oriented or evil-led inclusions and practices.

As we have already stated in previous chapters in whatever style or pattern or method prayer is performed it has to be textured with necessary ingredients for making it a qualityprayer to yield qualitylife. In this chapter we will treat about different settings usually humans pray and how Jesus and the Church deal with them; plus we will get into some details of a genuine and fruitful and pragmatic method of praying to reap its endresults.

A. Settings of Qualityprayer in Jesus' life

Surely we are asked to pray unceasingly, at every moment of our lives. From the prayer experiences of great prayerwarriors, like Biblical heroes and heroines, plus all our saints this unceasing-prayer habit gets into their system only by their frequent and regular prayer habits in daily life at specific times and definite places. When we look into Jesus' habit of prayer, though he was praying at every beat of his heart, we observe him praying silently, vocally, using gestures and with all his human resources in four of his life's specific settings: 1. In Solitude; 2. in public; 3. with the community; and 4. with his chosen ones.

1. **Personal Prayer in solitude**: All the Gospel writers point out this pattern of praying in Jesus' life as his priority. In his public life, according to their references, his standard form of prayer was prayer of solitude. All of them write about his forty-days staying alone in the desert in praying and

fasting before he started his public ministry. *"Once when Jesus was praying in solitude, and the disciples were with him."* (Lk. 9:18) He spent hours of both days and nights in praying alone. *"Rising very early before dawn, he left and went off to a deserted place, where he prayed."* (Mk. 1: 35) *"In those days he departed to the mountain to pray, and he spent the night in prayer to God".* (Lk. 6: 12) *"Then going out he went, as was his custom, to the Mount of Olives, and the disciples followed him".* (Lk. 22: 39) *"During the day, Jesus was teaching in the temple area, but at night he would leave and stay at the place called the Mount of Olives."* (Lk. 21: 37)

2. **Personal Prayer in public:** In public at the bank of River Jordan Jesus was praying after his baptism; during his qualityprayer he was overwhelmed with the power of the Spirit and was given a loving and public recognition of his glorious identity: *"After all the people had been baptized and Jesus also had been baptized and was praying, heaven was opened and the holy Spirit descended upon him in bodily form like a dove. And a voice came from heaven, "You are my beloved Son; with you I am well pleased."* (Lk. 3: 21-22) Sometimes Jesus was praying publicly in admiration and awe for his Father's accomplishments through and in him, praising his Father, being charged with full anointing and emotions:*"At that very moment he rejoiced [in] the holy Spirit and said, "I give you praise, Father, Lord of heaven and earth, for although you have hidden these things from the wise and the learned you have revealed them to the childlike. Yes, Father, such has been your gracious will."* (Lk. 10: 21-22). Some other times Jesus was praying in public before any astounding miraculous deeds he did. *"So they took away the stone. And Jesus raised his eyes and said, "Father, I thank you for hearing me. I know that you always hear me; but because of the crowd here I have said this, that they may believe that you sent me."* (Jn. 11: 41-42)

3. **Communal Prayer with the community:** He esteemed the Temple as 'House of prayer': He did not permit anyone to carry anything through the temple area. Then he taught them saying, *"Is it not written, 'My house shall be called a house of prayer for all peoples'? But you have made it a den of thieves."* (Mk. 11: 16-17); and he was burned with zeal for it because it was his Father's House.*"When his parents saw him, they were astonished, and his*

mother said to him, *"Son, why have you done this to us? Your father and I have been looking for you with great anxiety." And he said to them, "Why were you looking for me? Did you not know that I must be in my Father's house?"* (Lk. 2: 48-49)

Moreover, Jesus participated every year the Jewish Passover in the Temple as his custom from his early childhood. *"Each year his parents went to Jerusalem for the feast of Passover, and when he was twelve years old, they went up according to festival custom."* (Lk. 2: 41-42) He was accustomed to go to local synagogues as well as to the Temple for attending Prayer Services and involved actively in them. *"After three days they found him in the temple, sitting in the midst of the teachers, listening to them and asking them questions, and all who heard him were astounded at his understanding and his answers."* (Lk. 2: 46-47) *"He came to Nazareth, where he had grown up, and went according to his custom into the synagogue on the Sabbath day. He stood up to read."* (Lk. 4: 16) *"And every day he was teaching in the temple area."* (Lk. 19: 47a)

4. **Group prayer with his chosen ones**: As we see in the Gospel accounts, Jesus prayed in group. In the synoptic Gospels we see Jesus at the Last Supper conducting a group liturgy of the Eucharist; John in his Gospel portrays Jesus praying to his Father with his Apostolic team, presenting human wishes and petitions to the Almighty God.

Jesus prayed in group with his selected friends, those who were in one mind and one heart with him frequently, especially at the time of impending trials and perils his chosen ones were facing. Whenever he went to pray in the Garden of Gesthemane, especially just before he was captured by his enemies for sentencing him to death, all Gospel writers narrate that he took his friends with him to the Garden to conduct group prayer with them. One special occasion in his three years of public ministry Jesus organized a very special group prayer on a hilltop for a special reason: *". . . He took Peter, John, and James and went up the mountain to pray."* (Lk. 9: 28-36)

> Jesus prayed in group with his selected friends, those who were in one mind and one heart with him frequently, especially at the time of impending trials and perils his chosen ones were facing.

Just before they climbed up to the mountain Jesus was talking with them about his future journey to Jerusalem. They hated to hear about suffering and defeat from their leader, the Superman. Jesus tried his best to make them understand what he was preaching, the Gospel of the Cross. They could not digest his predictions about his ignominious death either because of ignorance or pride or fear for trials and tribulations.

That was the reason as Peter they rebuked him for his daredevil entering into deathzone and they too were like dead men walking in shock and shake. Many of them would have even begun to have second thoughts: Is Jesus really the expected Messiah? Should we go along with him to the showdown in Jerusalem or should we back off before it is too late? At that critical environment Jesus thought a group prayer would help his friends and in fact it did.

Truly the close friends of Jesus were praying with him on the mountain. Though they were weak in praying, got sleepy, they tried to be awakened; once they woke up they had marvelous encounter of Jesus' transfiguration and the hilltop experience of seeing the divine glory plus hearing God's voice from heaven. All happened in group prayer Jesus organized.

Being aware of the importance of group prayer Jesus advised his disciples to continue this group-oriented qualityprayer where he promised to be present and assured its power to bring God's helps to them: *"Again I say to you, that if two of you shall consent upon earth, concerning anything whatsoever they shall ask, it shall be done to them by my Father who is in heaven. For where there are two or three gathered together in my name, there am I in the midst of them."* (Matt. 18:19-20)

When believers gather together, they have the opportunity to pray with and for each other. It is to the benefit of each believer to have others pray with them. For example, in Mathew 9:2 the paralytic was healed because of the faith of his friends. This concept is throughout the scriptures, that our faith can positively effect change in others. In the Gospel we notice Jesus doing his miracles whenever he finds faith-filled approach toward him not only from individuals but also from groups. One of such miracles is mentioned in Matthew: *"And there people brought to him a paralytic lying on* a stretcher. When Jesus saw their faith, he said to the paralytic, "Courage, child, your sins are forgiven."

B. Church's Traditional Prayer-settings

In today's Christianity prayers are diverse and may vary among Christian denominational traditions. But all in unison come under four categories of prayer settings: Personal prayer in solitude; Personal prayer in public; community prayer in public; and group prayer among friends as family and associations. The Church, which is the community of Jesus' followers, from her early days, strictly kept Jesus' prayerlife-pattern as its own but as Jesus' Spirit inspired her and plus according to the signs of the time she tried to change the application of Jesus' pattern of qualityprayer. In the Acts and in the Letters of Apostles we notice early Christians prayed the same way as Jesus prayed and taught:

They, individually, prayed in solitude as Paul in his letters exposes to us his own private prayer experiences. He, before he became too busy in his ministry of preaching to the Gentiles, spent qualitytime with the Lord alone in solitude as soon as he was converted by the crucified Lord: "But when [God], who from my mother's womb had set me apart and called me through his grace, was pleased to reveal his Son to me, so that I might proclaim him to the Gentiles, I did not immediately consult flesh and blood, nor did I go up to Jerusalem to those who were apostles before me; rather, I went into Arabia and then returned to Damascus. Then after three years I went up to Jerusalem to confer with Cephas and remained with him for fifteen days." (Gal. 1: 15-18)

There abound so many interpretations regarding the reference of Paul on his going to Arabia. I personally love to accept some notable scholars' views that he went there and spent three years in qualityprayer of solitude: "In Arabia, he was alone with God, thinking through the implications of his encounter with the risen Christ on the Damascus Road." (Charles Ryrie) "He went into Arabia," says John R. W. Stott, "for quiet and solitude. He seems to have stayed there three years. In this period of withdrawal . . . he had Jesus to himself, as it were, for three years of solitude in the wilderness."

As Charles R. Swindoll emphasizes, in those three years of solitude in Arabia, 'Paul learned about the real Saul-the Saul God had uniquely called and chosen for a ministry of grace to the world. It was also there he saw the darker side of himself-the ugliness of his depravity. But against that bleak backdrop shined the greatness of God's mercy and love. Arabia became a temple where he worshiped the Lord in a way he had never experienced in his life. Solitude helped. The scales of spiritual blindness fell from his heart as he gained a fresh glimpse into the marvelous mystery of God's plan.'

In his daily life, in which he 'prayed unceasingly', Paul's qualityprayer consisted of praying in solitude as he describes in his preaching and Letters: "After I had returned to Jerusalem and while I was praying in the temple, I fell into a trance and saw the Lord saying to me, 'Hurry, leave Jerusalem at once, because they will not accept your testimony about me." (Acts 22: 17-18) "I must boast; not that it is profitable, but I will go on to visions and revelations of the Lord. I know someone in Christ who, fourteen years ago (whether in the body or out of the body I do not know, God knows), was caught up to the third heaven. And I know that this person (whether in the body or out of the body I do not know, God knows) was caught up into Paradise and heard ineffable things, which no one may utter." (2Cor. 12: 1-4) Apostle Peter used to pray in solitude. "The next day, while they were on their way and nearing the city, Peter went up to the roof terrace to pray at about noontime." (Acts 10: 9)

Following the Apostles early church members, like disciple Ananias who in his time of private prayer got a vision from the Lord: "There was a disciple in Damascus named Ananias, and the Lord said to him in a vision, "Ananias." He answered, "Here I am, Lord." The Lord said to him, "Get up and go to the street called Straight and ask at the house of Judas for a man from Tarsus named Saul. He is there praying, and [in a vision] he has seen a man named Ananias come in and lay [his] hands on him, that he may regain his sight." (Acts 9: 10-12) There is also another reference of a vision in the private prayer of a Christian named Cornelius. "Cornelius replied, "Four days ago at this hour, three o'clock in the afternoon, I was at prayer in my house when suddenly a man in dazzling robes stood before me and said, 'Cornelius, your prayer has been heard and your almsgiving remembered before God." (Acts 10: 30-31)

Church history contains numerous testimonies about private prayer experiences of individual Christians; they are not only those of saints like Theresa of Avila or John of the Cross or monks and religious priests and nuns but even the ordinary Christians like some of my friends, single as well as family people, I met in my ministry. These lay people spend a few minutes daily in solitude with the Lord; during the Days of the Lord, besides community services, more minutes they give to private prayer; amazingly as priests like me, they take time, usually a week or atleast a weekend, to spend in a monastery environment or retreat-houses where they are alone; pray in solitude; read and meditate Scriptural passages. They testify they come back, to their life's humdrum chores, calm, quiet, serene and poised and surely well-balanced.

> Personal prayer is a form of prayer whereby one loves God through dialogue with him, meditating on his words, and contemplating him. It is a time of silence focused on God and one's relationship with him.

In the Catholic tradition personal prayer has been positioned as a source for personal spiritual strength, just as Jesus was strengthened during prayer in Gethsemane (Luke 22:43). Personal prayer is a form of prayer whereby one loves God through dialogue with him, meditating on his words, and contemplating him. It is a time of silence focused on God and one's relationship with him. It is distinguished from vocal prayers which use set prayers, although mental prayer can proceed by using vocal prayers in order to improve dialogue with God. According to Saint Alphonsus Liguori "all saints have become saints by mental prayer".

There are some salient truths about this 'personal prayer' as we go into the historical background of development of Christian prayer. 'In the early Church worship was', Malcolm B. Yarnell indicates, 'inseparable from doctrine as reflected in the statement: *lex orandi, lex credendi*, i.e. the law of belief is the law of prayer.' Over time, a variety of prayers were developed as the production of early Christian literature intensified. Thanks to the writings of Origen Scripture became an intrinsic portion of Christian prayer as a sacrament and source of qualityprayer. Saint Ambrose and Saint Augustine were the pioneers in introducing the Origen's method of Scriptural prayer into the monastic traditions. These early communities, as Christopher Johnson writes in *Globalization of Hesychasm and the Jesus Prayer: Contesting Contemplation*, gave rise to the tradition of a Christian life of "constant prayer" in a monastic setting which eventually resulted in meditative practices in the Eastern Church during the Byzantine period.

During the Middle Ages, the monastic traditions of both Western and Eastern Christianity moved beyond vocal prayer to Christian meditation. According to the form of prayer called, *Lectio divina* monks read, meditated, prayed and contemplated God's words from the Scriptures. It is very interesting to observe how the Church kept faithfully its tradition of performing qualityprayer genuine but pragmatic. All the reforms taken in connection with prayer in the Church took seriously the main patterns of praying: vocal, meditative and contemplative.

However they took into consideration of the limitations of human members of the Church, especially those who are committed to life of prayer in monasteries and pastorates. Consequently, as Louis Barbo stated in his treatise on prayer titled *Forma orationis et meditionis*, otherwise known as *Modus meditandi*, Christian prayer was differentiated as 'vocal prayer, best suited for beginners; meditation, oriented towards those who are more advanced; and contemplation as the highest form of prayer, only obtainable after the meditation stage.

Following the Western Christianity's efforts of enhancing the performance style of prayer, as Mattá al-Miskīn and Igumen Chariton contend, the Eastern Churches too had a similar three level hierarchy of prayer: Level-I: vocal prayer, level-II: meditation "inward prayer"; and level-III: contemplative prayer in which a much closer relationship with God is cultivated.

Personal prayer that is conducted in solitude has been labeled as recollective prayer, meditative prayer and contemplative prayer. It has a more interior character than vocal prayer. In some Christian theology, this type of prayer is intended to help obtain some knowledge and love of God.

In the Catechism of the Catholic Church we read: "Meditation is above all a quest. The mind seeks to understand the why and how of the Christian life, in order to adhere and respond to what the Lord is asking."

One thing, we should be very clear about, on qualityprayer: Any prayer in any settings, in any styles, must contain a certain amount of interior recollection and meditative character; even in vocal prayer, for example, the Church advises us to include this interior reflection and meditation. In the public liturgical or sacramental prayers of the Church we come upon many places where the congregation is led to be silent for reflective prayer. Obviously every formal prayer—prayers found in the Bible, prayers constructed and used by our Saints, contains beautiful and thought-provoking words or verses that must be recited in recollection for the expected results; thus vocal prayers can turn out into qualityprayer. Meditation for meditation-sake is not the norm of genuine prayer in the mind of the Church.

> Any prayer in any settings, in any styles, must contain a certain amount of interior recollection and meditative character; even in vocal prayer, for example, the Church advises us to include this interior reflection and meditation.

She never shakes off her balance, received from her Master Jesus, in using the sacred tool of prayer. In every prayer she emphasizes the active involvement of both body and soul of humans must be present. In the document of the Congregation for the Doctrine of the Faith we read that 'Christian prayer is at the same time always authentically personal and communitarian. It flees from impersonal techniques or from concentrating on oneself, which can create a kind of rut.' New Catechism of the Catholic Church sums up very succinctly the Church's age-old attitude about qualityprayer that blends both the interior and exterior prayer as one: "Vocal prayer, founded on the union of body and soul in human nature, associates the body with the interior prayer of the heart, following Christ's example of praying to his Father and teaching the Our Father to his disciples." (2722)

No wonder then, we notice all the devotions, proposed and approved by Roman Catholic Church are basically prayers of solitude; and they were originated at the qualitytime of holy people's qualityprayer. For example, devotion to the Sacred Heart of Jesus was initiated by Saint Marguerite Marie Alacoque, who reported a series of visions of Christ, at her prayer in solitude, speaking to her which led her founding this devotion; devotion to the holy Face of Jesus was founded by Sister Marie of St. Peter, a Carmelite nun who had a vision in her private prayer in which Jesus told her :"*Those who will contemplate the wounds on My Face here on earth, shall contemplate it radiant in heaven.*" Devotion of reciting the Rosary of Blessed Mary was developed in Middle Ages as a substitute for the Liturgy of the Hours. After so many wonderful miracles occurred by the recitation of the Rosary it was recommended by numerous saints and Catholics were encouraged to pray it by almost every pope since then.

These Catholic devotional practices can be performed either privately or communally but in whatever situation they are performed it should contain, as Saint Louis de Montfort emphasized, *purity of intention* before the devotion begins, the need for *attention, focus* and *reverence* during the prayer and the necessity of *fighting distractions*. Although many promises are associated with devotional prayers, in his book *"The Way to Christ"* Pope John Paul II warned against "mechanical prayer" and pointed out the need for self reflection before prayer. This means, all devotions should have the ingredients of qualityprayer of solitude. However they, due to human weakness and misinterpretation, have been misused and even abused by members of the Church. Even in this modern world, people continue to be very shallow and emotional in their prayer habits. Richard Foster, in his famous book *Celebration of Discipline*, shouts out his painful thoughts about today's generation's disgraceful pitfall in this matter: "*Superficiality is the curse of our age. The doctrine of instant satisfaction is a primary spiritual problem. The desperate need today is not for a greater number of intelligent people, but for deep people.*" The source of becoming ourselves into people of in-depth is the qualityprayer conducted in solitude.

From early days of the Church **personal prayer in the public** has also been encouraged and practiced as a sign of witnessing the Lord's heavenly connections with humanity. Deacon Stephen's qualityprayer personal but in the public before his martyrdom is a proof of all the persecuted Christians' similar prayers as mentioned in Church's Martyrology. *"But Stephen, filled with the holy Spirit, looked up intently to heaven and saw the glory of God and Jesus standing at the right hand of God, and he said, "Behold, I see the heavens opened and the Son of Man standing at the right hand of God . . . As they were stoning Stephen, he called out, "Lord Jesus, receive my spirit." Then he fell to his knees and cried out in a loud voice, "Lord, do not hold this sin against them"; and when he said this, he fell asleep."* (Acts 7: 54-60)

Communal Prayer with the community has been a full-bloomed Christian practice grown out of the Jewish religion. As Jesus took it in his life very seriously so did his followers. In the Book of Acts we read the first Christian community gathered together as one community and prayed in Temple area. *"Every day they devoted themselves to meeting together in the temple area* (Acts 2: 46a). Prayer was frequently found in the gatherings of the early church, offered frequently throughout the worship service with the Lord's Prayer taking its place as the anchor—a common ritual in each gathering.

Elements of the oldest Christian liturgies may be found in liturgies such as the Roman Catholic Tridentine Mass, the modern Mass, the Orthodox Divine Liturgy, the Anglican Holy Eucharist service, and Lutheran Divine Service. Seasonal prayers are found in the Roman Catholic Breviary, which provides prayer for each liturgical season including Advent, Christmas, Easter, and Pentecost, as well as the other parts of the liturgical year. The Breviary developed and recited over the centuries. Today's Catholic Catechism proclaims that 'the Church invites the faithful to regular prayer: daily prayers, the Liturgy of the Hours, Sunday Eucharist, the feasts of the liturgical year.' (2720)

As the subject of catechetical teaching in one of his general audiences Pope Benedict XVI took St. Matilda of Hackeborn, an outstanding member of the German convent of Helfta. Describing about her active and committed involvement in Church Liturgy he highlighted the role of communal liturgy in Christian life: *"This saint,"* he said, *"allowing herself to be guided by Sacred Scripture and nourished by the Eucharistic bread, followed a path of intimate union with the Lord, always maintaining complete fidelity to the Christ. For us too, this is a powerful call to intensify our friendship with the Lord, especially through daily prayer and attentive, faithful and active participation in Mass. The liturgy is a great school of spirituality".*

All that we speak of qualityprayer apply to individual and communal prayer as well. While all prayer springs from individual acts, praying in community may wonderfully enhance the efficacy of prayer. The key factor is the degree to which the participants share the same intention and pray in unison. In my pastoral and sacramental ministries I discovered that any disorganized communal prayer, where people merely mill about and chat inside a house of worship, has little real value. The deeper the shared intention and the more unified the awareness, words, and actions, the more powerful the communal worship.

According to Book of Acts at the onset of Christianity **group prayer** was the powerful source of strengthening faith, bringing down the power of God's Spirit and enlivening the oneness of elite group of Jesus. Unhesitently we can declare that the Church was born at the Upper Room where a group of disciples with Mother of Jesus assembled in one heart and mind and prayed for ten days uninterruptedly. *"All these devoted themselves with one accord to prayer, together with some women, and Mary the mother of Jesus, and his brothers."* (Acts 1: 14)

The team of Jesus performed this group prayer in accordance with the Master's advice. He ordered them to conduct qualityprayer in group so that they could receive the power of the Spirit: *"While meeting with them, he enjoined them not to depart from Jerusalem, but to wait for "the promise of the Father about which you have heard me speak; for John baptized with water, but in a few days you will be baptized with the holy Spirit."* (Acts 1: 4-5) For Luke the climatic effort on the part of Jesus' team to be fully entering into the redemptive ministry of their Master was 'group prayer of waiting'. In his 3-years public life plus forty days after his resurrection, Jesus tried all his best to train and groom this team according to his Father's will. As his final effort he instructed them to go to upper room, not to be distracted by any other matters, and pray in group intensively: *"Jesus did and taught until the day he was taken up, after giving instructions through the holy Spirit to the apostles whom he had chosen, He presented himself alive to them by many proofs after he had suffered, appearing to them during forty days and speaking about the kingdom of God."* (Acts 1: 1-3) Thus Jesus showed the importance of group prayer in the disciples' lives.

Apostles and the early Church found the importance of group prayer and therefore they met in groups in their houses, prayed together as Eucharistic celebration." *. . . And to breaking bread in their homes. They ate their meals with exultation and sincerity of heart, praising God and enjoying favor with all the people. And every day the Lord added to their number those who were being saved."* (Acts 2: 46b-47) Group prayer was the regular pattern of prayer among early Christians. *"When he realized this, he went to the house of Mary, the mother of John who is called Mark, where there were many people gathered in prayer".* (Acts 12: 12) They knew well enough what the OT Wise man had written: *"Two are better than one: They get a good wage for their toil. If the one falls, the other will help the fallen one. But woe to the solitary person! If that one should fall, there is no other to help . . . Where one alone may be overcome, two together can resist. A three-ply cord is not easily broken."* (Eccl. 4: 9-12) Therefore they were always praying and performing other religious and spiritual exercises in group.

Though all disciples of Jesus followed their Master in praying personally and individually in solitude through the movement of Jesus' Spirit they came to a realization of the special significance to group prayer. At a time when the Church was threatened the Jesus' group was praying (Acts 4:5-37); the same group prayed when it was persecuted (Acts 12:1-23); the early Christian groups were praying at some important occasions in their Church life such as: sending disciples for missionary work (Acts 13:1-4); appointing new church leadership (Acts 14:21-23); bidding farewell to workers with prayer (Acts 20:17-38). In a special way as James instructs in his Letter early Church members as groups went to the side of any sick persons and prayed together for their healing (James 5:13-18).

Group prayer is a prayer of agreement of a team of single-minded people as Jesus indicates. It has been so powerful in the Church of today in bringing down many blessings from heaven.

C. Capsulated Method of qualityprayer for today's Christian

Cindy Jacobs, in her book *'Possessing the gates of the enemy'*, compares the variety of using prayer to the symphony Orchestra. She says, *"When a symphony plays, many instruments perform, each adding its own quality to the blend heard by the composer. In a similar manner the Scripture is telling us that God uses many types of prayers and people praying to orchestrate His divine melody of prayer."* To her descriptive comparison of prayer-patterns with Symphony we should add there is an important role of a conductor in using these prayer styles as needed in any music orchestra. In an orchestra we would hear only cacophony in the absence of a well-trained and experienced conductor. For the proper formation and application of various styles of prayer there should be a conductor who is none other than the Triune God. His grace is sufficient most of the time in prayer as Paul was instructed by the Lord.

On Jesus' behalf the Church takes the responsibility of conducting those different forms of prayer generated by settings, cultures, needs and other backgrounds of human pray-ers. Following always the prayerlife and teachings of Jesus as well as the day-today inspirations of the Holy Spirit, the Church created a fixed prayer-pattern to help all her members. In the Catechism of the Catholic Church (2644) we are taught that our prayer must contain as the basic forms: blessing, petition, intercession, thanksgiving, and praise. Most of the other denominational churches propose similar elements in prayer: petition (or intercession), thanksgiving, blessing (or benediction), praise or confession. The prayers recorded in early

Christian literature as well as throughout the centuries are categorized into above-mentioned elements.

> Following always the prayerlife and teachings of Jesus as well as the day-today inspirations of the Holy Spirit, the Church created a fixed prayer-pattern to help all her members.

In order to get its true quality and to reap its ultimate upshot every form of prayer at every human setting is to be methodically planned, prepared, and implemented. As any communication student would recognize the most result-oriented communication activity—especially interpersonal, can be prepared formally but implemented informally. In this way of communicating there is not any dramatization. It is the reality of every matured human behavioral act. A communication act from a communicator cannot be performed fruitfully if it is done in a formal way-for example, a young man cannot start communicating his love to his friend, saying, 'dear, this is first stage, let us sit down and talk.' After the first stage of act over, he cannot again tell, 'darling, as a second phase of love I am going to hold your hands warmly'. Thus if he goes on listing all his plan of love action while they are courting, it is ridiculous and will end in disaster. At the same time, if the same man, before he approaches his friend for love sharing, didn't prepare himself earlier and plan out appropriate moves he should do toward his lover, all his love actions will end in vain.

Similarly in our qualityprayer efforts, which we already described as a dating with our divine Spouse, we may be disappointed with getting no profit or only unfavorable and sometimes harmful results. Therefore let us now educate ourselves in the methodology of qualityprayer, how to prepare for it and implement our prayer plan for maximum fruits.

1. Plan spending qualitytime and quantitytime in prayer

There is not any right and wrong time for prayer. As Paul writes Christian prayer is ceaseless and continual state of communion with Our Father. In Jesuit spirituality I was taught about the 'sacred time' that starts from night bedtime upto next morning breakfast time during which we have to keep the rule of 'sacred silence.' It might be an instruction based on the words of Isaiah. He talks about the morning as the time when God gives the desire to pray on a daily basis and about renewed confidence in God. *"The Lord GOD has given me a well-trained tongue, that I might know how to answer the weary a word that will waken them. Morning after morning He wakens my ear to hear as disciples do."* (Is. 50: 4) However many other passages in the Bible endorse all times of the day. No part of the day is set apart as being more sanctified than another.

In making a prayer schedule for our life we should first be concerned with choosing appropriate times—be they minutes, hours, and days as **qualitytime** for qualityprayer. As we said earlier, prayer is the necessary means of union with God in every circumstance. Unquestionably union and communication with God is possible anywhere, anytime as God is omnipresent in and around us. Since our time is in the hands of God, as St. John Chrysostom writes, *'it is possible to offer fervent prayer even while walking in public or strolling alone, or seated in your shop, . . . while buying or selling, . . . or even while cooking.'*

Anytime we can talk to our Father. Knocking at the door at midnight may be some kind of shameful activity. Jesus demands such ill-mannered perseverance *"Ask, seek, knock at midnight and the door will be opened to you"*. In our prayerdeal with God time is not a barrier. No one time is more opportune than another, because God always listens. We can pray at midnight; pray at dawn; pray when we are happy and when we are sad; we should pray especially when are frustrated and fed up.

However as I have pointed out earlier God in Jesus claimed us as His lovers from whom He demands specific hours of our lives to commune with us. Look at Jesus who in his three-year public life not a few but many times he almost spent all night praying; when he fed the 5000 he went up on the mountain to pray during a rainstorm. he did not come down till the fourth watch so we know he prayed for over 9 hours; he was up on the mount of transfiguration all night; he got up a great while before day means at least

4am; the day he chose his twelve he had been up all night praying; and the night in the garden was almost all night.

As Jesus chose specific hours both at day and night we are expected to be in front of God consciously, exclusively and privately at a qualitytime of day or night. In qualityprayer we give God our qualitytime during which we are fully engaged in interaction with Him, giving full attention and total surrender to the Supreme Lover. We would be foolish if we distract ourselves with other earthly matters; and that means we do not want to spend qualitytime with our God.

We too must at the same time plan of our **quantitytime**, namely abundant time. The idea here is that "quality" in limited proportions does not suffice. It is certainly possible for quality to be absent from large amounts of time we spend in prayer; but the most pleasing schedule of prayer is that we spend *ample* quality time together with the Lord.

There are prayer warriors who do pray mightily and long; but due to their daily chores some have very little time to pray. In all our choices of spending time in qualityprayer God wants qualitytime and not quantitytime. In qualityprayer we need not spend hours as some of us think the best prayer life. Every one of us is filled with earthly life commitment to family and community and business and other social interactions. God just wants our heartfelt prayer and not too many hours of prayer.

One of my parishioners, a single parent, working double shifts of his job to earn his livelihood portrayed his qualityprayer style: "I am steadfast in praying daily but not spending long hours. When I do my family laundry I sing some ejaculatory prayer and that way I am elated to even raying in tongues. Before my children wake up, I get out of my bed and give to God little more of His time and listen to His voice; the same thing I do at night after my children go to bed; sometimes when I take my children to a playground or park while I sit watching them my heart beats for my God and I am connected to Him. Thus I have made it my daily routine to flinch some of the so-called 'my time' and give to God. As a matter of fact I do go with my children for Sunday Mass and pray with my congregation; surely I take a day off once in 6 months, entrusting my kids to their grandparents, I go to a nearby monastery and sped long hours with my God. It is these two holy breaks of the year that keep my longing for God ever on fire and both becoming close friends even a few minutes of daily life are sufficient to knit us together. God knows well my "I love you," to Him is spontaneous and sincere even if it only takes a few seconds to say."

That was very inspiring to me. I immediately thought my friend's way of giving qualitytime for God made his prayer undoubtedly a qualityprayer; God created us individuals and designed different roles and responsibilities to every one of us; He expects each one of us choose our own ways to give our precious time for Him. We shouldn't care about time limit.

Let us select any day or any hour disposable in our lifeschedule; but never should we give God only our surplus-time or extra-time. As any loving couple would do for preserving their life partnership intact, let us include into our regular schedule specific days and hours for prayer as necessities. Herebelow are some tips, on the typical prayer schedule of qualitytime and quantitytime, which I have gathered from my mentors and from my life:

1. We must give minimum 20 minutes a day to private qualityprayer.
2. Weekly let us schedule an hour for the Lord.
3. Let us arrange for a quiet morning/noon/evening at the church alone in front of the Eucharistic Lord once a month.
4. It is a praiseworthy practice to participate an annual retreat of either a week or atleast a weekend. It will be the most desirable qualityprayer where we individually would be slain by God's Spirit.
5. Let us make our close relatives and friends fully aware of the exact time of our daily/weekly/ annual schedule with God. It takes little more time for us to train and educate them not to disturb us in those precious times and days.
6. Besides being alone with God, as its followup, these holy minutes, hours or days can also be scheduled as a family or community member. For example as family we can give our qualitytime for the Lord through participation of Sunday Service during which

our private qualityprayer would add more spiritual flavor to it and make the ordinary ritual Service a qualityprayer.

2. Choose right Place for qualityprayer

People, belonging to natural religions and those, who endorse spiritualism with its wrong approaches, consider all human endeavors and surely all environments humans live and move as sacrosanct. We, the disciples of Jesus, too uphold this view. But while they never bring God and religion as the sources for such factor, we, on the other hand, hold God as its basic reason and His Scriptures and religion are the resources to enlighten us in this matter.

Every place we live and move is a sacred place; and the best suitable place of qualityprayer is nothing but our own interior sanctuary. As Paul would claim, our body is the temple of the Holy Spirit; the kingdom of God is within us; that means we carry within us a castle exclusively as God's residence. The advocates of 'centering prayer' insist this point and instruct us to give more importance to concentration in all our prayers. From this full belief in the immanent presence of the Lord and from the conviction that we are made in the likeness and image of God flows the greatness of personal prayer in solitude. To esteem our interior spirit as the abode of God is the priority not only for our personal private prayer but also for the qualityprayer performed at any life's settings.

> Every place we live and move is a sacred place; and the best suitable place of qualityprayer is nothing but our own interior sanctuary.

Such a belief and view of our interior castle does not overlook the necessity of choosing an exterior locale for qualityprayer. Primary purpose of selecting a proper place for our qualityprayer is for enhancing our concentration totally to our Lover God. From the prayer-pattern of Jesus as well as in the light of his teachings on qualityprayer, we understand the importance of picking out an undisturbed place for spending qualitytime with our God as loving parent and children and as intimate friends. *"When you pray, do not be like the hypocrites, who love to stand and pray in the synagogues and on street corners so that others may see them. Amen, I say to you, they have received their reward. But when you pray, go to your inner room, close the door, and pray to your Father in secret. And your Father who sees in secret will repay you."* (Matt. 6: 5-6)

While Paul teaches us to pray anywhere unceasingly, the Savior says 'go into your inner room'. Jesus, as he was always praying uninterruptedly, does not deny the 'heartbeat-prayer' pattern. As regards his suggestion of choosing a 'room' all scholars would agree that this "room" is not the room with four walls that confines our body when we are in it, rather, the secret space within us in which our thoughts are enclosed and where our emotions arrive. That is our prayer-room, always with us wherever we are, always secret to others but not to us and God.

Hilltop is the suitable place for qualityprayer

Undeniably any place can become an appropriate location for qualityprayer. That depends solely upon us. We take the trouble of making a place into the House of prayer. In this preparation time human effort is very much expected from our God. When He sees us seeking and striving for getting a place modified into His meeting place, as He desires, He starts sanctifying our efforts and consecrating our hard work. Any location we choose for our qualityprayer must turn out to be a sort of 'hilltop.'

If we flip through the pages of any religion's Scriptures and traditions we notice most of the extraordinary spiritual, religious experiences, visions, and other mystic events would have taken place on the hilltops. In our Scriptures, and our Christian traditions such hilltop experiences are numerous. We read about so many events, in which God interacted with his chosen ones, happening on the top of the mountains. In the Old Testament it starts with Abraham; Abraham sacrifices his son Isaac and gets him back from God on the top of the mountain; Jacob, in one of his hilltop prayers, held a nonstop fighting with the messenger of God to get what he prayed for and saw the vision of heavenly ladder; Moses met God most of the time on the top of the mountain; Prophets were used to hold historical interactions with God mostly on the mountain-pinnacles; God of Israel wanted His House to be built on the top of Zion, one of the hills of Jerusalem. In this connection very interestingly Jerusalem, the Holy City of God, was situated on the top of the hill.

In the Gospels we find Jesus went often to the mountain, especially the Mount of Olives (Jn. 8:1) to pray alone or with his Apostles. He preached his first sermon on the mount. Many revealing events, such as Transfiguration, Ascension, occurred on the top of the mountain. As we read in Mark (3: 13ff), Jesus went up the mountain and summoned those whom he wanted and appointed them as Apostles to be with him and to be sent for his kingdom-cause. Moreover Jesus' paschal events of God's handing Jesus over to crucifixion, death and resurrection and ascension for the salvation of humanity happened on the top of the hills. Even in this modern world so many apparitions of our Blessed Mother are recorded occurring on the top of the hills like Lourdes and Fatima. Many saints of our Church either have been converted, or inspired, or transformed while they were praying on the mountaintops.

Since there are many qualityprayer experience of ecstasy described in the Bible as happened on the hilltops Christians began naming qualityprayer experience as 'hilltop experience'. There are many reasons why God chooses the hilltop as his meeting place. It is not the literal top of a mountain that is preferable to God. Rather He wants to see us away from worldly distractions and climb up to the higher level of our humanness. When we go up the hill, we are *'off ourselves.'* We are alone with God. We choose a day-off, a situation-off, and a pleasure-off, TV-off, Internet-off and self-off for being with the Lord. So the right location for our qualityprayer is not a matter of place but that of human situation physically, psychologically and spiritually set apart for God and ourselves to be alone.

Construct a Sacred Zone for qualityprayer

To make any place as a sacred zone of God and us we have to take the trouble of modifying and renovating the environment of our choice. The first phase of this modifying process is to be continuously longing for it: As the Psalmist we have to crave for a House of His preference. *"One thing I ask of the LORD; this I seek: To dwell in the LORD's house all the days of my life, to gaze on the LORD's beauty, to visit his temple."* (Psalms 27: 4) We should also recite intensely with the same Psalmist: *"Blessed the one whom you will choose and bring to dwell in your courts. May we be filled with the good things of your house, your holy temple!"* (Ps. 65: 5) Once we discover the genuine Location of our meeting place with God, we will certainly exclaim with the Psalmist: *"How lovely your dwelling, O LORD of hosts! My soul yearns and pines for the courts of the LORD. My heart and flesh cry out for the living God. As the sparrow finds a home and the swallow a nest to settle her young, my home is by your altars. Better one day in your courts than a thousand elsewhere. Better the threshold of the house of my God than a home in the tents of the wicked."* (Ps. 84: 1-4, 11)

The Catechism of the Catholic Church clearly instructs us regarding prayer location: "The church, the house of God, is the proper place for the liturgical prayer of the parish community. It is also the privileged place for adoration of the real presence of Christ in the Blessed Sacrament. The choice of a favorable place is not a matter of indifference for true prayer." (2691) The Catechism also says, 'for personal prayer, this can be a "prayer corner" with the Sacred Scriptures and icons, in order to be there, in secret, before our Father. In a Christian family, this kind of little oratory fosters prayer in common.'

We can select any place we prefer, provided the rest of our lives and our world don't get in the way. Still there is a need for a specific place to go, set aside for the purpose of praying. For some it may be indoors like churches, prayer chapels, shrines at homes, or simply at the small tiny little living room where they would pray in front of a holy icon, especially the cross with crucified Savior. For many others it is an outdoor area such as a riverside as Paul went to pray for group prayer in his mission journey or a hill or a planted garden, or under large shady trees, as Jesus loved to pray frequently like the Garden of Gethsemane.

> 'The proper place for personal prayer can be a "prayer corner" with the Sacred Scriptures and icons, in order to be there, in secret, before our Father. In a Christian family, this kind of little oratory fosters prayer in common.'

In order to make any environment of prayer into sacred zone and consequently achieve the ultimate goal of qualityprayer-*the ecstatic environment* or *the mystic moment* we have to pass through four kinds of environments and zoom in to a climatic environment of God and make our abode there. We have to withdraw firstly from the *outer environment* that can be noisy, crowded and other social and even geographical conditions and situations. Secondly we depart from our *physical environment* in which we make use of formal and spontaneous prayers, devotions, and other liturgical and sacramental practices. Thirdly we pull out ourselves from our *mental environment* which includes memories, dreaming, imagining, probing, analyzing and planning. Fourthly we vacate ourselves from even our *spiritual environment* where we see our own achievement and our victory, and we feel as if we have earned comfort, satisfaction and fulfillment.

The sole purpose of all the efforts of specifying and fixing qualitytime and qualityplace before praying is to become totally present to God. In all forms of prayer whatever we apply as tools for its enhancement, be they vocal, various bodily gestures and positions, singing, and silence, they must sources of disciplining ourselves for being total to the chemistry of qualityprayer. There was a sage whose religious and spiritual behavior attracted thousands of men and women in his time. One of those devotees one day approached him and asked, "what's your path, what's your way?" The sage responded, "My path is very simple. When I am hungry, I eat; when thirsty, I drink; when sleepy, I sleep, and that is all." The devotee was astounded. He said, "What are you saying? I also eat and I also sleep, and everyone does the same. So what is in that to be called a new path". The wise man said, "When you are eating, you are doing many things, not just eating. And when you sleep, you do everything else except sleeping. But when I eat, I simply eat; when I drink, I simply drink; when I sleep I simply sleep. Every act of mine is total."

This story reminds us the rhyme we learned in out kindergarten years: *"Work while you work; play while you play; that's the way' to be merry and happy."* For our purpose here in this book we can add to it: *'pray while you pray.'* We can say a true prayer is an act riveted in one single direction and all senses being fixed on God and God alone. *"Little man, rise up! Flee your preoccupations for a little while. Hide yourself for a time from your turbulent thoughts. Cast aside, now, your heavy responsibilities and put off your burdensome business. Make a little space free for God; and rest for a little time in him. Enter the inner chamber of your mind; shut out all thoughts. Keep only thought of God, and thoughts that can aid you in seeking him. Close your door and seek him. Speak now, my whole heart! Speak now to God, saying, I seek your face; your face, Lord, will I seek.* (St. Anselm)

3. Qualityprayer Process

I always love to compare qualityprayer-process to a 'walking through' the inside portions of a Catholic Church building: **Phase-I: Narthex-Sensual Purification of self; Phase-II: Nave-Physical Concentration; Phase-III: Sanctuary-Intellectual Interaction; and Phase-IV: Tabernacle-Spiritual Intimacy.** Let us go over each phase of qualityprayer and perceive clearly our actions and God's own as well at each phase.

Phase-I: 'Narthex'—Sensual Purification of self:

Narthex is usually the first room or hall we enter when coming into the church. It is also called foyer, lobby, where originally penitents and Catechumens were confined to this area until their reconciliation with or initiation into the Church. In Narthex section we may find a Baptistery, a pool of water where people and children are baptized; in most of the churches a bowl of water, a holy water fount, mainly at the entrance door as well as in other church doors. Baptized Christians are recommended to sprinkle the holy water from those bowls and make the sign of the cross in order to remind themselves of the cleansing they had received through Baptism. In many modern churches this entrance area is used to welcome worshipers and guests into the Lord's House; some churches ask guests to fill out visitor forms in this area; in addition an information table or booth may also be located here to direct people to appropriate areas within the church building; plus church bulletins or any other handouts for any parish activity are kept on the tables or bookracks; almost in all the churches we see people using this Narthex site as a forum where they can exchange greetings or share their needs and special requests for prayers from each other.

> While we are in 'Narthex' stage of prayer all our senses should be disciplined in such a way that they all cooperate with us and detach themselves from our consciousness.

At the first phase of qualityprayer we perform similar acts but with difference. As we are entering into the sacred place we have already selected and scheduled proper time for connecting ourselves to the Holy, Holy, Holy, Lord God of hosts, first we try cleaning ourselves through certain ablutionary acts for purification. Though God's presence is not to be felt by our human senses, with our spiritual source we should be consciously fully present before his invisible presence. While we are in that stage all our senses should be disciplined in such a way that they all cooperate with us and detach themselves from our consciousness. It has been possible for all humans who have tried their best to go through such systematic and well-ordered procedure. For this, we have to first start from our body and purify it. The word 'purification' means 'to rid something of harmful, inferior, or unwanted contaminants, or get rid of harmful, inferior, to free somebody of sin, guilt, or defilement.

To commune with the Deity the Jewish Tradition commanded its people to purify themselves before they go to the Lord or He comes to them. This system had two objects. One, they had to cleanse their body from impurity by **physical ablutions:** *"The LORD said to Moses: Go to the people and have them sanctify themselves today and tomorrow. Have them wash their garments 11and be ready for the third day; for on the third day the LORD will come down on Mount Sinai in the sight of all the people."* (Ex. 19: 10) *"I will wash my hands in innocence so that I may process around your altar, Lord."* (Ps.26:

6) According to Sibylline Books, iii 591-593 God-fearing Jews are the ones who, *'rising from their bed early in the morning, wash their hands in water to lift them ever pure to heaven in prayer."* And two, they must sanctify their bodies by some rituals. *"The Lord said to them: "Listen to me, you Levites! Sanctify yourselves now and sanctify the house of the LORD, the God of your ancestors, and clean out the filth from the sanctuary."* (2 Chron. 29: 5)

Since the first followers of Jesus came from the Judaic culture the early church, adopting the Jewish custom of washing the hands before divine services and prayers, began providing the worshipers with fountains or basins of water for their ablutions. In the *Apostolic Constitutions* viii, 32, we read: *"Let all the faithful, whether men or women, when they rise from sleep, before they go to work, pray, after having washed themselves."* Jesus of Nazareth in his life has never shown any dislike over the ritualistic ablutions performed before entering into the House of His Father as prescribed in the Law. Surely as a typical Jew he would have followed this tradition, especially when he went to Jerusalem Temple or synagogues in Galilee to fulfill His Jewish prescriptions and to discuss with the elders. His main concern was with what spirit these rituals were performed. He insisted the true worship is one that was performed in spirit and truth.

In the Jewish Prescriptions one of the most stringent religious and social rituals was performing regular ablutions, especially before private and community prayers, before temple sacrifices and before every meal. Most of those 'washing rituals' were not done with the sincerity of heart by many Jews of Jesus' time. Therefore we read in the Gospels too many references Jesus making against those phony practices. He insists like Isaiah said that there is very large gap between what they do and say to God and what they hold in their hearts.

Jesus wanted his disciples to be sincerely performing any kind of religious practices in spirit and in truth-especially the ablutions before prayers. He is very candid in this regard when he said: *"Oh you Pharisees! Although you cleanse the outside of the cup and the dish, inside you are filled with plunder and evil. You fools! Did not the maker of the outside also make the inside?"* (Lk. 11: 39-40)

To People, who belong to Abramic religions like Judaism and Islam and in other eastern religions, qualityprayer depends on some ablutions before going to prayer of any kind as recommended by their Sacred Books and Traditions. In common all make use of their Scriptural words and traditionally-formulated prayers. Mainly they are to purify themselves physically, mentally and spiritually as well before they begin their prayer.

> Jesus wanted his disciples to be sincerely performing any kind of religious practices in spirit and in truth-especially the ablutions before prayers.

In this first phase of purification we clean first our body with an ablutionary ritual. According to Islam qualityprayer begins with physical cleanliness by eating no impure food, especially meats of any animal and birds. The base requirement for devotees to enter into the House of God is that they should be very careful on what they eat. *"Forbidden to you is that which is already dead, and the blood, and the meat of pig, and what was sacrificed to other than God, and that which has been strangled, and that which has been beaten to death, and that which has fallen from a height, and that which has been gored, and that which the wild animals have eaten from except what you managed to rescue, and what has been slaughtered on alters, and what you divide by the arrows of chance. This is all vile".* (Al Quran Chapter 5 verse 3) The second dimension of preparation of the devotees for qualityprayertime is to purify their bodies with codified ablutions: *"O ye who believe! When ye prepare for prayer, wash your faces, and your hands (and arms) to the elbows; Rub your heads (with water); and (wash) your feet to the ankles. If ye are in a state of ceremonial impurity, bathe your whole body . . ."* (Al Quran Chapter 5 verse 6)

Following the Abramic religious culture but with purity of intention Christ's followers continued to perform the washing rituals before their prayertime and later for pragmatic reasons, as the replica of a pool of water for washing ceremonies, the holy water fount was invented and is still maintained in the Roman Catholic Church. As the Lord reiterated in his life these washing ceremonies **are only mere rituals** signifying our commitment to be purified in all our life's dimensions—physical, emotional, intellectual, social and spiritual.

As a second part of purification we perform a ritual of **mental ablution** by distilling our intentions. In the first book of the Kings, Hannah, who is a type of the Church, observes that she prays to God not with loud petitions but silently and modestly within the very recesses of her heart. She spoke with hidden prayer but with manifest faith. She spoke not with her voice but with her heart, because she knew that that is how God hears, and she received what she sought because she asked for it with belief. The divine Scripture asserts this when it says: *She spoke in her heart, and her lips moved, and her voice was not audible; and God listened to her.* And we read in the Psalms: *Speak in your hearts and in your beds, and be pierced.* Again, the Holy Spirit teaches the same things through Jeremiah, saying: *But it is in the heart that you should be worshipped, O Lord.* (St. Cyprian) We therefore have to empty ourselves to be filled by God.

One day a man approached a holy monk, and asked if the monk would give him spiritual direction. To impress the monk, the man gave a lengthy recital of all his accomplishments—his several degrees, his importance in the business world, his many volunteer activities in the community. As the man talked, the monk began to fill a teacup with water. The water reached the rim of the cup, and the monk kept pouring, until the water spilled onto the table. The man said, "Stop, the cup will hold no more water!" The monk answered, "Neither can I teach you anything. You are too full of yourself now. Come back when you have some room for God." Isn't that also our problem? No room for God. No time to listen to God. Not that we do not want to listen to God. We would not be at Mass right now if we did not want to listen to God. But, from every side, we are bombarded. Our attention is drawn this way and that.

> We try to clean our mind from doubt, not doubting the existence of God; from fear, not fearing the worst to come; from low self-esteem, not feeling unworthy as a creation of God; from anger, not feeling anger toward anyone, and from hate, not feeling hatred toward anyone.

As a proper preparation for qualityprayer we are to purify our intentions of our hearts. Human heart is the most important part of the body. Therefore just before the prayer we should purify our hearts by filling them with two important thoughts: While we hold a negative thought about present earthly life as the hell-environ where there is scorching heat and no water facilities to drink, and makes feel like dying in hunger and thirst, we should cling to a positive thought that we are entering into the House of God which is going to be heavenly. We have to approach prayer as an oasis that would suddenly quench our thirst. We must rush toward God in prayer with such hope-filled happiness. In Islamic Scriptures we read:"*God will not call you to account for thoughtlessness in your oaths, but for the intention in your hearts; and He is Oft-Forgiving, Most Forbearing*" (Al Quran Chapter 2, verse 225)

We try to clean our mind from doubt, not doubting the existence of God; from fear, not fearing the worst to come; from low self-esteem, not feeling unworthy as a creation of God; from anger, not feeling anger toward anyone, and from hate, not feeling hatred toward anyone. These negative emotions and thoughts are the gifts of the Devil and therefore before entering into communing with Holy God we should get rid of them consciously.

The traditional way of confessing our sins before God or before the congregation as our penitential rite is the formal act of this mental and spiritual purification. All that happen at the church's Narthex would be surely entering into our mind as we start our prayer. The daily warfare, problems and trials in life, needs and dreams for successful life, family and community members' requests and desires, hot news we hear on TV or other media earlier, and so many other worldly issues will enter into our brain in a subtle way as if they are greeters and wellwishers to us. We should never permit them to overcome us. As much as we can we should try to be off from them through the ablutionary rituals we perform at our main entrance Narthex Phase of qualityprayer.

Phase-II: 'Nave'-Physical Concentration

Once we accomplish our preparation efforts of setting up qualitytime, quantitytime and qualityplace for qualityprayer and at the Narthex of qualityprayer purify body, mind, heart and soul by ritualistic and intentional ablutions, we enter now into the Phase-II of our prayer: "Nave".

As we pass through the Narthex of the Church we find ourselves in a large open space, the church's large 'body', which is traditionally called 'Nave'. Referring to the "Boat of Peter" and "Noah's Ark," the word "nave" is derived from the Latin word for ship, *navis*. It is in this area people sit or stand or kneel as the Order of Service demands from them. In Catholic churches we find the pictures or figures of 'Stations of the Cross', and statues or portrays of saints either with small altars like shrines with votive candles of prayer requests. Unlike the Western churches in many churches in the Third-world countries there are no pews or chairs, fixed or flexible.

> Nave-Phase of qualityprayer is the central portion of praying. In many traditional churches their prayer pattern consists of adoration, praise, thanksgiving, intercession, and communion.

In that open Nave their postures and positions vary according to the prayers they utter or as their Liturgical rubrics instruct them or in according with the movement of the Spirit. They sing, dance, and clap their hands, using gestures like lifting up their hands, holding hands together and bowing, kneeling, squatting and sitting as it is needed. They behave in the Nave, not as an audience in an auditorium as mere listeners but as doers, performers, active participants or actors.

Nave-Phase of qualityprayer is the central portion of praying. In many traditional churches their prayer pattern consists of adoration, praise, thanksgiving, intercession, and communion. Some others follow the acrostic 'A.C.T.S' (Adoration, Confession, Thanksgiving and Supplication) as regular pattern for their praying. Basing on this pattern herebelow are the **slots or segments of prayer at this Phase-II:**

Slot-1: We begin using all our physical abilities to get in touch with the Supreme Spiritual Being, more than controlling, to discipline our five senses, especially hearing, seeing, touching, smelling and tasting according to our purpose of totally surrendering ourselves to the Lord. Catechism of the Catholic Church (2702) instructs that *"The need to involve the senses in interior prayer corresponds to a requirement of our human nature. We are body and spirit, and we experience the need to translate our feelings externally. We must pray with our whole being to give all power possible to our supplication."* First we should select a bodily **posture** before we use our physical potentials.

> This does not mean we should stay put in those postures throughout prayertime; unless otherwise there are certain rubrics to be followed for the sake of community or group discipline, we can use any gesture appropriate to qualityprayer's spirit and truth. This is so important when we are at the setting of personal prayer in solitude.

At the onset certain disciplined physical gestures is good for letting us to the proper mood of prayer. A variety of body postures may be taken up, often with specific meaning associated with them: standing; sitting; prostrating on the floor; hands folded or clasped; hands upraised; holding hands with others; a laying on of hands and others. Some of them may be medieval gestures such as genuflection or making the sign of the cross; kneeling, bowing and prostrations. Some are very traditionally followed such as: the hands being placed palms together and forward, depicting our trust and conviction of faith; posture like 'with palms up and elbows in' expressing our 'receiving' mood. They are truly more productive and conducive for prayer. This does not mean we should stay put in those postures throughout prayertime; unless otherwise there are certain rubrics to be followed for the sake of community or group discipline, we can use any gesture appropriate to qualityprayer's spirit and truth. This is so important when we are at the setting of personal prayer in solitude.

In prayer eyes can be opened or closed. However, closing of eyes is commonly encouraged by those who propose prayer of recollection, of meditation and prayer of contemplation. They tell us this gesture of closing our eyes offers us an advantage of being silent, serene and even helps controlling other senses. Thus it supports us to renounce distractions. Before we begin our prayer at any settings we should be physically disciplined by any of those postures and gestures we indicated above; this is why before any public communal prayer, we are advised by our priests or preachers to come few minutes earlier to the Mass or Service, and stay silent and spend some time in 'stay-put' position, not to move our body and mind.

Slot-2: Once the appropriate posture is chosen and used, It is largely advised in the circle of prayer warriors to start repeating prayers that are vocal, short phrases like ejaculatory prayers and either they can be formal already taught and memorized and instructed by the Church; these vocal prayers include the Lord's Prayer; the Psalms; the Jesus Prayer; the Hail Mary; the Canticles throughout the Old and New Testaments; and prayers associated with the rosary and the prayer rope. One thing we should be very clear about, namely these prayers are supposed to receive the full mental and spiritual effort of those involved. Even if a standard wording is used, mechanical recitation is to be discouraged. Vocal prayer usually subsumes prayer of adoration, praise, thanksgiving, intercession, and communion.

Prayers may be recited from memory, read from a book of prayers, or composed spontaneously as they are prayed. They may be said, chanted, or sung. They may be with musical accompaniment or not. There may be a time of outward silence while prayers are offered mentally. Often, there are prayers to fit specific occasions of individual's or community's life-the birth or death of a loved one, natural disaster or diagnosis of terminal sickness, other significant events in the life of a believer or days of the year that have special religious significance.

In this connection we have to remember that Churches hold various manuals for praying rightly according to their traditions. There is no one prayerbook containing a set of liturgy used by all Christians; however many Christian denominations have their own local prayerbooks. For example, Catholic Church uses the books like 'Sacramentary, Roman Missal, Prayerbook, Book of Blessings, *The Roman Breviary* and so on; *Book of*

Common Prayer is a traditional Anglican prayer book; *Agenda*, a book used in liturgies of Lutheran Church; *The Upper Room*, a United Methodist Church daily devotional. They are sort of workbooks containing prayer organization, rubric suggestions of applying rightly and appropriately human silence, bodily gestures and movements during prayer. According to most of the churches these instructions have to be followed in all environments of prayer, especially in communal settings.

Though all those formal prayers with appropriate rubrics and guidelines prescribed by the Churches are most useful, sometimes very necessary, for organizational purposes of congregational and group prayer efforts, they too help in individual prayer efforts in solitude. Those prayers and guidelines as we mentioned earlier would discipline our body, emotionality, mind, heart and above all our human spirit.

In qualityprayer we try to concentrate and become conscious of God-and-me presence. To achieve this goal at this time slot of prayer we say some formal prayers to the Father, to the Son and to the Holy Spirit. We offer this hour to God consciously with the Holy Spirit whom we beg to stay with us till the last minute of this prayer time. The Spirit of Jesus Christ within us, the Holy Spirit, unites every aspect of our being into a complete person with reason for existence. We become spiritual. True prayer is prayer in the Spirit. As Paul says, "*God, who searches the heart, knows what is the mind of the Spirit, because the Spirit intercedes for the saints according to the will of God.*" (Rom. 8: 27) "*Pray in the Spirit at all times in every prayer and supplication.*" (Eph. 6: 18) "*Pray in the Holy Spirit.*" (Jude 20)

> In qualityprayer we try to concentrate and become conscious of God-and-me presence. To achieve this goal at this time slot of prayer we say some formal prayers to the Father, to the Son and to the Holy Spirit.

During this phase we too dedicate this particular prayer time to the Father **through, with and in** the exalted Jesus' Spirit. 'Through' Jesus' Spirit who is our mediator who is interceding to his Father; 'With' Jesus' Spirit who is our counselor and comforter; 'In' Jesus' Spirit who is the vine of which we are branches. We entrust to the Spirit of Jesus every effort we take in this prayer time; we should never stop this begging from the Spirit; every other minute of prayer we remind ourselves that we are weak in faith so we ask the Spirit to help us. That is what Paul indicates in his Letter: " . . . *the Spirit too comes to the aid of our weakness; for we do not know how to pray as we ought, but the Spirit itself intercedes with inexpressible groanings.*" (Rom. 8: 26) Many Christians belonging to mainline Churches take few minutes to pray to their favorite saints for their intercessory support because they believe as they recite in the Creed, the 'Communion of Saints.'

At the same time slot we keep our prayer continuous, not only through formal prayers (which would surely support when our mental setup gets wearied and tired) but also mainly through our heartbeats. This needs certain amount of training and formation. Once we get into the divine rhythm of spirituality we will find out quickly that a true prayer of a matured Christian is not a package of words but a band of heartbeats.

Slot-3: It is a time for offering our past and present life with all its wrong choices, habits and doings. This helps us to feel humble ourselves before: God, Family, World, Community, Universe, Nature, The valiant and talented, Social and physical structures, Scientific discoveries, The Saints, and My true self, which is so much disintegrated within itself. If we want our prayer being effective, if we desire our prayer being a bombshell to tear down the hurdles and terrors of our lifesituation; and if we dream of our prayer being enhanced to the status of qualityprayer becoming fruitful and result-oriented this slot time of prayer should be considered serious.

We must start prayer with the recognition of ourselves as flawed, dependent, needy, and in continual need of guidance, repentance and divine merciful forgiveness as the tax collector in Jesus' parable prayed. Standing off at a distance and not even raising his eyes to heaven but beat his breast he prayed, '*O God, be merciful to me a sinner.*' While the prayer of the Pharisee was all started and ended with "I" which left little room for the divine 'YOU', the tax-collector's prayer was God-centered. And the latter's prayer was esteemed great in the eyes of Jesus (Lk. 18:9-14). In a qualityprayer we should celebrate God as nameable, addressable, reachable, and knowable and near. So our praying should be less of 'I' and 'me' and more of 'You' and 'we'. When we confess to the Lord all our flaws and sinfulness we are not selfpitying, or brooding and groaning over our weakness and limitation; rather the greatness and mercifulness of God in focus; the Lord Jesus' loving face and interceding presence before our mind; and the Spirit's movement is testifying.

> While the prayer of the Pharisee was all started and ended with "I" which left no room for the divine 'YOU', the tax-collector's prayer was God-centered. And the latter's prayer was esteemed great in the eyes of Jesus

I personally believe that when I perform act of confession I do twofold proclamation: I profess and celebrate God as nameable, addressable, reachable, and knowable and near; and I declare in front Him that I am unworthy and a sinful servant. The same thing is true in what we do at the Nave-Prayer time slot. With all humility first we compare and contrast our outward masquerading with our inner ideals; our private secret dealings with our outside projection of our personality. And thus we stand naked before the Holy of Holies with our unholiness and wrong choices we have made and continue to make. In every qualityprayer-time surely there is an exchange of challenges between God and us. Our primary intention, interest, wish and goal for all prayers we say, sing or lisp at this moment should be a personal conversation with God. Prayer is for God to be glorified in us and us to be glorified by God as well. In prayer we seek only the Giver and not his gifts. Prayer is to be connected to the heavenly and eternal intercession of Jesus. This a time is one of confessional for begging God's mercy as we state our sins before Him; we too expose to God our hurts; plus we express our willingness to forgive those who hurt us.

Slot-4: In this time our humble self leads us gradually to be conscious of God's permanent and active presence throughout our past and present. We back-travel to our past life and discover the marvelous deeds of God, most of them being surprises; we start first feeling ashamed of our coldness toward Him but then getting convinced of the truth 'He is always faithful.'

At our early childhood we were unconscious of His presence; yet He held us. At our youth we were following willingly or unwillingly what our elders told us to do. But He was there still for us. As we had grown adults, we chose our own way. Consciously we withdrew from Him. Many times we would have hurt Him by our imprudent and silly choices. Still He supplied everything we needed but always waiting for us to come back to Him with our filial intense and conscious love. Now at this prayer slot we return home to Him. He embraces us. He prefers this state of our conscious and willful love and union with Him.

Slot-5: Feeling sorry or mere remorse of conscience is not sufficient for the standard of qualityprayer. We use this time for begging God's pardon and express our gratitude for His patience and acceptance. Moreover considering this time as a precious slot, we willfully promise our fidelity to His love and remind ourselves the promises we had made to Him in the past and renew them. We too surely ask God to help us.

Slot-6: As we notice in the Church's Nave votive candles burning and shrines of saints, plus as we remember the needs and requests of our friends we had heard at Narthex, we spend some minutes in interceding for others, including our enemies. It is because our Master has said: Before entering into prayer, *'Forgive your enemies; Pray for them; and Love them.'*

Phase-III: 'Sanctuary'-Intellectual Interaction:

The sanctuary in the church is like the stage in proscenium theaters, a raised platform, elevated with usually three steps and separated from the nave either by rood (meaning 'cross') screen or iconostasis or altar rails or as in most of the churches only by a distance of few feet away from the nave. Though the entire church area is holy this elevated platform has been labeled as sanctuary which means holy. It echoes the Judeo tradition of the Temple's special area the 'Holy of Holies' but in Christian tradition the place is considered holy because of: 1. The altar which is the holy table upon which the Lord's Supper is celebrated; 2. the lectern that holds the lectionary, the book of readings from Sacred Scripture; and 3. The pulpit, from where the celebrant breaks the Word of God and shares it with the congregation as homily or sermon. Not all churches have both a lectern and a pulpit; some just have one single speaker's podium called an ambo. In addition, there is a presider's chair and seating for the other ministers, which express the specialty of the functions performed by the ministers at this holy place.

During this phase of qualityprayer we should be actively silent telling God to speak to us as His servant listens. While the first 1/3 of our qualityprayer time is only a preparation time for this 2/3 of our prayer as precious moment of sitting at the feet of the Lord or on His lap or shoulders. This is the apt time for using any of those advanced prayer forms: Meditative prayer; prayer of recollection; contemplative prayer; and even charismatic prayer. As St. John of the Cross says in his *Ascent of Mount Carmel*, these types of prayers may be used as "obtaining some knowledge and love of God"; or we may seek, like St. Theresa of Avila, to "concentrate entirely on God present within us, and there at His feet will be able to converse with Him to our heart's delight"; or as Catechism of the Catholic Church (2724) instructs us, it can be a "Contemplative prayer, which is the simple expression of the mystery of prayer. It is a gaze of faith fixed on Jesus, an attentiveness to the Word of God, a silent love. It achieves real union with the prayer of Christ to the extent that it makes us share in his mystery"

Sometimes at this moment of prayer many prayer warriors may get into the free stream of the Spirit and start praying in tongues. They may make unusual sounds or adopt unusual postures. For example, a person may emit shrieks, or may lie on the floor face-up with the hands in an askew posture. It is a prayer pattern that resembles mysticism. If the Spirit of Jesus moves us we pray in tongues; if He offers a deep sleep we would willingly accept it but make sure that we are not drowned in it fully. Surely He wakes us up.

> "Contemplative prayer is the simple expression of the mystery of prayer. It is a gaze of faith fixed on Jesus, an attentiveness to the Word of God, a silent love. It achieves real union with the prayer of Christ to the extent that it makes us share in his mystery"

In this regard we should follow certain orderliness in the beginning and being conscious of how fragile and weak we are in this heaven-related practice. After we pass through ablutions of purification and physical and mental concentration phases we should not immediately jump into these advanced prayer styles. First we may open this time slot by reading from a holy book of some kind, perhaps the Gospels or any spiritual book that seems suitable; we too can read passages from the works of the Saints; subjects for meditative, recollective prayer can include any of the mysteries of Jesus or the events described in the Gospels, or the presence of God in the subject about which one has been reading. or even rereading the vocal and formal prayers we have been using during Nave phase. Then, when a suitably affective recollection takes hold, the book will be gently laid aside, and we should commence praying interiorly. The person may form sentences mentally, or may simply relax in the love of God.

This is an august moment in our qualityprayertime which is the last volitional stage where the soul can endeavor to be still and know that *God Is*. St. John of the Cross teaches that this phase of prayer begins with purifying aridity that marks the beginning of *infused passive love* that is stronger than the love corresponding to the period during which the soul received *consolations*, i.e. the prior experiences of prayer. Here, God does the work of reaching to the soul, yet we must be sufficiently mature to grow without requiring constant consolations. Many of the Saints, like St. Therese of the Child Jesus, St. Padre Pio, and blessed Mother Teresa, experienced years of dryness and spiritual desolation, as God effectively tested their love for God. These people became saints because their love for God gave them perseverance, and they continued uninterruptedly their efforts of qualityprayer, for the one and only reason that God is Love and they longed to be assumed and consumed within it.

Phase IV: 'Tabernacle'-Spiritual Intimacy

The English word "tabernacle" is derived from the Latin *tabernāculum* meaning "tent" or "hut", which in ancient Roman religion was a ritual structure. It reminds us the Biblical Tabernacle, which was used as the portable dwelling place for the divine presence and accompanied the Israelites on their wanderings in the wilderness and their conquest of the Promised Land. It contained the Ark of the Covenant which was eventually placed in the First Temple in Jerusalem. It is described as an inner shrine, named 'Holy of Holies'. It was a strong belief of the Jewish that the in-dwelling Presence of God, the *Shekhina* dwelt within this divinely ordained structure.

The most befitting position and encouraged by today's Church is to be kept in the main Sanctuary, behind the Altar, placed over an elevated pillar or another small altar. The other place where the Tabernacle might be kept can be a separate, conspicuous, well-adorned side chapel in churches in which the Altar area is used for the solemn conduct of the Divine Office or for Pontifical ceremonies.

Wherever the Tabernacle is placed there is always burning a tabernacle light. It is to remind us the real presence of the Eucharistic Lord in a sacramental way. The Catechism of the Catholic Church, paragraph 1374 says: *"The mode of Christ's presence under the Eucharistic species is unique. It raises the Eucharist above all the sacraments as "the perfection of the spiritual life and the end to which all sacraments tend." In the most blessed sacrament of the Eucharist "the body and blood, together with the soul and divinity, of our Lord Jesus Christ and, therefore, the whole Christ is truly, really, and substantially contained." "This presence is called 'real'—by which is not intended to exclude the other types of presence as if they could not be 'real' too, but because it is presence in the fullest sense: that is to say, it is a substantial presence by which Christ, God and man, makes himself wholly and entirely present."*

As the Israelites believed in the immanent Presence of God inside the Tabernacle Catholics uphold the faith in the real presence of God's Son in the new Tabernacle at every Catholic church.

Qualityprayer's ultimate goal is to enter into the real presence of the Lord and encounter His Love in a mystical way and consequently being led into the ecstasy of being one with the Supreme Being. We don't know when and how the Lord let us into His Tabernacle Experience. It is all in His Hands to take us into His Holy of Holies where we, as Paul and other Saints were encountering, would be intimately present with Him. But we should be fully positive that we will one day hit a holy Jackpot in His Abode. Until then we will be continuing our qualityprayer efforts that may take us even to His Sacrificial Altar. We are ready for it. Let God let go.

The true end of any qualityprayer is 'we live happily thereafter.' We would have achieved the ultimate upshot of qualityprayer as hilltop mystic experience; or we would have been failing throughout those phases of prayer not doing justice to the genuineness of prayer; or we would have ended up in aridity and darkness. Whatever be the result that particular day of prayer, we should always end with grateful heartbeats. We have tried; we have worked hard in prayer. God wants our process of pleasing Him rather than its product. He is the One who bestowed the grace of faith, hope and perseverance and good will. Truly we were with the Triune God. With these positive thoughts we should say aloud to the Lord, as Jesus instructed us, *"So should it be with you. When you have done all you have been commanded, say, 'We are unprofitable servants; we have done what we were obliged to do.'"* (Lk. 17: 10) Also at the last few minutes we should offer our schedule of that day, our activities, our contacts and plead for God's blessings on them; in addition we will beg Him to be with us in unexpected challenges our life and nature are going to offer us on that day.

> We don't know when and how the Lord let us into His Tabernacle Experience. It is all in His Hands to take us into His Holy of Holies where we, as Paul and other Saints were encountering, would be intimately present with Him. But we should be fully positive that we will one day hit a holy Jackpot in His Abode.

In all our endeavors regarding qualityprayer we should keep in mind the fundamental principle of how the Church worships: *"lex orandi, lex credendi,"* a Latin axiom, meaning "the law of prayer is the law of belief". It denotes two important factors in Christian practice of prayer: One, the way that we pray largely depends on what we believe in; and the other, the manner we pray declares our way of believing and living the faith. That our prayers and ritual actions bear very definite meaning in light of Sacred Scripture and

Tradition serves us in how we understand the truth of Christian faith and how we live that truth. Adding a final note to the discussion on the method of qualityprayer, this is what I claim as the secret of learning how to pray fruitfully: As in any other human endeavors, we have to practice it to be accomplished in it. If we want to improve in qualityprayer we have to pray and pray and pray without being discouraged.

Some Salient Points on QualityPrayer

A. The Power of Qualityprayer

QUALITYPRAYER HAS MORE power than physical force. Christianity holds prayer primarily as a force for seemingly non-physical effects such as peace, forgiveness and pardon. According to WikiQuote, Mother Teresa is quoted saying: *"When I was crossing into Gaza, I was asked at the checkpost whether I was carrying any weapons. I replied: Oh yes, my prayer books."* We know what Mother Teresa would not have meant prayer as a threatening force but a force for service, love and peace. This is testified by her writing: *"The fruit of silence is prayer; the fruit of prayer is faith; the fruit of faith is love; the fruit of love is service; the fruit of service is peace."* Cardinal John Henry Newman said: *"If there is anything which distinguishes religion at all, which is meant by the very word, it is the power of prayer."*

The title of this section 'the power of prayer' may mislead many humans to consider prayer as some sort of magical tool-a Harry Potter's Stick—through which they can attain anything they ask for. The ability of prayer is to be perceived properly as highlighted in the Scriptures.

> In qualityprayer as the Spirit of the resurrected Christ defines there is no power in itself. It is not something like rolling beads or reciting formulas of 'mantras' continuously and thus achieving what we demand in the 'Gei-Boomba'-style of Genie. Prayer is not the source of power; it's God who is the sole origin of it.

In the OT we read so many references regarding the effects of prayer. Especially in Psalm 107:28-30 we hear that: *"Then they cried out to the LORD in their trouble, and he brought them out of their distress. He stilled the storm to a whisper; the waves of the sea were hushed. They were glad when it grew calm, and he guided them to their desired haven."* As I have quoted in my introduction of this book, the author of the Book of Sirach writes: *"The prayer of the lowly pierces the clouds; it does not rest till it reaches its goal, nor will it withdraw till the most high responds, judges justly and affirms the right".* (35:17-18) Jesus too is quoted saying: *"I tell you the truth, if you have faith as small as a mustard seed, you can say to this mountain, 'Move from here to there' and it will move. Nothing will be impossible for you"* (Matthew 17:20).

Unfortunately people in the past as well as today are made to misunderstand the Lord's words about prayer. 'Anything' to them includes largely their material and earthly needs. In qualityprayer as the Spirit of the resurrected Christ defines there is no power in itself. It is not something like rolling beads or reciting formulas of 'mantras' continuously and thus achieving what we demand in the 'Gei-Boomba'-style of Genie. Prayer is not the source of power; it's God who is the sole origin of it. Our attempts of hard-worked prayer are not the causes of bringing down super-power from heavenly places.

Qualityprayer is a moment when the Divine and human meet; a place where loving dialogue is held between the two lovers; and once their interaction reaches its climax they are pleased with each other—as God the Father was pleased with Jesus in his qualityprayer at Tabor: "You are my beloved son in whom I am well-pleased"; and as Jesus had many moments in his life such joy flowing from him because of the Father (Lk. 10: 21).

In Jesus' time people were approaching prayer as something resourceful for doing good for themselves and others. He came forward to correct and enhance their views. Once his disciples who returned from their preaching and healing ministry were going on bragging about how powerful they had been in their performances. He immediately corrected them saying: *"Nevertheless, do not rejoice because the spirits are subject to you, but rejoice because your names are written in heaven."* (Lk. 10: 20)

Though Jesus never denied the power of prayer he neither endorsed the view about prayer as the means of producing any tangible benefits. One thing is certain that qualityprayer, if properly handled, it will be empowering us in Jesus' Spirit; we will accomplish wonderful things in life. However as I have mentioned in the chapter on the Upshot of Qualityprayer, the empowerment, the joy and our names being written in God's Book of Life are the secondary (I call them shortterm goals) to the ultimate goal, namely the mystical encounter with God.

When our act of prayer turns out to be a qualityprayer it is a real, living power; it is not a vague ideal, a bartering system, or a quickfix to material gain or an easy life as many consider. It is the song that enables our souls to blossom and release their magic, an alchemical force by which we can transmute our basic selves into the gold of our higher natures. Qualityprayer, used with a pure heart and motif, is that "energy" called love in its higher octaves. It is the most powerful key to unlock the limitless potential, such as radiant spiritual power and strength, which is hidden within us. Through qualityprayer we can consciously use the universal life forces that flow freely through the universe to bring miracles into our lives and to the world around us.

Mystics of all religions know it is impossible to think certain thoughts without invoking our spiritual energy. If we charge our thoughts with love and dynamism and give them direction, we can then send them anywhere in the world. This is what the endresult of qualityprayer. From a genuine prayer a person gets power in life like St. Paul (2Tim.4: 6-18) to run the race, to compete the odds and hurdles, to fight the good fight, and to make the most and best of life.

This power is generated from the 'tripod-base' prayer builds up in the inner sanctuary of the person who prays genuinely: 1. A strong belief that he/she stands, moves, dances, and fights (sometimes stumbles and fails but most of the time wins) always on the solid rock of Godhead. 2. A well-substantiated hope of receiving one day a crown or mansion from the Lord the just Judge somewhere outside of this earthly life. 3. An uninterrupted trust that the Lord stands by him/her and gives him/her strength in the midst of calamity, terror, problem, disappointment, failure, and trial. To make my prayer as a powerful weapon/ammunition and as a strong catalyst we should follow the following action-plan already catalogued in the IV chapter.

QualityPrayer is 'mining' incredible power from within

Almost all religions emphasize the importance and the need of prayer in human life. However prayer is one of the most misunderstood spiritual sciences on Earth But every disciple of Jesus deems it as a tremendous tool that every man, woman, and child can use to become a modern miracle maker. Indeed prayer to him/her, as Charles Capps wrote, is *'a key to heaven's storehouse.'*

Theophan the Recluse says, *"Prayer is the test of everything; prayer is the source of everything; prayer is the dividing force of everything; prayer is the director of everything. If prayer is right everything is right. For, prayer will not allow anything go wrong'.* With the right technique—and a little faith and effort—there are no limits to what can be accomplished through QualityPrayer. With QualityPrayer, we consciously draw the great universal life forces down into us, imbue these forces with the deepest aspects of our love, and then consciously direct this spiritual power out into the world. This is an act of the highest spiritual potency. We become like a "magical instrument" radiating divine light out into a world that desperately needs it. This is not merely a means of asking God for things but a powerful tool by which we can bring about personal and global transformation, as well as healing and self-mastery. It is a tremendous tool that every man, woman, and child can use to become a modern miracle maker; through qualityprayer they can preserve nature, stop wars, transform, transmute, inspire, and uplift. Through prayer we can heal one person or help to heal a thousand.

> All disciples of Jesus strongly believe that when their prayer develops into QualityPrayer it is a very powerful instrument, weapon and resource for their daily lives.

Mahatma Gandhi was an orthodox Hindu who tried to change not only his own lifestyle but also his country's political situation only through prayer and sincere adherence to both his religious Scriptures and the Gospel of Jesus. He is quoted saying: *"Prayer . . . properly understood and applied, is the most potent instrument of action."*

All disciples of Jesus strongly believe that when their prayer develops into QualityPrayer it is a very powerful instrument, weapon and resource for their daily lives. This is because they know Jesus believed it: *Rising very early before dawn, he left and went off to a deserted place, where he prayed.* (Mk. 1: 35) *Then he made his disciples get into the boat and precede him to the other side toward Bethsaida, while he dismissed the crowd. And when he had taken leave of them, he went off to the mountain to pray.* (Mk. 6: 45-46) *After doing so, he went up on the mountain by himself to pray. When it was evening he was there alone.* (Mt. 14: 23) *. . . great crowds assembled to listen to him and to be cured of their ailments, but he would withdraw to deserted places to pray.* (Lk. 5: 16)

Jesus' disciples are convinced in the power of qualityprayer because their Master has promised so: *"Ask and it will be given to you; seek and you will find; knock and the door will be opened to you. For everyone who asks, receives; and the one who seeks, finds; and to the one who knocks, the door will be opened. Which one of you would hand his son a stone when he asks for a loaf of bread, 10 or a snake when he asks for a fish? If you then, who are wicked, know how to give good gifts to your children, how much more will your heavenly Father give good things to those who ask him."* (Mt. 7: 7-11) *"Therefore I tell you, all that you ask for in my prayer, believe that you will receive it and it will be yours"* (Mk.11:24).

In one of CNN talk show interviews Mr. David Sacks told Mr. Larry King: "Some people have a tremendously condescending attitude about religious people and prayer. Although, they take pains not to use the word crutch, that's what they have in mind. Prayer to them seems like a weakness. To be kind, they'll say, it's so great that prayer and religion give you comfort. This is a fundamental misconception about prayer and about God. Prayer is not like a baby aspirin—it arises from an understanding of who God is. When you understand that God created the world and is sustaining the world, then prayer becomes an obligation and a necessity; it is not a weakness but a strength." David is obviously correct in his statement on the force of prayer; I go little further and always love to say to my congregations, "Qualityprayer, in the hands of Christians, is like a bombshell and not just an aspirin."

Since qualityprayer is powerful we can call it a bombshell—the sacred ammunition to shake and shape first our own life and then others' and the entire world system. This is not just a bedtime story we heard from my grandma. Rather it is a his(s)tory and her-story of humanity in every part of the world. Prayer is simply an instrument and source of power from on High and from the immanent presence of the Supreme Being within.

Jesus made it very clear that we alone can do nothing even with our prayer; on the other hand if we change ordinary human prayer to qualityprayer through:

1. "Seeking in prayer God's kingdom as our primary benefit: "*But seek first the kingdom (of God) and his righteousness and all these things will be given you besides.*" (Matt. 6: 33)
2. Abiding in Jesus and in his words we will do all impossible things through the act of praying: "*If you remain in me and my words remain in you, ask for whatever you want and it will be done for you.*" (Jn. 15: 4-8.)
3. Building up our prayer pattern or style on the Word of God: "*Everyone who listens to these words of mine and acts on them will be like a wise man who built his house on rock.*" (Matt. 7: 24)

From a qualityprayer a person gets power in life like St. Paul (2 Tim.4: 6-18) to run the race, to compete the odds and hurdles, to fight the good fight, and to make the most and best of life. This power is generated from the 'triple-base' on which qualityprayer is built up in the inner sanctuary of individuals who pray genuinely: They strongly believe that they stand, move, dance and even fight always on the solid rock of Godhead; they live with a well-substantiated hope of receiving one day a crown or mansion from the Lord the just Judge somewhere outside of this earthly life; and they possess an uninterrupted trust that the Lord stands by them and gives them sufficient strength in the midst of calamity, terror, problem, disappointment, failure, and trial.

> Since qualityprayer is powerful we can call it a bombshell – the sacred ammunition to shake and shape first our own life and then others' and the entire world system. This is not just a bedtime story we heard from my grandma. Rather it is a his(s)tory and her-story of humanity in every part of the world.

Qualityprayer settles us in an anxiety-free zone. In qualityprayer we feel full. It inspires us and dissuades us to quit. It drags us into a concrete planning to use this 'present.' We start feeling greater and more genuine self-esteem, a clear and well-balanced view about ourselves. It makes us to go beyond. It brings home to us the real and mysterious presence and activity of the devil—"*Even Satan disguises himself as an angel of light.*" (2 Cor. 11: 14)

Qualityprayer is a powerful force primarily to change 'us' and then 'we' change the things outside of us. Through qualityprayer efforts, as many of us who are committed to it, would testify that our view of life is changed; our personal prejudices are changed; our esteem of our fake self is changed; and our handling of every moment of life is changed. Very surprisingly our God has so constituted things that prayer on the basis of Redemption alters the way in which we look at things. We ultimately come to a realization that prayer is not a question of altering things externally, but of working wonders in our inner disposition. Consequently we settle ourselves in peace.

It happened while I was in Houston. I was there with an idea and vision to get away from this form of ministry as pastor to a ministry of chaplaincy in hospital environment. One day I lost my billfold that was so much needed for my life as I was a new beginner in a totally new environment of profession. I searched and searched for two days. I couldn't find it. Finally I knelt before God one morning in despair and grief. It was a Sunday. I did pray every day. But this time it was with difference. I proposed to God this way. I made a deal with Him. 'God', I said, 'if you get that billfold and hand it over to me today, as I am praying **now**, then I promise, I let you do in whatever way you want me to do. I will go back again to the diocese and be a sincere, simple and committed pastor in a rural parish you fix through the bishop. I will obey you.' Amazingly as soon as I prayed this way, I heard my phone ringing. I answered the phone. Guess who spoke what? On the other end one of my friends from the hospital where I was working said, 'hey, Vima. Good news. You got your billfold. I give you the phone number. Just contact this man. He will tell you all details about this. I think you lost it some place in the downtown area.'

There are so many such prayer experiences like this in my life. And so it is in many of my friends' lives too. Prayer is powerful. It is very productive. It is fruitful. It pays us back all that we wish as magic sometimes, but most of the time in a reasonable way. Undoubtedly prayer possesses a certain power to bring God's hands over our lives.

When we pray for justice to be done to us and uproot injustice oppressing us, God hears the cry of the oppressed. '*When the just cry out, the Lord hears them, and from all their distress he rescues them.*' Prayer redeems the lives of God's servants. The lives and words of holy people, especially in the Scriptures attest to the efficacy of prayer. Jesus' main purpose of his life was to make us convinced of the power of prayer. In today's Gospel he emphasizes it by telling us, 'ask you will receive, seek, you will find, knock, and the door will be opened to you. For everyone who asks receives; and the one who seeks, finds; and to the one who knocks, the door will be opened.'

In the responsorial Psalm we said, when I call you answer me'. This is the continuous claim of the Psalmist, and all heroes and heroines in Scriptures. In the Jabez prayer, you will find the final word, 'So God granted him what he requested'. It was the conviction of all religious people that as God's word cannot return back without yielding its fruits, so the prayer of a broken heart will never go unheard. It will yield its fruits, as the word of God, to some hundredfold, others fifty, to some others thirty.

As Paul writes, prayer helps us to run the life's race and complete it successfully, to fight the good fight and finally get the crown of victory. Also, when we are left alone without anyone to defend us, when everyone deserts us, through prayer the Lord will stands by us and gives us enough strength as He gave to Paul.

The power of prayer should not be underestimated. James 5:16-18 declares, "... The prayer of a righteous man is powerful and effective. Elijah was a man just like us. He prayed earnestly that it would not rain, and it did not rain on the land for three and a half years. Again he prayed, and the heavens gave rain, and the earth produced its crops." God most definitely listens to prayers, answers prayers, and moves in response to prayers.

The Word of God is full of accounts describing the power of prayer in various situations. The power of prayer has overcome enemies (Psalm 6:9-10), conquered death (2 Kings 4:3-36), brought healing (James 5:14-15), and defeated demons (Mark 9:29). God, through prayer, opens eyes, changes hearts, heals wounds, and grants wisdom (James 1:5). The power of prayer should never be underestimated because it draws on the glory and might of the infinitely powerful God of the universe! Daniel 4:35 proclaims, "All the peoples of the earth are regarded as nothing. He does as he pleases with the powers of heaven and the peoples of the earth. No one can hold back his hand or say to him: 'What have you done?'"

B. Powerlessness of Some Prayer ventures

While we are convinced from the light of our Scriptures and Church members' experiences that prayer is a powerful tool why then many people's prayer efforts remain powerless and unproductive? I have heard the cry and complain of many parishioners: "I pray and pray; nothing happens as I prayed for. Does God really hear me when I pray? Why does it seem as if my prayers just hit the ceiling and bounce back at me? Is God mad at me? Is that why He does not answer me? Why is prayer is so boring and fruitless for me?"

> The first reason is that their prayer endeavors are not based on the formulas Jesus gave to us through the Lord's Prayer.

Due to such disappointment and disillusionment many of them pray as merely a religious rote exercise, one that is not concerned with obtaining results. Consciously or unconsciously they become convinced that prayer is not very important to everyday life and that it does not apply to the real world; and prayer is not an instrument of support to their burdensome life better than themselves or other people around them. Prayer lost its priority-role in majority people's lives. Other activities are more exciting, fruitful and necessary. Some people use prayer as an 'out-sourcing' scheme in their life or crisis management. Because of unanswered prayers many turned out to be atheists or constant doubters about God and His Presence. As the consequence of unanswered prayer, they begin asking the question posed in Job 21: 15: *"What would we gain by praying to him?"*

From my personal life as well as from spiritual authors and Saints' writings I enlist a few reasons for such powerlessness found in many people's prayer efforts: The first reason is that their prayer endeavors are not based on the formulas Jesus gave to us through the Lord's Prayer and they don't contain three important qualities of prayer which were elaborately discussed in previous chapters: Prayer must have a strong, familial, and intimate connection with God. Perseverance is another important quality of effective prayer; the effort of persevering in prayer is one of the means to straighten out our connections with God. And the third quality to put in to prayer the boldness; we should be daring enough to ask God even if the situation seems one hundred percent hopeless and grim.

Secondly the powerless prayer is oriented toward silly and irrelevant results. Many are afraid to ask for miracles from the God who is a God of miracles. Every day He is performing thousands of miracles to millions of His people. Unfortunately all his miracles are easily taken for granted or just ignored and denied. The main reason for this human attitude is that humans think every miracle can be explained by natural causes; for example, the miracle of Jesus walking on the water. Many make a joke out of it. They say that Jesus knew well where the stones were in the lake, but Peter unfortunately did not know it. This is why Peter sank. Even the miracle of the multiplication of the loaves is being explained by the sudden opening of the generosity of people present at that time. They all shared with each other what they were hiding in their bags.

So many miraculous deeds of God are thus overlooked and ignored by us in our day-today lives. And this is why we stopped asking God for His great miracles. We try to limit His capacity or put a boundary for his intervention telling ourselves: "It's enough. Let me not disturb the Lord. He had done His best in His creation and redemption. Now it is my time to show my worth." This is how Peter thought when He got out of the boat and began walking on the water. He said to himself: "Jesus my master has initiated me. I have now enough power. So let me walk by myself." Peter at that moment lost the psychological connection with Jesus though he was very close to him physically. Then we know what happened. Despite the providence and guidance of the Lord, Peter sank. This event of sinking and failing happens in most of our lives even we pray regularly; it is due to our indifference in expecting almighty miracles from God for our ordinary vulnerable lives.

> So many miraculous deeds of God are thus overlooked and ignored by us in our day-today lives. And this is why we stopped asking God for His great miracles.

'Ask it will be given.' That is true. But we should ask for proper things. Tertullian wrote: *"Prayer is the one thing that can conquer God. But Christ* has willed that it should work no evil and has given it all power over good." This means our prayer can work even evil to ourselves, to others and even to God. This is why my spiritual fathers always advise me, 'better be careful in what you pray and surely in how you pray.' For example, we can pray for our prosperity. No problem but do we pray for the prosperity that does not take us away from God? Do we pray for pleasures that do not blind us for heavenly joy? Do we pray for good future that goes in line with God's will?

For too many of us our greatest problem in our prayer is to find its ineffectiveness. We have asked, we have knocked and we have sought in prayer as the Lord advises us. Yet why has nothing has been occurring as we demanded in prayer? In one of my retreats the preacher, responding to my personal question about the ineffectiveness of my prayer splendidly, told me: 'All the Scriptural passages that promise wonderful effects of prayer are truly true. No doubt about it. But you should have read them in connection with the other words the Lord has uttered and with the behavior and way he dealt with this earthly situation and our relationship with God.'

Hence I began reading some other pages of Scriptures in relation to prayer and its power: First *"If you remain in me and my words remain in you, ask for whatever you want and it will be done for you."* (Jn. 15:7) How to remain in God's love? *"If you keep my commandments, you will remain in my love, just as I have kept my Father's commandments and remain in his love."* (Jn. 15: 10) I came across another saying of Jesus which was not directly targeted to prayer but I thought it was ruthlessly attacking me. *"Do not give what is holy to dogs, or throw your pearls before swine, lest they trample them underfoot, and turn and tear you to pieces.* (Mt. 7/6) I felt ashamed of myself being named as a useless and harmful pig and being incapable of receiving gifts from God through prayer.

The author of James' letter pinpointed rightly the reason why I do not get what I pray for. *"You do not possess because you do not ask. You ask but do not receive, because you ask wrongly, to spend it on your passions. Adulterers! Do you not know that to be a lover of the world means enmity with God? Therefore, whoever wants to be a lover of the world makes himself an enemy of God.* (James

4: 2-4) The writer of Sirach positively points out that "He who serves God willingly is heard; his petition reaches the heavens." (Sir. 35:6)

I read also from the OT why God considers most of our religious practices, especially our prayerful acts: *"What care I for the number of your sacrifices?" says the LORD. "I have had enough of whole-burnt rams and fat of fatlings; in the blood of calves, lambs and goats I find no pleasure. When you come in to visit me, who asks these things of you? Trample my courts no more! Bring no more worthless offerings; your incense is loathsome to me. New moon and Sabbath, calling of assemblies, octaves with wickedness: these I cannot bear. Your new moons and festivals I detest; they weigh me down, I tire of the load. When you spread out your hands, I close my eyes to you; though you pray the more, I will not listen. Your hands are full of blood! Wash yourselves clean! Put away your misdeeds from before my eyes; cease doing evil; learn to do good. Make justice your aim: redress the wronged, hear the orphan's plea, defend the widow."* (Is. 1: 11-15)

I too read in OT about King Solomon who had a dream one night in which the Lord told him, "Ask something of me and I will give it to you." If the Lord had directly asked me as He did Solomon, I might have told Him, "Lord, make me wealthier (in no time with no sweat and no hard labor); or more famous (adored by others); or thinner (despite swallowing more than 3000 calories worth of snacks); or taller (so that my peers are beneath me); or more intelligent, talented, and beautiful (because that would make me feel good). I would also have written down a litany of my desires and presented to him: 'Lord, give me the power to foretell the future, the power to right the wrongs in the world, the opportunity to quit my nagging job and travel the world, friends who make no mistakes, and give me assurance that I could live a long, healthy, safe and secure life. Lord, help me to run a successful business and be my own boss, and make me a world class athlete, artist, singer, dancer, writer.'

> I am careful what I pray for. I do not ask for small things, not trivial gifts, but bigger blessings, a fuller life of God, the 'qualitylife'. Going a little further, I desire and pray to possess Him. Indeed, the Giver is greater than the gifts.

Obviously, this wish litany could go on and on, because the desires of the human heart are legion. King Solomon put all these earthly desires aside and requested God give him an understanding heart. The king wanted to possess the wisdom of God in order to know His presence, to understand God's precepts, and to perform his worldly affairs according to God's Will. Solomon got what he prayed for, plus abundant prosperity and happiness, and he was granted an opportunity to build God's Temple, an unfinished project of his father David. I therefore must keep in mind that I get, not what I deserve, but what I ask for.

That time on I am careful what I pray for. I do not ask for small things, not trivial gifts, but bigger blessings, a fuller life of God, the 'qualitylife'. Going a little further, I desire and pray to possess Him. Indeed, the Giver is greater than the gifts. This is the greatest of all the dreams I long for. It needs miraculous intervention of God and countless blessings, including earthly, will follow thereafter.

From that moment I came to realize that the power of prayer is not the result of the person praying. However much we pray passionately and purposefully unless we pray according to God's will nothing works as we expect. Rather, the power of prayer resides in the God who is being prayed to. 1 John 5:14-15 tells us, *"This is the confidence we have in approaching God: that if we ask anything according to his will, he hears us. And if we know that he hears us—whatever we ask—we know that we have what we asked of him."* No matter who prays, what passion behind the prayer or the purpose of the prayer—God answers prayers that are in agreement with His will. His answers are not always yes, but are always in our best interest. When our desires align with His will, we will come to understand that in time.

We cannot access powerful prayer by using "magic formulas." Our prayers being answered is not based on the eloquence of our prayers. We don't have to use certain words or phrases to get God to answer our prayers. In fact, Jesus rebukes those who pray using repetitions, *"And when you pray, do not keep on babbling like pagans, for they think they will be heard because of their many words. Do not be like them, for your Father knows what you need before you ask him"* (Matthew 6:7-8). Prayer is communicating with God. All you have to do is ask God for His help. There is power in prayer!

Although we can definitely say that prayer always works, it does not, however, always work as we might wish. This is especially true with what is called personal prayer. This is because our desires are not always aligned with our Higher or God. Prayer will always help; it will always be beneficial, it will always strengthen and uplift the recipient if said with good intentions from a loving heart. However, prayer does not always bring the results we would like, but sometimes it brings the results that we need. Herebelow are the sincere findings of an unknown Confederate soldier between 1861 and 1865 about his own prayer experience

"I asked for strength that I might achieve;
I was made weak that I might learn humbly to obey.
I asked for health that I might do greater things;
I was given infirmity that I might do better things.
I asked for riches that I might be happy;
I was given poverty that I might be wise.
I asked for power that I might have the praise of men;
I was given weakness that I might feel the need of God.
I asked for all things that I might enjoy life;
I was given life, that I might enjoy all things.
I got nothing that I had asked for, but everything that I had hoped for.
Almost despite myself, my unspoken prayers were answered; I am, among men, most richly blessed."

C. The misuses of prayer

It is not part of the life of a natural man to pray. Probably that may be one of the reasons why prayer is one among the most misunderstood spiritual sciences on Earth. We hear it said that a man will suffer in his life if he does not pray; as a disciple of Jesus I question it. What will suffer is the life of the Son of God in him, which is nourished not by food, but by prayer. When a man is born from above, the life of the Son of God is born in him, and he can either starve that life or nourish it. Prayer is the way the life of God is nourished.

Our ordinary views of prayer are not found in the New Testament. We look upon prayer as a means of getting things for ourselves. A priest asked a little boy: "Do you say your prayers every night?" "No, Sir," replied the boy. "Some nights I don't want anything." Certainly to most children, prayer means asking God or the Absolute for various things, just as they would ask their parents. This concept of prayer is often carried over to adulthood. Many people look upon the Creator as a great benevolent figure like Santa who gives them things. They ask for this and that, and then, if their prayers aren't answered, they doubt God's very existence.

Prayer is also being handled as a form of bargain in our deals with God. 'If you give me this, I'll do that.' There is a story of two men adrift at sea on an open boat for thirty days. One man decided that he had had enough and prayed: "Oh God, if you save us, I'll stop gambling, drinking, swearing, will donate more to my church, and . . ." "Stop, stop, stop!" screamed his companion. "Watch what you're saying, don't go too far. I think I see a ship coming!" Then there is a sort of Agnostic prayer prevalent among the prayer-users who are tempted to tell their God: "Oh God, save my soul—if I have a soul!"

When I first came to the United States, I was shocked to see the empty pews at Sunday services. I asked one of my colleagues at University of Illinois, in Chicago about it. He himself never went to church nor prayed anytime. He said to me, 'why go? And why pray? I have everything I need.' After my studies, I went back to my mission diocese in India, and to my astonishment, I found in some of our city churches the same empty pews. I asked one of the youngsters who stopped going to church what had happened with him. He answered, 'Why go to God who does not give me what I need when I ask for it.' This is how we are divided in our prayer practices. Many of us don't need God because we possess everything we need. Others don't like God because he does not answer their prayers instantly.

As one author beautifully defined prayer, it is 'earthly license for heavenly interference.' Its effect is seen in two ways: a) When prayer does not bring results, it is an indication that something is wrong. b) When prayer does bring results it is an indication that we are building intimacy with God; we bring honor to His nature and character; we cause respect for his integrity; we are able to believe fully in his word; we begin to trust in his love; we affirm more and more his purposes and will in our lives; we appropriate his promises.

D. Qualityprayer in Sufferings

Sometimes, on the darkest days of our lives, all we do is either we behave like the Apostles did while their Master left them and ascended to heaven, looking intently to the sky, surely feeling sad and lonely (Acts 1: 10) or we stand still, looking sad as the Disciples of Emmaus did in their travel. (Luke 24:17) Certainly all these Apostles and disciples were moving in dark and grim situation; their hearts were in tatters and their minds were in confused status; they had no strength and courage to pull themselves out of despair and dare to hope again; they possessed no wisdom to look at the same facts in a different light and see a whole new world. However acutely they were thrusted into chaotic lifesituation they emerged champions of the world by one and only instrument and that is becoming praying persons. The Spirit of the resurrected Lord assisted them in his own way. He brought an angel to the Apostles and directed them to come to reality of life and start praying together in the Upper Room waiting for the Power from on High. To the Emmaus disciples on the road he appeared like a co-traveler and changed them prayer-persons by his enlightening conversation, establishing trustworthy friendship with them and conducted the Eucharist celebration where he showed his identity to point out the real upshot of prayer.

During their acute suffering time and at the beginning stage of the Church, Apostles and disciples have spent days and hours privately and in group discussing, meditating on the crucifixion and death of the Lord. This was the primary purpose of their prayertime; when they joined with the people their mouths couldn't but preach and teach about Jesus' passion and death and his final victory. This probing reflection helped them clarify and deepen their questions. We should do the same when we pray in times of anguish.

When we pray in sufferings we tell God our story and prepare ourselves to listen to God's response. In this regard the Psalmist is a wonderful model. Almost 2/3 of his Psalms are his communicating with God, especially his downfalls, perils, sufferings, trials, failures, disappointments and desolations. He expressed to God his greatest afflictions that came from, besides other outside enemies, his own family members as worst foes; his nagging temptations of poverty and wealth, of honor and reproach, of health and weakness, which tried their power upon him; his peaceless state of mind; his continuous seasons of despondency and alarm, bringing him into the lowest depths; and all God's waves and billows rolling over him. At the same time we should notice him crying out like a baby for help and support from God who alone his Protector and Rescuer. Here are a few samples of the Psalmist's prayers in his sufferings:

Lord! My foes are too many; they rise against me; they too say of me, "God will not save that one." But my God! Arise and save me. (Ps. 3: 2-3, 8)

Answer when I call, my saving God. show me favor; hear my prayer. How long will you people mock my honor, love what is worthless, chase after lies? (Ps. 4: 2-3)

Hear my words, O Lord; listen to my sighing. Hear my cry for help, my king, my God! To you I pray, O Lord; Guide me in your justice because of my foes; make straight your way before me. For there is no sincerity in their mouths; their hearts are corrupt. Their throats are open graves; on their tongues are subtle lies. Declare them guilty, God; make them fall by their own devices. Drive them out for their many sins; they have rebelled against you. Protect them that you may be the joy of those who love your name. For you, Lord, bless the just; you surround them with favor like a shield. (Ps. 5: 2-3; 9-11; 13)

Lord! I am wearied with sighing; all night long tears drench my bed; my couch is soaked with weeping. My eyes are dimmed with sorrow, worn out because of all my foes. Do not reprove me in your anger nor punish me in your wrath. Have pity on me for I am weak; heal me for my bones are trembling. In utter terror is my soul—and you, Lord, how long . . . ? Turn, Lord, save my life; in your mercy rescue me. (Ps. 6: 2-8)

Lord, my God, in you I take refuge; rescue me; save me from all who pursue me, lest they maul me like lions, tear me to pieces with none to save. I spared even those who hated me without cause. If I am at fault in this, if there is guilt on my hands, if I have repaid my friend with evil. then let my enemy pursue and overtake me, trample my life to the ground, and leave me dishonored in the dust. Rise up, Lord, in your anger; rise against the fury of my foes. Wake to judge as you have decreed. Have the assembly of the peoples gather about you; sit on your throne high above them, Lord, judge of the nations. Grant me justice, for I am blameless, free of any guilt. Bring the malice of the wicked to an end; uphold the innocent, O God of justice, who tries hearts and minds. (Ps. 7: 2-10)

Have mercy on me, Lord; see how my foes afflict me! You alone can raise me from the gates of death. Arise, Lord, let no mortal prevail; let the nations be judged in your presence. Strike them with terror, Lord; show the nations they are mere mortals. (Ps. 9: 14, 20-21)

We should observe here that it is not despite of his faith in confidence in God as his Shepherd as he exposes in Psalm 23, *"Even when I walk through a dark valley, I fear no harm for you are at my side"*, but because of such 'Chutzpah' a virulent and audacious faith he comes back again and again to his Shepherd, complaints, implores and resigns to the God's will in every prayertime.

The Psalmist inserts in almost all of his Psalms words of praise and thanks toward God: *"I praise you, LORD, for you raised me up and did not let my enemies rejoice over me. O LORD, my God, I cried out to you for help and you healed me. LORD, you brought my soul up from Sheol; you let me live, from going down to the pit."* (Ps. 30: 1-4) And he too asks his friends and those around him to join in his praising and thanking the Lord: *"Sing praise to the LORD, you faithful; give thanks to his holy memory. For his anger lasts but a moment; his favor a lifetime. At dusk weeping comes for the night; but at dawn there is rejoicing."* (Ps. 30: 5-6)

> We should notice here that the suffering Psalmist behaves exactly like babies who, when they are hungry and need food from their moms, cry aloud; they know from their previous experience how effective this 'strategy of crying' wins over their moms.

We may be little leery of his sincerity in his composition of Psalms: Is it some sort of fake prayer or a kind of showoff hiding inside his foaming and restlessness against God's deeds against him? Certainly it is not so. This sufferer, as all of us experience by the unfairness of earthly life, was continuously thwarted by many trials as nonstop trail of events. At every time he was caught and strangled by crisis he prayed and he experienced a relief and rescue from that trial: *"Complacent I once said, "I shall never be shaken." LORD, you showed me favor, established for me mountains of virtue. But when you hid your face I was struck with terror. To you, LORD, I cried out; with the Lord I pleaded for mercy: "What gain is there from my lifeblood, from my going down to the grave? Does dust give you thanks or declare your faithfulness? Hear, O LORD, have mercy on me; LORD, be my helper."* (Ps. 30: 7-11)

After his pleading he was liberated from his tribulations and felt so happy and thankful about the Lord's goodness: *"You changed my mourning into dancing; you took off my sackcloth and clothed me with gladness. So that my glory may praise you and not be silent. O LORD, my God, forever will I give you thanks."* (Ps. 30: 12-13) We should notice here that the suffering Psalmist behaves exactly like babies who, when they are hungry and need food from their moms, cry aloud; they know from their previous experience how effective this 'strategy of crying' wins over their moms. He knew his qualityprayer was the most effective strategy to bring down the Almighty into his life with all His absolute power and love.

In any qualityprayer this is what is happening. After describing our critical situation and our hurt-feelings to the Almighty (Lk. 24: 18-24), we start listening intently as He explains to us His will as He had revealed in the scriptures (Lk. 24: 25-27). We then allow ourselves to fall into a receptive, contemplative state during which we leave space for God. This humble but sacred space enables us to hear the word of God in a new way. Our hearts will be burning within us. (Lk. 24: 32) Our world that is shattered by our grief, sickness, and other trials will now be broken open again, but with spiritual strength and joy.

If we are truly the disciples of Jesus, the instinct to pray becomes natural and abides within our heart. When suffering comes, Jesus will be with us and will invite us to tell him about our pain. As Paul was convinced we too are fully swayed by the unconditional help of the Holy Spirit in our praying during sufferings. *"In the same way, the Spirit too comes to the aid of our weakness; for we do not know how to pray as we ought, but the Spirit itself intercedes with inexpressible groanings. And the one who searches hearts knows what is the intention of the Spirit, because it intercedes for the holy ones according to God's will."* (Rom. 8: 26-27)

During our suffering times we too must be conscious of the loving and healing presence of our Lord Jesus in us and in our midst. Scriptural passages always invite us to recognize Jesus as our Healer sent by God to continue his wok of healing in our midst. Jesus, in his short term of life, was preoccupied with human sicknesses and tried to heal them as much as he could within his human limitation. He was a busy man round the clock, 24/7. Wherever he was found he was preaching, teaching and curing the sick and driving out demons. He did all these at daytime. His power went out of him to offer sudden and dramatic healings. He did not do only these liberating activities. He spent most of his nights and early hours of daily life in praying, in being alone with God. While he was so busy round the clock performing his ministry of preaching, healing and loving, moving, rather running up and down, north to south, east and west of Palestine to fulfill his mission as today's Gospel says: he slipped away from the crowd and found for himself sufficient time of rest, solitude and prayer. *'Rising very early before dawn, he left and went off to a deserted place, where he prayed.'* Whether he was resting or actively preoccupied Jesus was always in union with His Father.

We always think that he brought salvation to the humanity by his death and resurrection. Surely that is the climatic acts of Jesus. But from Scriptures we know that the whole life of Jesus was the reason for our salvation: his whole of 33 years in this world. Out of those thirty three years he spent 30 years in a hidden way, being obedient and lovable son to his parents, who always prayed together, fulfilled all community religious rituals with him. Even during those three years of his public life he divided his day and night into 50/50. Half of his daily life was preoccupied with hectic services to his fellowmen whereas the other half was totally to be in prayer. This means the salvation he brought to us depended largely on his obedient, surrendering and praying life.

> This spirit of prayer continued even in the inactive life of the Disciples that was thrusted on them due to their sickness, old age, social situation or any other natural causes. This saved them from being tensed, worried and humiliated.

Another truth we learn from Jesus' life is this: At the final week of his life he underwent ignominious sufferings, rejections, betrayal and disowning and horrible death. During those days and nights he could hold on to his religious and spiritual adherence to his Father only by his heart-to-heart prayer. Operation accomplished by Jesus mostly again by his obedient, surrendering and praying hours. He won the victory largely by prayer.

When we reflect on Jesus' life of healing and praying we understand Jesus himself is a healer in our midst; plus he taught us how to get this healing power only through our regular and persistent praying habit. As he got power to heal others and himself through prayer he expects us doing the same. Paul and other disciples of Jesus truly followed him in this regard. They spent night and day in preaching, teaching, healing, caring, sharing, administering and leading in the kingdom of God. While they worked hard tirelessly they always kept themselves united with their Master. This spirit of prayer continued even in their inactive life that was thrusted on them due to their sickness, old age, social situation or any other natural causes. This saved them from being tensed, worried and humiliated.

To be active onetime and to be quiet and inactive at other time is the normal process of human life. These two stages are inevitable for any human person. Job, whose mourning and groaning we hear in the Book of Job had had his stint of busyness and intense preoccupation. He had raised seven sons and three daughters. He was responsible for a large estate, which included "seven thousand sheep, three thousand camels, five hundred yoke of oxen, five hundred she-asses, and a great number of work animals." Suddenly a misfortune occurred in his life. He loses his livestock, his children were swept away by a storm, and he himself was stricken with the skin disease. It was very hard on him. He could not accept this critical situation of loss, sickness and inactivity. At this horrible stage of his life Job enters into the hell of bitterness. While he feels very negative about his personal life he cries: *'I am filled with restlessness until the dawn'*, and he views also the entire human life the same way: *'Is not man's life on earth drudgery?'*

This is how most of us approach our own lives. While we are active we are so much plunged into the deep stream of material life. We forget God and his well-set love expecting us to be closely attached to Him. But when the life calls us for another critical stage of retirement, sickness or any other inactive life situation, we are shocked; we begin to curse God, others and ourselves. Our beautiful life of retirement turns to be sorrow-filled drudgery as Job remarks. We fall into deep despair and depression.

> "Mom, don't worry about it; God considers your bedroom as His sanctuary and your bed as His Son's Altar. As you lie down in bed, just think of the Lord's love and offer all your sufferings, including your disappointments, to God with the sufferings of His Son. This is the most precious sacrifice of the Mass God would have received ever in His Life."

We must follow the example of Jesus and his disciples in order to be peaceful, joyful and content and very positive. During our times of success, and victory we need to spend sufficient qualitytime with the Lord, either personally or in group and with community. Our hearts must swell with gratitude and love for our Master during those times of glory. We too must continue to hold on to such spirit of prayer during our times of darkness, isolation, sickness, disappoint and sorrows. Not like Job but like Jesus and his disciples we should unite ourselves with our God continuously and persistently. For this, one of the preachers suggested (may be in one of his blogs) five ways of praying to God during our dark days:

Lord of Compassion, have pity on me. I hate myself wasting my time in selfpitying. You are a compassionate God. You know me in and through. If these sufferings are the outcome of my sinfulness you forgive me. I am a limited being; I cannot save myself unless and until you extend your hands. Have pity on me.

Let this bitter chalice pass away from me; however let your will be done and not mine. Behold the handmaid of the Lord; be it done unto me according to your word.

Into your hands I offer up my sufferings. I am aware of my presence in you and yours in me. I leave everything in your hands. You take care of me more than me. I shall relax and lie on your lap.

Let not my sufferings go in vain. I should not suffer in waste. Kindly make the best use of them according to your wish. It can be for my personal salvation or for my family members' renewal or for the salvation of the whole world as you used your Son Jesus' sufferings.

My powerful God! Snatch victory for me from the jaws of sorrows. This victory can be temporary, temporal, and physical healing and winning in this world or it can be my eternal resurrection."

When we are suffering afflictions most of us don't to know how to pray as we ought. But because they are hard to endure and painful, we, pray to have our afflictions taken from us. Having great respect for God in Jesus, even if he does not take our afflictions away, we should not consider ourselves ignored and neglected, but should hope to gain some greater good through our patient acceptance of suffering. For we believe what Jesus said to Paul: "*My power is at its best in weakness.*"

When my mother, in her venerable old age of 100 years, was complaining to me about her inability to attend Mass in our parish church, I told her very gently, "Mom, don't worry about it; God considers your bedroom as His sanctuary and your bed as His Son's Altar. As you lie down in bed, just think of the Lord's love and offer all your sufferings, including your disappointments, to God with the sufferings of His Son. This is the most precious sacrifice of the Mass God would have received ever in His Life."

According to the Lord's suggestions, we should not be proud of ourselves if our prayer is heard rather we should acknowledge God's absolute power over us and rejoice that we are counted among those chosen by Him. When the Apostles were thrilled with excitement that they had performed wonders in their apostolate Jesus instructed them: *"Nevertheless, do not rejoice because the spirits are subject to you, but rejoice because your names are written in heaven."* (Lk. 10: 20) Jesus too ordered them to uphold always a servant attitude in their dealings for the Supreme Being. He is quoted saying, *"So should it be with you. When you have done all you have been commanded, say, 'We are unprofitable servants; we have done what we were obliged to do.'"* (Lk. 17: 10)

The same Lord expects us not to become utterly dejected if we are not given what we ask for, despairing of God's mercy towards us. Who knows, it might be that what we have been praying for could have brought us some still greater affliction. It may be because we have not prioritized our prayer requests or it could have brought us the kind of good fortune that brings corruption and ruin. In such cases, it is clear that we cannot know how to pray as we ought.

Even in time of sufferings and especially when we feel our requests for healing and rescue are not granted we should thank and praise the Lord. As St. Augustine says, *"if anything happens contrary to our prayer, we ought to bear the disappointment patiently, give thanks to God, and be sure that it was better for God's will to be done than our own."*

E. The Hardships faced in QualityPrayer

The following of Jesus as our Master and Teacher is like 'going through the narrow gate.' *"Enter through the narrow gate; for the gate is wide and the* road broad that leads to destruction and those who enter through it are many. How narrow the gate and constricted the road that leads to life. And those who find it are few."(Matt. 7: 13-14) Any religious as well as spiritual practices we perform in our Christian life are to be as if walking through a narrow gate. Number one disturbing factor in praying efforts is the duality existing within us: Spiritual and physical dimensions. Though we are made 'little less than the angels', it is very difficult to get out of our physical dimension and totally become spiritual. Qualityprayer in a certain way demands this from the disciples of Jesus who enlisted certain requirements for making our prayer into qualityprayer.

The first requirement Jesus proposed is to pray in secret: *"When you pray, go to your inner room, close the door, and pray to your Father in secret."* (Matt. 6: 6) Certainly Jesus did not want us dreaming about our Father in secret but praying to our Father in secret. Act of praying is an effort of our will. After we have entered our secret place and have shut the door, the most difficult thing we face is to pray; we find it hard to discipline our mind into working order not wandering or fooling around. The great fight we fight in private prayer is the subduing of our mental 'wool-gathering'.

A secret silence Jesus indicates means a 'sacred silence' of shutting the door deliberately on our emotions and being present before God. This battle is nothing but hopping from physical dimension to spiritual realm. Though both realms are within us, we discover our inability to win over them. That awareness is another source of our suffering in prayer.

Because of the duality in humanness it is hard to 'pray unceasingly'. This is one of those elements that enhance Christian prayer into qualityprayer, namely living and breathing and walking and interacting and laughing and loving in a constant spirit of prayer. This is not that easy as many think. It is much easier to go on reciting by our lips some ejaculatory prayers or formal prayers continuously even throughout the day and night but people who are committed to efforts of reaching to the status of praying qualityprayer know how hard it is to connect and integrate both natural and earthly moments to heavenly deals. It is painful indeed.

Another demand from Christ to pray qualityprayer is: 'Pray perseveringly'. Albert Einstein once said, *"I think and think for months and years. Ninety-nine times, my conclusions are false. The hundredth time I am right."* President Calvin Coolidge put it this way, *"Nothing in the world can take the place of persistence. Talent will not. Genius will not. Education will not."* Though persistence and determination bring wonderful results in our human life their role in qualityprayer endeavors is very different. We have to persist with determination in getting into the deeper or higher level of humanity, the spiritual realm where unholy elements cannot be admitted; and no earthly and natural ambitions and dreams can play their rocking roles. Again we are pricked by another issue that is generated from our humanness.

Conflict in prayer arises and kills us from the important twofold facet of humanness: personal and social. Qualityprayer stipulates these two features are to be present when we pray. In Scriptures we are commanded 'love your neighbor as yourself.' This means first we love truly ourselves and in the same way love others. God created us individuals and bestowed His likeness and image to each person. In practical life we say 'share what you have'. Unless I individually possess certain things I cannot share anything with others. First I must be spiritually well-equipped and full of godly experiences through my qualityprayer and then I can start praying for others and with others. These thoughts are posed by people who esteem the human individuality greater than human social dimension.

> One more difficulty that stabs us in our qualityprayer efforts is to be indifferent to where we are. Whichever way God designs our circumstances of life our duty is to pray.

In a Christian prayer, as we hear from the Lord, no individualistic attitude should be present. We are advised always to connect ourselves to our fellow human beings and pray as, for and with 'us, our' and not 'I, and my'. That is the spirit of Jesus' prayer in which he never adds 'my' and 'me', rather only 'our' and 'us' as he starts the prayer: "Our Father". Here is the continuous battle we are engaged in when we pray. Though we are 'social animals', we are prone to be individuals, especially when we grow to a matured status of our humanness. The more we develop our personality greater the difficulty to forget our individuality and attend to 'we', 'us' and 'they' and 'them'.

One more difficulty that stabs us in our qualityprayer efforts is to be indifferent to where we are. Whichever way God designs our circumstances of life our duty is to pray. One spiritual author advises us: "Never allow the thought—'I am of no use where I am;' because you certainly can be of no use where you are not. Wherever God has dumped you down in circumstances pray, ejaculate to Him all the time."

It is painful also to read from the Scriptures and follow one more of its advice, namely to pray always, even if we don't get thrills, which is the intensest (extreme) form of spiritual selfishness. We have to labor along the line of God's direction. There is nothing thrilling about a laboring man's work, but it is the laboring man who wins ultimately.

Nevertheless there is one more capsule of hard factor we have to swallow regarding the results of prayer. We work arduously at prayer yet its results happen all the time from His standpoint.

Regarding the sufferings we bear to make our prayer efforts genuine and fruitful as qualityprayer, I love what Oswald Chambers with his enlivened mind says: *We are too much given to thinking of the Cross as something we have to get through; we get through it only in order to get into it. The Cross stands for one thing only for us—a complete and entire and absolute identification with the Lord Jesus Christ, and there is nothing in which this identification is realized more than in prayer.*

Our Lord insisted that we should pray to our Father for whatever we need; at the same time he is also quoted saying, *"Your Father knows what things you have need of, before you ask Him."* My rationality asks myself why then should I ask? The straight answer comes from the Scriptural Authors and from many of our Saints who declare that our prayer is not in order to get answers from God; prayer is perfect and complete oneness with God. In other words, we don't pray for getting results at its end, rather during prayertime we are in the process of getting more acquainted and closer to God in Jesus. Again to stomach such truth of prayer is very hard and sometimes painful. It is there I am carrying the Cross with the Lord.

F. Prayer of Petition in Qualityprayer

In prayer we always have a long list of needs to be submitted to God. But Jesus expects us to keep the following petition of the Psalmist as the first and the basis of those petitions: *"I have asked one thing from the Lord, this is what I will seek: to dwell in the Lord's house all the days of my life, to see the graciousness of the Lord, and to visit his temple."* In qualityprayertime our main concentration is to commune with God and inside of it there comes automatically a time when we make appeal, request and begging for certain things we are deprived of. Our **primary petition in tears and sighs** is for the grace from the Lord to see His face; to feel His presence continuously; and to fill us with His fuller Life and Light. When we face the Lord in qualityprayer we observe our own emptiness and we discover there is a vacuum within us which He alone can fill in. A litany of petitions starts pouring from our hearts for achieving this primary goal of qualityprayer. This means we put the petition before God for the Giver and not much for the Gifts.

Secondly in continuation of the primary petition we begin to feel for our own friends and family and community members who too, like us, very badly need of God's fuller Life and Light. We submit this petition to the Lord remembering each of our needy neighbors mentioning their names if possible. Above all, we pray for the whole Church and for the entire humanity. St. Ambrose, highlighting the importance of this prayer-petition for community, says: *"You must remember that more grace comes to one who prays for others than to any ordinary sinner. If each person prays for all people, then all people are effectively praying for each. In conclusion, if you ask for something for yourself alone, you will be the only one asking for it; but if you ask for benefits for all, all in their turn will be asking for them for you. For, you are, in fact, one of the "all." Thus it is a great reward, as each person's prayers acquire the weight of the prayers of everyone."*

During the petitioning time slot of qualityprayer we should also add our petitions for various material and earthly needs of us, our family, our community, our nation and the entire world. It is true Jesus told us not to bother about all our earthly needs and he reminded us it is the habit of pagans who don't have any clue about the true God, Father in Heaven. He too promised once we seek God's kingdom and its principles the Father would grant them to us. *"So do not worry and say, 'What are we to eat?' or 'What are we to drink?' or 'What are we to wear?' All these things the pagans seek. Your heavenly Father knows that you need them all. But seek first the kingdom (of God) and his righteousness and all these things will be given you besides."* (Matt. 6: 31-33)

We may think we have asked and sought God Himself through our primary petition; now why to ask Him for the material needs? Plus Jesus proclaimed that our Father knows all that we are in need of and He is a very good all-knowing Provider and all-loving Giver; why then to disturb Him? Yet Church and all our spiritual mentors advise us to plead to God for all our material needs. The **reasons** behind our petitioning prayer are:

1. It is Jesus' order plus his prayerstyle. *"Ask and it will be given to you; seek and you will find; knock and the door will be opened to you."* (Matt. 7: 7) He himself was putting petitions to His Father: *"Father, if you are willing, take this cup away from me"* (Lk. 22: 42) Jesus' petition was very demanding: *"He raised his eyes to heaven and said, "Father, the hour has come. Give glory to your son, so that your son may glorify you . . . I glorified you on earth by accomplishing the work that you gave me to do. Now glorify me, Father, with you, with the glory that I had with you before the world began.* (Jn. 17: 1, 4-5) To perform miracles like raising Lazarus from the tomb he petitioned to his Father: *"Jesus raised his eyes and said, "Father, I thank you for hearing me. I know that you always hear me; but because of the crowd here I have said this, that they may believe that you sent me." And when he had said this, he cried out in a loud voice, "Lazarus, come out".* (Jn. 11: 41-43)

2. Our God in Jesus asks us to pray and place our petitions at his feet not because he wants to know what we really want; rather, he wants us to exercise our desire through our prayers, so that we may be able to receive

what he is preparing to give us. His gift is very great indeed, but our capacity is too small and limited to receive it. That is why we are told: *Enlarge your desires, do not bear the yoke with unbelievers.* The deeper our faith, the stronger our hope, the greater our desire, the larger will be our capacity to receive that gift, which is very great indeed. *No eye has seen it; no ear has heard it; and it has not entered man's heart.* Rather, our heart must enter into it. The more fervent the desire, the more worthy will be its fruit.

> Through prayer of petition we do not make God pay attention to our needs; rather we make ourselves pay attention to God and our desire for him.

When we read Paul saying: *"Make your requests known to God"* this should not be taken in the sense that they are in fact becoming known to God who certainly knew them even before they were made, but that they are becoming known to us before God through submission and not before men through boasting. However if we continue reading Paul in the same passage he refers to the result of such petitions not as 'all of them would be granted' but 'our hearts and minds would be settled in peace': *"Have no anxiety at all, but in everything, by prayer and petition, with thanksgiving, make your requests known to God. Then the peace of God that surpasses all understanding will guard your hearts and minds in Christ Jesus."* (Phi. 4: 6-7)

3. Through prayer of petition we do not make God pay attention to our needs; rather we make ourselves pay attention to God and our desire for him. In this regard John Calvin offers us some profound observations in his book *'The Institutes of the Christian Religion'*: *"It is very much in our interests that we be constantly supplicating Him, first that out heart might always be inflamed with the serious and ardent desire of seeking, loving, and serving Him 'as the sacred' anchor in every necessity. Secondly, that no desire, no longing whatever that we are ashamed to make Him the witness, enter our minds while we learn to place all of our wishes in His sight, and thus pour out our heart before Him. Lastly, that we might be prepared to receive all of His benefits with true gratitude and thanksgiving, while our prayers remind us that they proceed from His hand."* (Book 3, Chapter 20, section 3) Our prayer of petitions is like

everything we perform in our Christian life. It is primarily for God's glory and secondarily for our benefits.

There are a few **guidelines** Jesus has given regarding our prayer, especially that of petition: a) we should not spend lengthy time unnecessarily for the slot-prayertime of petitioning. It is not wrong or useless to pray even for a long time when there is the opportunity. To pray for a longer time is not the same as to pray by multiplying words. Surely too much talking should be excluded from prayer. This doesn't mean that one should not spend much time in prayer so long as the fervent qualityprayer-spirit and attitude continuously accompany his prayer. Agreeing fully the right place of qualitytime in qualityprayer St. Augustine very reflectively writes in his letter to Proba: *"To spend much time in prayer is to knock with a persistent and holy fervor at the door of the one whom we beseech."* b) Besides, we need not pray in many words as though speaking in a stylish way could gain us a hearing. After all, we pray to One who, is Almighty, All-knowing and immanently present with us. Only pagans, as Jesus indicates, use such useless lengthy form of prayer: *"In praying, do not babble like the pagans, who think that they will be heard because of their many words. Do not be like them. Your Father knows what you need before you ask him."* (Matt. 6: 7-8) The act of petitioning can be accomplished more through sighs than words, more through weeping than speech. c) In previous chapter we discussed about the kind of faith 'Chutzpah' as one of the necessary ingredients in qualityprayer. This kind of faith is more needed in the prayer of 'petitioning'. It should be held in shameless faith and trust; we must go on praying with persistence and persevere till the end at any cost. This is how the prayer warriors like Abraham did in their conversation with God. We read in Gen. 18: 20-32 about Abraham's prayer of interceding in a silly and childish way.

In that particular prayertime the Lord first spoke to Abraham that He has decided to destroy Sodom and Gomorrah; Abraham with humanistic concern for his neighbors interceded to God not to harm the cities; he negotiated with Him saying if there were fifty, forty five, forty and even ten righteous people found within those cities He should not bring destruction to the cities. God patiently heard his prayer and accepts his deal; unfortunately since even the minimum numbers of righteous people were not discovered He destroyed the cities. His prayer may seem like an ill-mannered daring in his dealing with God. Yet that is what God likes. We ask anything and in any way from him. He doesn't need any poetic/tidy/formal designs.

> During our time of petitioning we must not continue our outcry in a monologue style. We should also stop our petitioning and listen to what God thinks about our requests.

This peculiar and crazy manner of dealings in prayer is generated from the one fact of our impudent, shameless faith and trust in God who is our Abba, Papa. Just think of children's trust on their parents and parents' attitudes toward them. There is beautiful lullaby of a mother that depicts the parental goodness: *"Hush, little baby, don't say a word, Mama's going to buy you a mockingbird. And if that mockingbird won't sing, Mama's going to buy you a diamond ring."* As it continues, this popular lullaby expresses the unquestioning willingness of parents to satisfy their child's every need and desire, whether these are as necessary as food and shelter or as frivolous as a mockingbird and diamond ring. And this is why Jesus said: *"If you then, who are wicked, know how to give good gifts to your children, how much more will your heavenly Father give good things to those who ask him."* (Matt. 7: 11)

d) During our time of petitioning we must not continue our outcry in a monologue style. We should also stop our petitioning and listen to what God thinks about our requests. Therefore our prayer of intercession must be punctuated by many pauses and silences so that we might be open to hearing words and thoughts other than our own. We have to keep in mind that the goal of petitioning prayer is not to intervene in God's plan and design that is already in his blueprint of wisdom but to integrate ourselves and others and our action and situation with his plan and get adjusting to it.

Hence this is how we should pray when we pray for our needs: First we rationalize with God everything that is happening to us and people for whom we intercede. "*Why have you forsaken me?*" We must ask and ask, seek and seek, question and question him until he answers us. Secondly we plan with God in handling our situations, our challenges, our ambitions and our undertakings. "*If Jesus is in my situation, what would he do?*" Finally we surrender to God as Abraham and Jesus did. Abraham tried his best to put an end to the devastation of his neighbors but it was not possible so finally he relented and subdued to God. That was always his character and behavior. Jesus too in his life would have done the same. At the horrible sunset of his life he was loud enough. In the garden of Gesthemane he petitioned to his Father, '*let this bitter chalice of cruel death pass away from me*', but finally at the intense experience of God's intimacy he responded, '*yet not my will let your will be done.*'

e) We should be careful what we pray for. Human dreams are countless and the desires of the human heart are legion and so follow thousands of petitions to God. We hear in OT King Solomon put all these earthly desires aside and requested God in prayer to give him an understanding heart. The king wanted to possess the wisdom of God in order to know His presence, to understand God's precepts, and to perform his worldly affairs according to God's Will. He got what he prayed for, plus abundant prosperity and happiness, and he was granted an opportunity to build God's Temple, an unfinished project of his father David. We get, not what we deserve, but what we ask for. So let us not ask for small things, not trivial gifts, but bigger blessings, a fuller life. Going a little further, as we mentioned earlier, let us desire and pray to possess Him. Indeed, the Giver is greater than the gifts.

f) Our Prayer must seek for real needs of the hour. When I was a parish priest in an area where leprosy was prevalent, one day a leper knocked at my door for some financial support. I offered him what I could. But he gave that money back and said: "You keep that money with you. Is it for this small amount I came all the way from my home?" I was shocked for life. Later I pacified myself when I reflected over his condition and how it had changed his entire personality.

Invariably, most of us behave the same way as this leper because we too are as Paul and other Saints used to declare, are possessed some evil spirits of jealousy, envy, hatred, injustice, dishonesty and so on. We actually become sick out of them and beginning to hold some perverted views or esteem about ourselves and others. Consequently as that leper we are irritated by, and angered at, the life conditions we were and are in; we form our own system within ourselves (Jung called it 'complex') and try to deal with the life conditions, to face the outside world, or to relate ourselves with one another through that system we built in. Most of us are not aware that this system has been built on a sleeping Volcano of our wounded, irritated, and hurt spirit. This is why, when other people around us are hurt and affected by our peculiar behavior, we don't care about it and feel cool like cucumber.

Many of us therefore find it hard to go to the Lord and afraid to pray sincerely and to go deeper into ourselves because we feel we will be hurt by retrospection; this inner process of reflection will break our built-in system of fake prestige and self-glory. Naaman the leper, mentioned in OT behaved the same way with his denial-strategy and reused to go and pray to the Prophet. Then later the story tells us he yielded to the Spirit of God and was cured. We also see the same attitude and behavior in those nine out of ten lepers in the life of Jesus. When they were cured, the nine did not have the curtsy or heart to go back and say thanks to the one who gave cure to them. They were very much self-centered and self-preoccupied. Their only concern was their cure, their recognition in the society. But while those nine cured outside and not inside of them, the one who went and thanked Jesus was cured both outside and inside of his self.

> Many of us therefore find it hard to go to the Lord and afraid to pray sincerely and to go deeper into ourselves because we feel we will be hurt by retrospection; this inner process of reflection will break our built-in system of fake prestige and self-glory.

In the prayertime of petitioning many among us behave the way. They never bothered about getting all possible benefits for their true self and they beg the Lord to feed their fake self more and more and get sicker within them. Jesus wants us to use our religion not just for material blessings. He expects us to go beyond those blessings and seek for a persistent faith in staying with Him, thanking Him, giving first priority to Him, and giving witness to His healing power. This type of healing He calls Salvation. Our whole purpose of praying to God for blessings should be, as Paul says, *'so that we may obtain the salvation to be found in Christ Jesus and with it eternal glory.*

g) Interceding for others and their needs is an intrinsic part of prayer of petition. However we cannot perform this ministry of interceding if we do not believe in the reality of the Redemption; and our intercession will turn into futile sympathy with human beings. It will only make them more content to being out of touch with God. Their attitude would be complacent about their life without God and say to themselves, 'there is after all somebody out there to take care of our needs in front of God'.

In intercession we must bring the needy person, or the circumstance that urges us to God first. Intercession means filling up "that which is behind of the afflictions of Christ." Therefore intercession must "Put us in his place." And never should we try to put ourselves in God's place. Let's uphold the revealed truth with Oswald Chambers that *God creates something He can create in no other way than through intercessory prayer.* h) Maintaining a 'stay-put'-trust in God's eternal Silence; because, as one spiritual writer puts it, *'God's silences are His answers.'* In communication studies we are told one of most persuasive communication is by human silences. Family people more than anybody else know what this means. When one spouse keeps silent for hours, especially at some important daily chores the other gets the clue that he/she is not happy about certain words uttered or matters done by him/her at home or outside. Many spouses apply this strategy and most of the times they win.

> The admonition I have received from so many of my spiritual mentors is: God is waiting to give us the blessings we ask if we would not drift away from Him. So don't take it for granted. His silence is to be esteemed as the sign that He is taking us into a marvelous understanding of Himself.

Though the Silence we are talking here cannot be equated to the spousal silences still these human silences in communication may resemble as that of God's in bearing some meanings within them. God's silence both in His words and actions as well is meaningful but with difference. Let's think of those days of absolute silence on the part of God when we have been ceaselessly, persistently praying about certain petitions we have submitted to Him while Jesus seemed like not being ready to visit us with his blessings as he did when he was informed of the illness of Lazarus. *"Now a man was ill, Lazarus from Bethany, the village of Mary and her sister Martha. Mary was the one who had anointed the Lord with perfumed oil and dried his feet with her hair; it was her brother Lazarus who was ill ... Now Jesus loved Martha and her sister and Lazarus. So when he heard that he was ill, he remained for two days in the place where he was."* (Jn. 11: 1-2, 5-6)

Take another incident in the lives of the Apostles. Let's consider also those hours when we were being tossed around by the violent storms of unfair life and crying for help from above, God in Jesus seemed careless, as if sleeping tight on a cushion: *"A violent squall came up and waves were breaking over the boat, so that it was already filling up. Jesus was in the stern, asleep on a cushion. They woke him and said to him, "Teacher, do you not care that we are perishing?"* (Mk 4: 37-38)

The admonition I have received from so many of my spiritual mentors is: God is waiting to give us the blessings we ask if we would not drift away from Him. So don't take it for granted. His silence is to be esteemed as the sign that He is taking us into a marvelous understanding of Himself. Let's go back again to those Gospel incidents. In Lazarus' case the Lord is very sharp and clear in the motivation and meaning of his silence: *So the sisters sent word to him, saying, "Master, the one you love is ill." When Jesus heard this he said, "This illness is not to end in death, but is for the glory of God, that the Son of God may be glorified through it."* (Jn. 11: 4). About his sleeping while the Apostles were crying for help, again Jesus refers to their childish (not childlike) faith in him: *"He woke up, rebuked the wind, and said to the sea, "Quiet! Be still!" The wind ceased and there was great calm. Then he asked them, "Why are you terrified? Do you not yet have faith?"* (Mk 4: 39-40)

If God has given us a silence, we should praise Him because He is bringing us into His Vineyard business-deals. One more truth on this matter emerges from the Scriptures that the result-factor of the answer in time is a matter of God's sovereignty. Time is nothing to God. He is leading us to enjoy many times His 'timeless Time.' The ultimate result of God's silence is, as I can testify from my personal prayerlife, it silences my anxieties, my internal tension and turmoil, and get into the cave of serenity taking things one at a time and go with the flow. It may seem like I have subdued by some sourgrape attitude. I don't think so. I have settled and stayed put in the Hands of the Almighty.

And therefore I smilingly continue to place my petitions at His Feet day in and day out. *"If Jesus Christ is bringing you into the understanding that prayer"*, writes famous preacher Oswald Chambers, *"is for the glorifying of His Father, He will give you the first sign of His intimacy—silence."* The author Madeleine L'Engle adds: *"It is God's silence, the withdrawal which is so devastating. The world is difficult enough with God; without him, it is a hideous (ugly) joke"*.

G. Praying With Mary, Mother of Jesus

I know some of my Protestant friends may not like this section of my book. They have to forgive me on this, not just because I am a Catholic priest, or I am a cradle Catholic. Rather they should see my early childhood life in a tiny little village of India where our Catholic settlement was surrounded by thousands of Hindus and Moslems; my parents, especially my dad, were very much keen on my persevering in their faith and reach the goal intended and dreamt by them. Surely they brought me up, with the support of the priests and nuns and other Catholic teachers, in sincere adherence to every bit of Catholic teachings. One of those teachings as I learned and memorized in my Catechism classes is the verse, *'I believe in the communion of Saints.'*

Later in my life I came to know that it is one among many features in the 'Nicene Creed' which is the sum total of any Christian's belief. With Jesus, the eternal intercessor, these saints who are already admitted in heaven are also interceding on our behalf. When I was asked by my elders, my dad in a special way, to pray to Mary and some other of his favorite saints, I accepted it halfheartedly in the beginning. During my deep study on my own beliefs I understood clearly what it really means to pray to and with Mary. This is the main reason for my including this section in qualityprayer discussion.

Besides praying for the dead I am interested in praying with many of my deceased friends with whom I lived and moved and about whose lives and writings I read in Scriptures and historical, biographical and autobiographical books. There is an innate element in human nature to relate oneself to the dead. I am one in that club of remembering many of my favorite relatives and friends belonging to my both micro and macro families. If some of them in my view are truly dedicated disciples of Jesus I am accustomed to pray with them. For example, I consider my dad as an audacious prayerwarrior. Though in his lifetime he seemed, to my teenage eyes, a controlfreak, in my adolescent age I started loving him and all his advices and orders regarding religious practices. He was not a mere talker or pharisaical. What he told me he was already practicing.

> Besides praying for the dead I am interested in praying with many of my deceased friends with whom I lived and moved and about whose lives and writings I read in Scriptures and historical, biographical and autobiographical books.

I remember still how he attended and took me with him for daily morning prayer in the church as well as early Eucharist; he prayed with me before and after meals; and at evenings he brought me again to church for evening prayers; plus he organized daily at home a family prayer of reciting the Rosary, a prevalent Catholic prayer practice. And then, then only we all were allowed to eat our supper. My dad was truly a prayerwarrior. So after his demise, I firmly believe he is in heaven with the other of my favorite saints. I sincerely believe he is there praying for me. So when I began applying seriously the elements of 'qualityprayer' in my spiritual life I keep him at my side and pray with him. The same way I bring Mary into my qualityprayertime and pray with her.

Through the few Gospel references we can discover Mary as a 'Prayerwarrior'; by her behavior and words she seems to be a rolemodel for our qualityprayerlife; and therefore she can be the worthiest heavenly person to closer to us in all our prayer efforts.

First of all, as we discussed in previous chapters our qualityprayer efforts must be totally integrated with a personal relationship with Jesus and combined with the fidelity to God's Word. Mary is a model of such qualityprayer. She is the Mother of Jesus, our Savior and Lord. Surely she should be having a unique place in heaven; her heartbeats must be the same as those of her Son; hence our praying with her has got more power in front of the Almighty who has done great things for her in her life. More than a physical mother to Jesus she was connected to the Triune God intimately and spiritually by being very faithful to the Word of God. In Luke we read Jesus highlighting the high rank Mary possessed in God's kingdom. He included Mary in his inner close circle of disciples who hear the word of God and act on it. (Lk. 8: 19-21) Again in the same Gospel of Luke we find that Jesus praising Mary' blessedness not only because of her physical relationship with him as Mother, but also due to her obedient observance of God's Word. (Lk. 11: 27-28)

> Through the few Gospel references we can discover Mary as a 'Prayerwarrior'; by her behavior and words she seems to be a rolemodel for our qualityprayerlife.

Secondly Mary loved to pray in solitude of reflection and contemplation. Luke writes about Mary's behavior after the shepherds visit to the manger. While the shepherds and all who heard of the event of Jesus' birth were publicly praising and talking aloud about God's deeds, she was silently praying over them. *"All who heard it were amazed by what had been told them by the shepherds. And Mary kept all these things, reflecting on them in her heart. Then the shepherds returned, glorifying and praising God for all they had heard and seen, just as it had been told to them."* (Lk. 2: 18-20) In another place Luke also refers to Mary's recollective prayerlife when he describes the story of Jesus lost and found in the Temple. She was accustomed to pray in silence especially at the time of her life clouded with inability to understand God's mightiest deeds happening in her Son's life. *"And he said to them, "Why were you looking for me? Did you not know that I must be in my Father's house?" But they did not understand what he said to them. He went down with them and came to Nazareth, and was obedient to them; and his mother kept all these things in her heart."* (Lk. 2: 49-51)

She also prayed in group as we see her praying with the group of disciples at Upper Room (Acts 1: 14); she too prayed in public in praising and glorifying God as we notice her singing the prayer of Magnificat at the house of Elizabeth. (Lk. 1: 46-55) Her prayer was incorporated with action of love. While she brought joy and love to the elderly woman she too did all household works for her for three months. *"During those days Mary set out and traveled to the hill country in haste to a town of Judah, where she entered the house of Zechariah and greeted Elizabeth . . . Mary remained with her about three months and then returned to her home."* (Lk. 1: 39-40, 56)

One of the most striking points of Mary's qualityprayer pattern was that she included in it all its necessary ingredients and features. We notice this truth in the event of Annunciation. As matter of fact it was Mary's prayertime. As her usual practice in daily prayer she would have read and reflected on the Scriptures that are filled with the promises of God and His prescriptions, admonitions, advices, orders, instructions about how to covet all those promises being fulfilled in human lives. Her whole spiritual life, especially her qualityprayer was founded on God's promises as we hear in her prayer of Magnificat. She was enchanted not merely by the list of God's promises, but much more by the way God has fulfilled those promises in human history: "According to his promise to our fathers, to Abraham and to his descendants forever He has shown might with his arm, dispersed the arrogant of mind and heart. He has thrown down the rulers from their thrones but lifted up the lowly. The hungry he has filled with good things; the rich he has sent away empty. He has helped Israel his servant, remembering his mercy." (Ref. Lk. 1: 46-55)

At this particular prayertime Mary heard some more new promises from God's messenger. This first statement of greeting was entirely new to her as she was a humble and simple Jewish woman. Because this was about her glorious identity: "Hail, Favored one! The Lord is with you." More shocking to her was the bundle of promises of God about a baby she is going to carry in her womb:

1. "Behold, you will conceive in your womb and bear a son.
2. He will be great and will be called Son of the Most High,
3. The Lord God will give him the throne of David his father,
4. He will rule over the house of Jacob forever,
5. And of his kingdom there will be no end."
6. The Holy Spirit will come upon you, and the power of the Most High will overshadow you.
7. Therefore the child to be born will be called holy, the Son of God.

Mary respected and loved all God's promises. They were all esteemed by her as God's gifts. His promises were very positive and would bring to her and her community the petitions they were raising for thousands of years. However, what she was hearing about her baby was little too much for her. She would have been including in her prayer her longing for the coming of Messiah and for the arrival of new heavens and new earth. Her only aim of prayer was to see the face of God and dwell in the House of the Lord throughout her life. In this manner she would have prayed ceaselessly. Her faith got stronger, her hope became more formidable and her charity grew more astounding. A day came in her prayerlife when her qualityprayer reaped its fruit: an angel of God announced to her that the Messiah as she desired was coming, not somewhere in Palestine or anywhere in the world but in her womb. Her prayer was answered by God.

We observe in her prayer there was a wonderful dialogue between her and God's messenger. It all centered on her virginity, a commitment she had made to God as a gift of love and fidelity; also she was concerned about the disturbance to her family and social life this event of becoming a mother even before wedding would bring. Even if she did not see clearly all that implied in the greeting, statement, and promises of God's messenger, she accepted her mission to become the mother of the Savior. The most important and required element in qualityprayer is a final total surrender to God, the all-knowing and all-powerful Lover. Mary ends her prayertime with that: *"Behold, I am the handmaid of the Lord. May it be done to me according to your word."* (Lk. 1: 38)

This spirit of total surrender of qualityprayer had to continue in her life till its end. As people say, 'be careful what you pray for because you have to reap its consequences,' Mary reaped the fruit of her prayer that would be accompanied by trials and tensions; As Simeon predicted, she would face acute pain and suffering: *"Simeon blessed them and said to Mary his mother, "Behold, this child is destined for the fall and rise of many in Israel, and to be a sign that will be contradicted (and you yourself a sword will pierce) so that the thoughts of many hearts may be revealed."* (Lk. 2: 34-35)

Mary had miles to go, travel in earthly life, the valley of tears and darkness; she had to wait and wait with formidable hope as a pregnant woman waiting for the seed in her womb to grow. She waited with no doubts about those promises about her Son; even at the end she didn't see every promise being fulfilled. She saw her Son crucified, bleeding and dying ignominious death. It seemed a failure and the glorious promises of God unfulfilled. It was hurting her very much. Nonetheless she would have been praying in her heart as her Son did: "Behold, I am the handmaid of the Lord. Not my will but let Your Will be done."

> The most remarkable matter portrayed by John is that though the time for Jesus had not arrived to perform his miraculous deeds, he did it at the request of his Mother. This event is traditionally acknowledged and interpreted by the Church not only as the first sign of Jesus' glory manifested but also as a proposal from God to the disciples of Jesus to make use of Mary's role as an efficient 'catalyst' in their qualityprayer.

My final comment about my reason why I want to pray with Mary is generated from a Gospel incident, narrated by John, in which Mary proved her qualityprayer as the inspirational method for our prayer efforts. In a wedding at Cana when the wine, which was the important factor in any wedding ceremony as the sign of happiness and joy, ran out, all who attended the feast were very much disappointed and became gloomy and sad. When the Mother of Jesus noticed this critical situation of the people she reported it to her Son (a petitioning part of qualityprayer). The most remarkable matter portrayed by John is that though the time for Jesus had not arrived to perform his miraculous deeds, he did it at the request of his Mother. This event is traditionally acknowledged and interpreted by the Church not only as the first sign of Jesus' glory manifested but also as a proposal from God to the disciples of Jesus to make use of Mary's role as an efficient 'catalyst' in their qualityprayer.

This is why, in Acts we read, the Apostles took her to the Upper room and prayed with her for the outpouring of the Holy Spirit. *"All these devoted themselves with one accord to prayer, together with some women, and Mary the mother of Jesus, and his brothers."* (Acts 1: 14) At the apparitions of Mary, approved by the Church, Mary is reported her help and support in our prayer efforts.

H. Fasting in Qualityprayer

What does exactly 'fasting' mean?

In an encyclopedia we read: "For Christians fasting is not only a bodily expression of our need for God; the practice itself is a pathway which can lead us to the reality of God's kingdom." Msgr. James Mancini, a charismatic liaison for the Catholic Charismatic Renewal, referring to Paul's letter to the Romans, once said, 'fasting is a recognition that the Spirit and the flesh are in battle with each other. In fasting we try to limit or modify the demands of our appetites. The appetites are not wrong, God gave them to us for a purpose, but they definitely need discipline.' Fasting is simply the denial of our fake self to draw closer to God, and according to Abbot Jerome 'it is a way of putting God back in control'.

Church always contends that fasting is to make up for what we have lost by despising others. It is an offering of our souls in sacrifice to God. This is the most pleasing oblation that we offer to God, as we read in Scriptures: *"For you do not desire sacrifice or I would give it; a burnt offering you would not accept. My sacrifice, O God, is a contrite spirit; a contrite, humbled heart, O God, you will not scorn."* (Ps. 51: 18-19)

Through fasting our soul become a pure offering, a holy sacrifice, a living victim, remaining our own and at the same time made over to God. Fasting is one form of penances that a human being performs physically to enhance the spirit of one's soul. Biblically, fasting is abstaining from food, drink, sleep or sex to focus on a period of spiritual growth. Specifically, we humbly deny something of the flesh to glorify God, enhance our spirit, and go deeper in our prayer life.

Too often, our focus of fasting is on the lack of food. Although fasting in Scripture is almost always a fasting from food, there are other ways to fast. Any negation or denial of pleasurable, comfortable, convenient element done for the sake of God is fasting. Therefore the voluntary poverty, voluntary refraining of bodily pleasures, forgoing freely certain material possessions are wonderful forms of fasting.

> Through fasting our soul become a pure offering, a holy sacrifice, a living victim, remaining our own and at the same time made over to God.

This is how Jesus wanted his disciples to be enabled with spiritual power of healing. The main purpose of fasting is to take our eyes off the things of this world and instead focus on God. Fasting is a way to demonstrate to God and to ourselves that we are serious about our relationship with Him. Anything you can temporarily give up in order to better focus on God can be considered a fast. Fasting is not intended to punish our flesh, but to focus on God. As the Bible-heroes and heroines, saints and disciples of Jesus did, we have to add fasting to our qualityprayer to make it more efficacious and productive.

This kind of genuinely-understood fasting should go hand in hand with qualityprayer. It's possible we can pray without fasting from food, and fast from the same without prayer. But no prayer would become genuine if it is accompanied with the fastings: from the evil thoughts, words and actions; from regular customs and habits of chit-chatting by disciplined silence; and from watching TV, Twittering, listening or sending text messages to friends and so on. Thus by controlling the passions of the body, we free our souls for prayer.

However for special purposes and in specific occasions the restraining from satisfying our physical hunger and thirst is very much appreciated and endorsed by God in Jesus and through Church Traditions. The primary occasion, as the Church endorses, is the time of getting pardon from the Lord for all our sins. Our tears of sorrowful contrition must accompany with certain penances including physical fasting. Catechism of the Catholic Church (para <u>1434</u>) exhorts: *"The interior penance of the Christian can be expressed in many and various ways. Scripture and the Fathers insist above all on three forms, fasting, prayer, and almsgiving, which express conversion in relation to oneself, to God, and to others. Alongside the radical purification brought about by Baptism or martyrdom they cite as means of obtaining forgiveness of sins: effort at reconciliation with one's neighbor, tears of repentance, concern for the salvation of one's neighbor, the intercession of the saints, and the practice of charity "which covers a multitude of sins."*

Pope Benedict was quoted saying in one of his weekly general audiences during Lent, 2011: *"Fasting means abstaining from food, but includes other forms of self-denial to promote a more sober lifestyle. But that still isn't the full meaning of fasting, which is the external sign of the internal reality of our commitment to abstain from evil with the help of God and to live the Gospel,"*

In many church traditions the season of Lent being dedicated for concentrated observance of prayer, fasting and almsgiving. It is the duration of forty days before the Easter celebration following the Lord's example of praying and fasting forty days and forty nights in the desert. It is also a way of doing penance for past excesses. That is why the Church strongly recommends that Catholics fast during Lent.

Fasting is certainly part of the Christian life and has been from the very beginning. It enables us to unite ourselves with Christ in his own fast for forty days in the desert. Fasting focuses the mind. Fasting also helps us to be in solidarity with the poor. But perhaps the best description of fasting I've come across is that it is a "prayer of the body". The longing for food during a fast is offered to God in sacrifice and directly parallels the deep longing for God that is so much a part of our Christian life.

The Power of Fasting in qualityprayer

St. Peter Chrysologus wrote: *There are three things, by which faith stands firm, devotion remains constant, and virtue endures. They are prayer, fasting and mercy. Prayer knocks at the door, fasting obtains, mercy receives. Prayer, mercy and fasting: these three are one, and they give life to each other.* According to the saint fasting is the soul of prayer.

It is Biblical truth that when prayer and fasting are combined and dedicated to God's glory they reach their full effectiveness. Having a dedicated time of prayer and fasting is not a way of controlling God into doing what we desire. Rather, it is simply forcing ourselves to focus and rely on God for the strength, provision, and wisdom we need. Many spiritual and religious mentors point out that one of the main reasons why God does not answer our prayers is we are not yet ready, specifically our spirit and body are not ready, to receive God's gifts from heaven.

> Fasting inspires and enlivens our prayer efforts when it lacks of genuine faith 'without which it is impossible to please God.'

This is especially true in the case of our qualityprayer for qualitylife where we hunger, long and wait for the intimacy with the Divine. We continue to be incapable of receiving God's favors due to our spirit of pride and arrogance, our spirit of unforgiveness, our spirit of distraction and anxiety over too many material things and not fully focused on God and God alone. Our heart-cups either covered by such unwanted spirit or overflow with too many worldly cares. There is no room for getting the favors from the sky from where torrent-rain of God's favors fall down unceasingly. Fasting makes our heart-bowls empty so that God can fill it to the brim with His amazing graces.

Fasting inspires and enlivens our prayer efforts when it lacks of genuine faith 'without which it is impossible to please God.' (Heb. 11:6) Jesus said, "Therefore I say to you, whatever things you ask when you pray, believe that you receive them, and you will have them." (Mk. 11:24) Many may not understand the words of Jesus or may wrongly interpret them and yield to discouragement. But we understand Jesus very clearly and through our empty stomach, not filled by food and drink, we tell the Lord that we understand the true meaning of faith: We see everything not by sight, not by the physical and earthly feeling of contentment of having favors from God but believing in the reality of things, even though we cannot see them (Heb. 11:1) When we pray we believe in the finished results of our prayer, and not the immediate pleasure of getting what we pray; however we will eventually experience the tangible results sometime later.

In addition, we hold an unwavering hope and faith toward the Giver and His Gifts. We prove, through our fasting, our perseverance and audacity in front of God and tell Him we are able to even sacrifice our very life if needed in order to get the primary as well as secondary blessings of prayer from God.

Particularly in the cases of fighting with evil forces fasting becomes practical ammunition. Our prayers may many times need to engage in what we call "spiritual warfare" to obtain results. Paul writing to Ephesians emphasizes this prayer-warfare: *"For we do not wrestle against flesh and blood, but against principalities, against powers, against the rulers of the darkness of this age, against spiritual hosts of wickedness in the heavenly places"* (Eph 6:12). To fight with such demons and evil spirits our earthly and physical power alone cannot be helpful. In point of fact when Jesus' disciples couldn't do much in their ministry of driving out evil spirits he advised them to add fasting with prayer. (Mk. 9: 27-29 We need spiritual authority and strength, first from Jesus and His Spirit; plus from our spiritual power God in Jesus has already established within us through his Sacraments. As a deliberate belief and longing for such spiritual authority we make recourse to the practice of fasting and add it into prayer.

In the Bible there are so many references about the act of fasting playing great role in the prayerlives of holy people: According to the Jewish Law people are asked to fast on the 'Day of Atonement' considering it as the 'day of fasting.' (Jer. 36: 6) Besides that general custom of fasting individuals were praying with fasting for many impending needs to be fulfilled by God: Moses fasted during the 40 days and 40 nights he was on Mount Sinai receiving the law from God (Ex. 34: 28). King Jehoshaphat called for a fast in all Israel when they were about to be attacked by the Moabites and Ammonites (2 Chr. 20: 3). In response to Jonah's preaching, the men of Nineveh fasted and put on sackcloth (Jonah 3: 5).

Prayer and fasting was often done in times of distress or trouble. David fasted when he learned that Saul and Jonathan had been killed (2 Sam. 1: 12); Praying in fasting helped the confession and contrition of David to get pardon and blessing the Almighty. Esther, both by her personal continuous praying in fasting and by three days of prayer and fasting of the Israelites, got sufficient wisdom and strength to win her victory over king for the people of God; "*Go and assemble all the Jews who are in Susa; fast on my behalf, all of you, not eating or drinking night or day for three days. I and my maids will also fast in the same way. Thus prepared, I will go to the king, contrary to the law. If I perish, I perish!" Mordecai went away and did exactly as Esther had commanded.*" (Esther 4: 15-17) By fasting Daniel trained his mystic sight and delivered from the lions' might.

In the NT we read about John the Baptist teaching his disciples to fast (Mark 2: 18). Jesus Christ, by whom all things were made, himself added fasting to his qualityprayer for 40 days and 40 nights. He began his public ministry not with just undergoing certain religious rituals but with an intense preparation of spending those days and nights in the desert in prayer and fasting. (Matthew 4: 2) We also observe such practice of fasting in the midst of Jesus' friends: Anna, the widow, "worshipped night and day, fasting and praying" at the Temple (Luke 2: 37). The church of Antioch fasted and sent Paul and Barnabas off on their first missionary journey *"While they were worshiping the Lord and fasting, the holy Spirit said, "Set apart for me Barnabas and Saul for the work to which I have called them." Then, completing their fasting and prayer, they laid hands on them and sent them off.* (Acts 13: 2-3) Paul and Barnabas spent time in prayer and fasting for the appointment of elders in the churches: *"They appointed presbyters for them in each church and, with prayer and fasting, commended them to the Lord in whom they had put their faith."* (Acts 14: 23)

There were in the history of the church people prayed in fasting for important and critical occasions: Many saints continue to pray and fast for getting their requests granted by the Supreme Being. Many devotees of St. Anthony of Padua are familiar with the fact that he is a saint who can do many wonders in our lives by his intercession. The array of wonders attributed to Anthony's life is equally astounding in its variety. He was in two places at the same time; at his prayer, a donkey knelt before the Blessed Sacrament, after a dare by an unbeliever; fishes lifted their heads above the water to listen as he preached to them, after bored believers turned away; a foot severed by an ax was rejoined to its leg. Though these stories of miracles, happened during saint's lifetime, may sound legendary and imaginative,

Anthony's devotees continue believing in them as true for the main reason the same kind of miracles have been occurring even after his death to this day. Through the intercessory prayer of this Saint millions of people of different faiths keep on receiving the gifts from heaven. What is the secret to the power of St. Anthony's intercession? If we go back to his days of living in this world we can notice Anthony from his early youth days had strong faith in God and he firmly believed that any prayer, which is accompanied with fasting, would surely bring God's gifts.

The Perfect Fasting

Jesus insisted every bit of our spiritual exercises and religious practices must be only for the greater glory of God, keeping Him as our sole target to be attained in life. In Jesus' Sermon on the Mount we hear him say: *"When you fast, do not look gloomy like the hypocrites. They neglect their appearance, so that they may appear to others to be fasting. Amen, I say to you, they have received their reward. But when you fast, anoint your head and wash your face, so that you may not appear to be fasting, except to your Father who is hidden. And your Father who sees what is hidden will repay you."* (Matt. 6:16-18)

Jesus too connected his fasting and praying with his charitable actions, as the Gospels indicate, 'doing good wherever he went.' We should never separate fasting from charitable almsgiving. As Church Fathers like St. Chrysologus expounded, almsgiving is the lifeblood of fasting. If we pray, we need to fast; if we fast, we have to perform the act of almsgiving. When we fast, we should think of the fasting of others. If we want God to know that we are hungry, He wants us to know that some of neighbors are hungry.

In order to make our prayer and fasting acceptable to God, certainly we must add almsgiving to them. This is because 'fasting bears no fruit unless it is watered by mercy'. Here are some beautiful words of St. Chrysologus on the intrinsic connection between fasting and merciful almsgiving: *"Fasting dries up when mercy dries up. Mercy is to fasting as rain is to the earth. However much you may cultivate your heart, clear the soil of your nature, root out vices, sow virtues, if you do not release the springs of mercy, your fasting will bear no fruit. When you fast, if your mercy is thin your harvest will be thin; when you fast, what you pour out in mercy overflows into your barn."*

> In order to make our prayer and fasting acceptable to God, certainly we must add almsgiving to them. This is because 'fasting bears no fruit unless it is watered by mercy'.

By refraining from eating, we free up food or money that we can give to those less fortunate than ourselves. When we fast we actually save some food or drink or money; those savings are not to be considered as some surplus we can use later days; rather since they are the fruits of our fasting they should go again to the Lord. Nonetheless God, being a Creator and Possessor of abundance is not interested for such things: *"I will not take a bullock from your house, or he-goats from your folds. For every animal of the forest is mine, beasts by the thousands on my mountains. I know every bird in the heights; whatever moves in the wild is mine. Were I hungry, I would not tell you, for mine is the world and all that fills it. Do I eat the flesh of bulls or drink the blood of he-goats?"* (Ps. 50: 9-13)

On the other hand, being the champion of justice and compassion, he expects us to share everything with the needy and thus to offer the sacrifice of praise to Him: *"This, rather, is the fasting that I wish: releasing those bound unjustly, untying the thongs of the yoke; setting free the oppressed, breaking every yoke; sharing your bread with the hungry, sheltering the oppressed and the homeless; clothing the naked when you see them, and not turning your back on your own"* (Is 58:6-7). God tells us that fasting from food must go together with fasting from violence and fasting from oppressing people. In other words, when we fast from food it is to be accompanied by a loving and forgiving attitude towards others.

God's Son Jesus reiterated the same concept of performing the practices of fasting and almsgiving totally for the glory and will of God. Portraying the event of final judgment he would be rewarding or punishing us in accordance with the almsgivings and charities we would do in this world because he considers our needy neighbors are his 'proxies'. *"Amen, I say to you, whatever you did for one of these least brothers of mine, you did for me."* (Matt. 25: 40) Therefore all that we save from fasting must go to the hands of the poor and the needy who are the proxies of God.

St. Augustine summed up all that were said earlier: *"Let us by our prayers, add the wings of piety to our alms deeds and fasting, so that they may fly more readily to God."* In the Book of Ecclesiastes the Word of God esteems the triple practice of prayer, fasting and almsgiving as a 'three-fold cord': *"Where one alone may be overcome, two together can resist. A three-ply cord is not easily broken."* (4:12.) The evil will not prevail against all our spiritual efforts, if we follow the call of God in Jesus to use this three-ply cord of prayer, fasting and almsgiving, especially in our efforts of qualityprayer.

Conclusion

What should I say finally about qualityprayer? It stands still a mystery. It may be because prayer is something concerning with God and his spiritual realm. As a human being I am also carrying within me a component of God's Spirit and therefore I am also a mystery. Naturally prayer when it is performed at the level of spirit stands out as a phenomenon unfathomable. I conclude it will be the same till my last breath. I should then go on praying with my restless heart. St. Augustine rightly said, *'my heart is restless until it rests in God.'* Prayer is not after all a product but a process as my life-journey. In this mystery-process of Prayer here are some personal findings I finally disclose with my readers:

Self-Feedback

At the end of my qualityprayer I do sit back and get a feedback from myself about the genuineness of that particular prayer effort. The criteria I usually use to find whether my prayer is genuine and real or fake and imaginative is to closely watch whether the sense of longing for the same relationship with God stays intact even after my prayertime.

This is how most of my colleagues in the 'suffering church' in this world survive, breathe and move in joy, peace, contentment, power and victory. Some of them may not express their experience of the exalted Jesus in words but witness it through their handling of daily life. The Wheel of Christian Spiritual endeavors is rolling on. The searching and waiting continues in both God and fragile humans. We come and go; we are in and out. But God remains forever faithful and loving toward us.

Go with the Spirit's Blow

At the end of all my prayer efforts I came to a conclusion that in our spiritual journey we have to follow the promptings of Jesus' Spirit. People always advise me 'go with the flow.' I make little change to it in the light of the Bible: 'Let me go with the blow of the Spirit.' The main reason is: *"The Spirit blows where He wills."* What I really discovered in this matter is that sometimes the Spirit asks us to pray longer, sleepless; other times with lots of sacrifices and in the midst of irritating smoke. We have to obey His order.

> God is the One who invites us to enter boldly into His abode in prayer. Therefore we have to be very cautious in prayer efforts and never perform anything in the name of prayer superficially, haughtily or insolently.

We should always remember the sovereignty of God: God is God and he owes nothing to any human. *"Our God is in heaven and does whatever he wills."* (Ps. 115: 3) The Spirit of Jesus moves every human person, especially the disciple of Jesus, to go intensely through this process of qualityprayer. Difference comes only in the way we spent our time exclusively for God. For priests and religious, even some chosen lay persons because of their role of leading and witnessing to the fact of qualityprayer they have to spend more time in prayer, with greater power and intensity. This can lead them to ecstatic and mystic experiences. Other ordinary people are prompted to pray as their lives avail them: Workers, retired, bed-ridden, sick and dying, and suffering differ in their intensity and length of praying time. But all have only one goal: To be integrated and burnt by the fire of Jesus' Spirit and bear lasting fruits.

God is the One who invites us to enter boldly into His abode in prayer. Therefore we have to be very cautious in prayer efforts and never perform anything in the name of prayer superficially, haughtily or insolently. *"Be not hasty in your utterance and let not your heart be quick to utter a promise in God's presence. God is in heaven and you are on earth; therefore let your words be few. As dreams come along with many cares, so a fool's voice along with a multitude of words."* (Eccl. 5: 1-2)

Prayer with action of love

Another great truth I found out in the process of qualityprayer-efforts is that *'in God's Stadium double-track runners are the winners'*. Our life journey consists of two parallel lines. One: our engagements with God and the other: our dealings with the earthly things and persons. In both dealings our success consists in persevering, not losing heart at any time and in performing our hard labor at our best. It is true our secular studies and formation taught us that perseverance and hard labor are important tools for success in human efforts. Unfortunately the world and the age of Enlightenment have made us forget or ignore to use the same strategy in our successful dealings with God too.

Many times we hear people say in hospital surroundings: "They have done all they can, the only thing left is prayer." It tells us how our modern mind thinks about prayer: "Human efforts are what count. God doesn't make a lot of difference, but we might just as well pray. It certainly won't hurt. The underlying meaning is that prayer won't do any good."

That is not what Jesus thought nor did Moses. Victory in life can never go to the hands of people who are quitters and lazy bones. Here we are talking about our total victory, winning this world and the world to come. The only possible way to succeed is to persevere and put our hard labor both on our human efforts and in prayer. Let me quote what Madam Swetchine, a Russian Mystic said: *"There are two ways of attaining an important end—force and perseverance. Force falls to the lot of the privileged few, but austere and sustained perseverance can be practiced by the most insignificant. Its silent power grows irresistible with time."*

Prayer in, with, for Jesus alive

I was once praying earnestly inside of a Charismatic people's circle. I firmly believe with the prayer-help of one of my Protestant lay-Evangelists I was anointed by the Spirit and with humility I testify I was granted the Gift of Praying in Tongues. It happened some twenty years back. I still continue praying in the Spirit mostly in my personal prayertimes.

While I was intensively praying and preaching and closely connected with the Charismatic friends I used to hear their testimonies such as:

"Jesus is alive! Alleluia!"

"The resurrected Jesus is moving in our midst! Hi! Jesus!"

"I saw Jesus alive. He spoke to me. He touched me. He ate with me. He cured me."

"He appeared to me in bright light. He took me to his third heaven."

"He met me on my way while I was hurrying to perform a blunder. He stopped me there. While he was with me and talking to me my heart was burning within me."

"Many times he met me and greeted me saying 'peace be with you.' I could feel at that time certain kind of tranquility and peace."

"He opened my mind to understand the scriptures."

"He told me, rather he commanded me to go and witness all that I experienced."

"I was under zero religious influence of any kind. I was just routinely performing my duties to my children and my wife as a loving dad and husband. I permitted them to go to church, to CCD, and other fellowship meetings in their church. But I did not accompany them. One night I was awakened by what I could only describe as a 'yearning' to go to the living room with pencil and paper. When I walked into that room, I found myself 'surrounded with love,' and I knew the presence of Jesus Christ alive. I found myself writing over and over on the paper, 'I don't care! I don't care!' My concern about who this 'Jesus' was did not matter anymore in view of the presence I had encountered. I became totally a Jesus freak."

"I prayed earnestly many days, 'Oh God, if there be a God, show me the right way, and I will become a holy man; otherwise I will kill myself.' One morning at about a quarter to five my room was filled with light. I looked outside, thinking there must be a fire, but he saw none. Continuing to pray, I suddenly saw before me a glorious face filled with love. At first I thought it was Buddha or Krishna or some other deity. But a voice in my language said, 'How long will you persecute me? Remember, I died for you; I gave my life for you.' Seeing the scars on his body, I recognized Jesus and saw that he was alive, not someone who died centuries ago. I fell at his feet and accepted him as my master and worshiped him. Afterward I became a world-famous example of God's life present among human beings."

When I heard these testimonies on 'Jesus Alive experiences' first I did not believe. Those stories seemed like nonsensical. As St. Thomas the Apostle, I doubted about the authenticity of these people's statements. Like the same Apostle I myself wanted to see the 'Jesus Alive personally but out of curiosity. I wanted to touch him physically, and I wanted to encounter him as I walk or drive on my own high way.

I confess sincerely that for the past 25 years I have not been given that sacred opportunity of encountering Jesus Alive, rather I see only his 'empty tomb', may be, with some linen clothes, and added to it, one or two gardeners and some cemetery custodians. I mean I did not get so far as to have any such very dramatic or exciting encounters and visions of Jesus Alive. I stand near the empty tomb of my faith full of doubts, full of confusion, filled with agony and despair. In most of my prayertimes I behave literally like Mary of Magdala; I weep and cry out 'Where are you Master? Are you truly risen? Are you really alive among us? I want to see you, I love to hold you in my hands, I want to hug you, I want to host you and I want to abide in you. I too want to be gifted with power, love and wisdom so that I can be a wonderful instrument in your hands to witness to your Gospel.'

> I confess sincerely that for the past 25 years I have not been given that sacred opportunity of encountering Jesus Alive, rather I see only his 'empty tomb', may be, with some linen clothes, and added to it, one or two gardeners and some cemetery custodians.

Do you want to know his repeated and consistent answer to me? I call it his 'Alleluia Litany':

"My friend, why do you seek the living one among the dead? I am not in your empty tomb, I am risen, and I have become alive in the lives of your fellowmen. When they weep I weep, when they rejoice I rejoice, when they show love I do love. Unfortunately I also become sin very regrettably when they commit evil, thus I am crucified. I suffer with the sick and the dying. I am there in your midst till the end of time. When your humanity sinks I descend into hell and when it soars with Gospel's love I am risen."

Jesus Alive continues proclaiming to me,

"So the historical cross or empty tomb or any other Nazareth and Jerusalem stories about me is nothing compared to the realities of my present engagement among you. After my resurrection I have become one with humanity, one with the entire universe. So the gardeners you see in your life and the custodians you come across on your way as parents, elders, leaders, teachers, friends, spouses, preachers, and other helpers are all my physical presence until you are here in this world. Once you enter into my Father's house after your death, it's a different story."

He insists again and again the mode of his living presence in the world and consoles me:

"But as a faithful disciple here on earth you frequently enjoy its foretaste. Is it not? I mean my heavenly love in your loved ones, my heavenly *wisdom in your preachers, writers and teachers and my heavenly joy when you become committed hosts to the poor and the needy. I am alive my friend. Say Alleluia again and again. Use the linens I left at my empty tomb, I mean the sacraments, Scriptures and other traditions I left with my Church. Make the best use of them. You will encounter me not just one-time dramatic encounter, rather a permanent ecstatic and mystic experience of me, far away from the empty tomb!"*

> Therefore, as a weak but hardheaded person—only in my qualityprayer efforts, I continue performing my daily prayer practices, always keeping in mind, besides all that I have catalogued in this book: that my prayer is to be connected to the heavenly and eternal intercession of Jesus for its efficacy and authenticity.

One saint, whose name I don't know, gives us a beautiful description of what it means to pray: *"Insignificant man, escape from your everyday business for a short while, hide for a moment from your restless thoughts. Break off from your cares and troubles and be less concerned about your tasks and labors. Make a little time for God and rest a while in him. Enter into your mind's inner chamber. Shut out everything but God and whatever helps you to seek him; and when you have shut the door, look for him. Speak now to God and say with your whole heart: I seek your face; your face, Lord, I desire!"*

Therefore, as a weak but hardheaded person—only in my qualityprayer efforts, I continue performing my daily prayer practices, always keeping in mind, besides all that I have catalogued in this book: that my prayer is to be connected to the heavenly and eternal intercession of Jesus for its efficacy and authenticity; my prayer is to be treated as a confessional for begging God's mercy as we confess our sins before Him; my prayertime is as if fulfilling my regular doctor's appointment exposing to God, my heavenly Doctor and Healer, all my wounds and sicknesses; my prayer is an occasion to express my willingness to forgive those who hurt me as well as to beg God's grace for boldness and sincerity of going to those particular so-called 'my enemies' and say 'hello' to them.

Nothing is impossible with Jesus. I know the One—who called me to pray; and who joint me into his ministry of prayer, will never disown me. He will accomplish what He has begun in me. Until then I base my qualityprayer efforts on his departing words: *"Amen, amen, I say to you, whoever believes in me will do the works that I do, and will do greater ones than these, because I am going to the Father. And whatever you ask in my name, I will do, so that the Father may be glorified in the Son. If you ask anything of me in my name, I will do it."* (Jn. 14: 12-14)

BOOKS & AUTHORS REFERRED

Catechism of the Catholic Church, at the Vatican Website

Catholic spirituality, its history and challenge by James J. Bacik 2002 ISBN 0809140608

The Tradition of Catholic Prayer by Christian Raab, Harry Hagan, 2007 ISBN 0814631843

Catholic Family Prayer Book by Jacquelyn Lindsey 2001 ISBN 0879739991

Selected Writings of Saint Alphonse Liguori ISBN 0809137712

The Theology of Prayer by Monsignor Joseph Fenton 2009 ISBN 2917813008

An Invitation to Prayer, Pope John Paul II ISBN 0743449061

Everything Starts from Prayer, Mother Teresa, ISBN 978-1883991258

Primary Speech: A Psychology Of Prayer, Ann and Barry Ulanov, ISBN 978-0804211345

The Devotion to the Sacred Heart of Jesus Fr John Croiset, S.J. ISBN 0895553341

The Holy Man of Tours Dorothy Scallan. (1990) ISBN 0895553902

Saintly Men of Modern Times Joan Carroll Cruz, OCDS. (2003) ISBN 1931709777

Pope John Paul II's encyclical *Rosarium Virginis Mariae* at www.vatican.com

Marian apparitions, the Bible, and the modern world by Donal Anthony Foley 2002 ISBN 0852443137

Saint Augustine *"Confessions"* ISBN 978-0385029551

Vatican Messages of Pope John Paul II at the Vatican Website

Vatican Messages of Pope Benedict XVI at the Vatican Website

Releasing the Ability of God through Prayer, Charles Capps (Tulsa: Harrison House, 1978)

The Art of Prayer Igumen Charitan and Timothy Ware (London: Faber and Faber, 1966)

Jesus the Jewish theologian, Brad H. Young (Peobody, Massachustts: Henrichson, 1995)

Our Father Abraham, Marvin R. Wilson (Grand Rapids, MI: Eerdmans, 1994)

Prayer: A History, by Philip Zaleski, Carol Zaleski (2005), Houghton Mifflin Books. ISBN 0618152881.

Simple Ways to Pray by Emilie Griffin 2005 ISBN 0742550842

Christian Meditation for Beginners by Thomas Zanzig, Marilyn Kielbasa 2000, ISBN 0884893618

An introduction to Christian spirituality by F. Antonisamy, 2000 ISBN 8171094295

Christian Meditation by Edmund P. Clowney, 1979 ISBN 1573832278 *The encyclopedia of Christianity, Volume 3* by Erwin Fahlbusch, Geoffrey William Bromiley 2003 ISBN 9004126546

Personality Development in The Religious Life, JohnJ. Evoy, S.J. and Van F. Christoph, S.J. Sheed and Ward, New York, 1963

When the Well Runs Dry, Thomas H. Green, S.J., Ave Maria Press, Notre Dame IN, 1998

Prayer and Common Sense, Thomas H. Green, S.J., Ave Maria Press, Notre Dame IN, 1995

How to pray, R.A. Torry, Moody Press, Chicago

Powerprayer, Chrissie Blaze and Gary Blaze, Adams media, an F+W Publications Company, Avon, MA, 2004

The Tree of Life: Models of Christian Prayer, Steven Chase, Baker Academic, Grand Rapids, Michigan, 2005

Moment of Christ: The Path of Meditation, John Main, O.S.B., The Cross Road Publishing Company, New York, 1984

How to develop a Powerful Prayer Life, Dr. Gregory R. Frizzell, The Master Design, Memphis, TN, 1999

Intercessory Prayer, Dutch Sheets, The Regal Books, Ventura, California, 1996

Experiencing God by Henry T. Blackaby & Claude V. King, Walker and Company, New York, 1999

Opening to God, Thomas H. Green, S.J., Ave Maria Press, Notre Dame IN, 1992

Centered Living: The Way of Centering Prayer, M. Basil Pennington, OCSO, Liguori / Triumph, Liguori, Missouri, 1999

The Prayer of Jabez, Bruce Wilkinson, Multnomah Publishers, Inc., Sisters, Oregon, 2000

The Hidden Power of Prayer and Fasting, Mahesh Chavda, Destiny Image Publishers, Shippensburg, PA, 2000

Breaking Through God's Silence, David Yount, Touchstone Simon & Schuster, New York, 1997

Understanding the Purpose of and Power of Prayer, Dr. Myles Munroe, Whitaker House, New Kensington, PA, 2002

In Silence: Why we pray, Donald Spoto, Penguin Group, New York, 2004

Orthodox Prayer Life: The Interior Way by <u>Mattá al-Miskīn, St Vladimir's Seminary Press 2003 ISBN 0-88141-250-3</u>

Sermon notes of John Henry Cardinal Newman, 1849-1878 by John Henry Newman 2001 ISBN 0852444443

Themes in Old Testament Theology, William Dyrness (Dowers Grove, Ill.: InterVarsity, 1979)

The Soul of Prayer, P. T. Forsyth (Grand Rapids, MI: Eerdmans, 1916),

A New Testament of Devotion, Thomas Kelly (New York: Harper and Row, 1941)

The Old Testament and the World, Walther Zimmerli, trans. John J. Scullion (Atlanta: John Knox, 1976)

Berakhot, Mishnah

Berakhot, Babylonian Talmud

The History of Israel from Pompey to Bar Cochba, in *The New Jerome Biblical Commentary*, eds. Raymond E. Brown, Joseph A. Fitzmyer, Roland E. Murphy, (Englewood Cliffs, NJ: Prentice Hall, 1990)

Qumran Writings in *The New Jerome Biblical Commentary* eds. Raymond E. Brown, Joseph A. Fitzmyer, Roland E. Murphy.

The Scrolls and Christian Origins, Matthew Black (New York: Charles Scribner's, 1961)

Study or Action? Torah in Jewish life, Raphael Z. Werblowsky in *Jewish Heritage Reader*, ed. Lilly Edelman (New York: Taplinger, 1965)

Jesus of History: Origins and Ministry, John P. Meier, in *The New Jerome Biblical Commentary*, ed. R. E. Brown

The Jewish Background to the Lord's Prayer, Brad Young (Austin, Texas: Center for Judaic-Christian Studies, 1984)

The Collegeville Bible Commentary, eds. Dianne Bergant, and Robert J. Karris (Collegeville, Minnesota: Liturgical Press, 1989)

Judaism in the First Centuries of the Christian Era, George Foot Moore (Cambridge: Harvard University Press, 1927)

Contributions of Judaism to Modern Society, Abraham J. Feldman_(New York: The Union American Hebrew Congregation,n.d)

The Ryrie Study Bible, New American Standard Translation, Charles Caldwell Ryrie (Chicago, Ill,: Moody Press, 1978)

The Message of Galatians: Only One Way, John R. W. Stott (Downers Grove, Ill., and Leicester, England: InterVarsity Press, 1968)

Paul, a man of grace and grit, Charles R. Swindoll (The W. Publishing Group, Nashville, Tennessee, 2002)

Sermon notes of John Henry Cardinal Newman, 1849-1878 by John Henry Newman 2001 ISBN 0852444443

The Irrational Season, Madeleine L'Engle; Barnes and Noble, New York: 1977

Luke for Everyone, N.T. Wright, Westminster John Knox Press, Louisville, Ky.: 2004,

The Experience of Praying, Sean Caulfield, OCSO, Paulist Press, New York: 1980

Matthew Henry's Commentary on the Whole Bible: New Modern Edition, Electronic Database. Copyright © 1991 by Hendrickson Publishers, Inc.

Saint Paul, Michael Grant, Orion Publishing Group Ltd.

My Utmost for His Highest, Oswald Chambers, Barbour and Company, Inc. Uhrichsville, Ohio.

Sacred Companions: The Gift of Spiritual Friendship & Direction, Intervarsity Press, Downers Grove, Illinois, 2002

Prayer: Finding the Heart's True Home by Richard J. Foster.

Thoughts on the East by Thomas Merton

Practicing the Presence of God by Brother Lawrence

Celebration of Discipline by Richard Foster

The Coming of the Cosmic Christ by Matthew Fox

The Way of the Heart by Henri Nouwen

The Road Less Traveled by Scott Peck

Healing Light by Agnes Sanford

Book of Foundations by Teresa of Avila

Mysticism by Evelyn Underhill

Conversations with God by Donald Neal Walsch

Purpose-Driven Life by Rick Warren

Pray your Way to Happiness by Fr. Robert DeGrandis, S.S.J.

Life Wide Open by David Jeremiah

God's Joyful Surprise and "*When the Heart Waits*" by Sue Kid Monk

The Spiritual Man by Watchman Nee

The Contemplative Pastor by Eugene Peterson

How to Listen to God by Charles Stanley

Christian Meditation by Michael John Talbot

Be Still (DVD) by Max Lucado